To my friend —
a terrific guy!
With best regards
Frank Robinson

Life, Liberty, and Happiness

FRANK S. ROBINSON

AN OPTIMIST MANIFESTO

Life, Liberty, and Happiness

Prometheus Books
59 John Glenn Drive
Amherst, New York 14228-2197

Published 2006 by Prometheus Books

Life, Liberty, and Happiness: An Optimist Manifesto. Copyright © 2006 by Frank S. Robinson. All rights reserved. No part of this publication may be reproduced, stored in a retrieval system, or transmitted in any form or by any means, digital, electronic, mechanical, photocopying, recording, or otherwise, or conveyed via the Internet or a Web site without prior written permission of the publisher, except in the case of brief quotations embodied in critical articles and reviews.

Inquiries should be addressed to
Prometheus Books
59 John Glenn Drive
Amherst, New York 14228–2197
VOICE: 716–691–0133, ext. 207
FAX: 716–564–2711
WWW.PROMETHEUSBOOKS.COM

10 09 08 07 06   5 4 3 2 1

Library of Congress Cataloging-in-Publication Data

Robinson, Frank S.
    Life, liberty, and happiness : an optimist manifesto / by Frank S. Robinson.
       p. cm.
    Includes index.
    ISBN 13: 978–1–59102–426–2 (hardcover : alk. paper)
    ISBN 10: 1–59102–426–9 (hardcover : alk. paper)
    1. Life. 2. United States—Politics and government—2001– I. Title.

BD435.R594 2006
149'.5—dc22

2006009277

Printed in the United States of America on acid-free paper

*For Elizabeth—
Reach for the stars*

Acknowledgments

Everyone at Prometheus Books has done a splendid job and has been a pleasure to work with. I am especially grateful to my editor, Brian McMahon; to Jackie Cooke for the cover design; and to Editor-in-Chief Steven L. Mitchell.

Also, special thanks to David Hendin for his generous counsel.

Contents

INTRODUCTION	9
THE MEANING OF LIFE	15
REASON, SCIENCE, AND HUMAN VALUES	21
LIVING A GOOD LIFE	33
HAPPINESS IS A CHOICE	42
SATISFACTION	51
CONSCIOUSNESS, THOUGHT, AND PERSONAL RESPONSIBILITY	59
ALWAYS QUESTION	69
RELATIVISM AND NONJUDGMENTALISM	82
THE MYSTERY OF CREATION	95
FREEDOM FROM FEAR	101
LOVE, MARRIAGE, AND SEX	109
POLITICAL VOCABULARY	119
THE SOCIAL CONTRACT	126

INDIVIDUALISM AND SOCIETY	131
GOVERNMENT IS THE PROBLEM	137
THE FORCED MARCH TO PARADISE	152
THE ERA OF BIG GOVERNMENT	159
BUT WHAT ABOUT THE TRULY NEEDY?	169
WRONGFUL RIGHTS	175
AMERICA THE BEAUTIFUL	182
THE MORALITY OF FREE-MARKET CAPITALISM	202
GLOBALIZATION AND WORLD POVERTY	217
WHY CORPORATIONS ARE NOT TOTALLY EVIL SCUM	231
TERRITORIALITY AND TRIBALISM	241
WHY THE GLOOM AND DOOM CROWD IS WRONG	251
MAN, TECHNOLOGY, AND NATURE	264
HISTORY AND ITS LESSONS	272
FREEDOM OF EXPRESSION	280
RACE	287
PRO-LIFE AND PRO-CHOICE	298
ANIMAL RIGHTS	306
CRIME AND PUNISHMENT	311
HOMOSEXUALITY	321
THE WAR WITH ISLAMIC EXTREMISM	328
CODA	337
INDEX	343

Introduction

We all know the bleak litany: humankind is beastly; hatred, violence, and war are bred in the bone; man's inhumanity to man; ignorance, bigotry, oppression, exploitation, overpopulation; a sick society perverting nature, a materialistic capitalist economy controlled by evil corporations; the rich get richer while the poor get poorer; we are killing ourselves with pollution and wantonly destroying the planet.

We hear it endlessly. And it's so wrongheaded.

Anne Frank was someone who directly experienced our darkest side. Yet even while falling victim to one of history's worst horrors, she continued to insist, "in spite of everything, that people are truly good at heart." And she was right. This book shares her positive vision. It aims to counter the poisonous pessimism the first paragraph portrays. Despite all the human race's undeniable faults, I'm proud to be a member. For the most part, people *are* fundamentally good. And we are getting better all the time while we make a better world.

Human history has only just begun. Ahead of us, a long and bright future beckons. It's morning on planet Earth.

Let me explain how this book started. One day, retired, lounging around a pool with my family, I was thinking that all my life's work was done. My wife, noting my past literary efforts, casually asked if I had any new ones in mind. I answered that no particular topic motivated me. Then, referring to our young daughter, she said, "Why not write for Elizabeth everything you want her to know?"

Well, *that* motivated me!

I opened a file on my computer labeled "Letter to Elizabeth," imagining that that was all it would be. As I wrote, I found more and more to say, and the "letter" grew to book length. While at first I was writing for only my daughter, this project turned out to be no children's book, and I soon decided it should be shared with a wider audience.[1]

So, who am I to write such a book? I'd like to say I'm an all-seeing genius. But in truth I am an ordinary mortal and cannot claim entirely original insights. However, what I *can* say is that a great deal of thought, indeed a lifetime of thought, has prepared me to write this book. I believe it stands unique in weaving an extraordinarily wide spectrum of ideas into a coherent whole, and if these ideas are not altogether new, many are rarely discussed and will likely seem surprising to most readers. Does that suggest I am some kind of crackpot? I hope instead your reaction will frequently be "Wow! I never saw it that way before!" Or maybe you'll hurl the book against the wall in anger. Either way, at least it will have engaged your mind.

What I want for my daughter is a happy and successful life—as I have. Happiness and success require a positive outlook on life and a clear view of the world. I have always stressed to Elizabeth that the more you know, the better you understand the world and its people, the better you will do at everything. To travel a road without getting lost you need a roadmap. To make your way in the world, you must know how the world actually is, and how it came to be this way. This means cultivating an understanding of history and civics, science and culture, and the ways of other nations and peoples. Equally important is an under-

---

1. I must admit that I was also writing for myself. It required coming to grips with what I truly believe—and whether those beliefs could withstand critical examination. This made for a lot of hard work. It was an edifying process and I think I am better for having gone through it.

standing of literature and all the other arts, which are so important in the human project. Finally, it means developing a coherent philosophy as a lens for viewing all this and putting it into perspective.

This is what education is really about—not just earning good grades and a fancy diploma. Nor is it even about knowledge for knowledge's sake. Education provides the equipment for living a full and rich life. Someone who knows little of history, of literature and science, of the wider world, and who lacks an intellectual framework to filter it all, cannot taste fully of life, just as without taste buds you can't enjoy food. I want my daughter to have fully developed taste buds for life.

You must also know yourself. People in business must know their customers, and in living your life you are your own customer. This book cannot shine a light into your personal heart and soul, but I do hope to say some things about the human condition that will help you to shine that light into yourself.

Different religions offer varied perspectives on what life is about. There are plenty of books covering that ground. This one instead is centered outside of and apart from religious ideas. You will not be told here to believe, or not to believe; rather, I will endeavor to speak to believers and nonbelievers alike. For readers who are religious, I hope to present some ideas that may supplement what faith offers, providing a broadened and enriched outlook; and for nonbelievers, a pathway for understanding life and the world that stands on its own, independent of any religion.

The focus of this book will be not upon facts but *ideas*. I will try to offer a coherent viewpoint on the big questions, starting from a foundation of first principles and building upon them. We will begin with the meaning of life, and of a good life. We will consider morality, consciousness, thought, free will, love, and more. After covering the personal, we will move out to discuss what human society is all about. This will lead us into political philosophy and economics so as to provide a framework for grappling with public issues. There will also be chapters on some particular topics such as race, homosexuality, abortion, and others.

One common failing of human thought is not seeing the forest for the trees. We are bombarded with facts and impressions and too easily react to them in isolation from their larger context. We get so caught up in issues and details that we forget the big picture. This book aims to keep the big picture always firmly in view.

I did not write this book hoping that my daughter will read it and simply copy my mind-set, and I don't expect anyone else reading it to agree with everything I have written. While parts of the book may reflect elements of libertarianism, humanism, objectivism, and so forth, I am not a mouthpiece for any one dogma, doctrine, or ideology. Instead, everything here comes from within me, from a lifetime of observing, pondering, and responding to the world. And while the book presents my own particular vision, yours will inevitably be different, because no two people ever think exactly alike. If everyone did, life would be awfully boring. The uniqueness of every human mind is to be celebrated and this is part of why I put the primacy of the individual at the center of my own worldview.

Portions of this book may seem idealistic. I hope so. I consider myself both an optimist and an idealist, though not a pie-in-the-sky dreamer. To the contrary, I believe equally in realism; that is, in confronting the world as it truly is. It is a mistake to assume that idealism cannot be consistent with realism. I've tried to approach both my life and the writing of this book with a soft heart but a hard head. Looking at reality, I see much that's bad, but even more that's good. And my idealistic vision for mankind[2] is grounded in reality.

One of these realities is human imperfection. Though perfection, of course, can never be attained, my idealism insists that we must strive toward it. I admit to being imperfect myself. I don't do everything I

---

2. Some may deem the words "man" or "mankind" sexist and a slight to women; however, those words have traditionally been understood to include women and banning them diminishes our linguistic tool kit. This book will occasionally use these words as referring to all humanity, women equally with men; similarly, "he," may sometimes be used as a shorthand for "he or she," and so on, with no disrespect to women intended.

know I could and should to be better. I have done some things I'm not proud of. But that I am not perfect, that I don't always practice what I preach, does not invalidate the idealism that says we must try.

This book's philosophy can be summed up in the four words "live and let live." While this may seem simple-minded, I believe that this simple little phrase truly encapsulates everything.

The first word embraces the age-old philosophical debates on the meaning of life and how to live the good life. The essence of it is that life is a gift, we have a right to be happy, and we can rightly live in ways that make us happy.

The "let live" part concerns relations among people, which also encompasses all politics and social issues. "Let live" means freedom, and that has everything to do with happiness as well. Life, liberty, and happiness are really all of a piece. Not only is freedom crucial to our self-realization as individuals, but to "let live" makes a better world for everyone.

In short: live the best life you can, and let others do the same.

The rest of these pages will use up much ink discussing all these ideas in greater depth. But if you keep before you the core idea, "live and let live," you will never go far wrong.

The Meaning of Life

I once met a man who said his main interest was philosophy.

"So," I asked, "what's the meaning of life?"

He answered with a chuckle.

What he meant was that, while the question may seem simple, the answer is not.

Of course, one can go through life without ever stopping to ponder its deep meaning. In fact, the French writer Albert Camus said that if you are searching for the meaning of life, you will never live it.[3] On the other hand, Socrates held that the unexamined life is not worth living. The fact is we are inveterately curious creatures. We seek answers to everything, and surely to understand our own lives is an inescapable challenge. We are compelled to grapple with it.

Many look to religion for answers to life's questions. Spiritual ideas do satisfy a deep human craving to make sense of the universe and to find meaning in one's life. And many people feel that without God they would be adrift in a bleak and meaningless existence. Like philosophy and science, all religion is a product of human thought. In

---

3. And F. H. Bradley suggested that "the philosophical search for truth is like looking in a darkened room for a black cat which is probably not there."

our effort to grasp life's meaning, we use our capacity to think and reason.

The starting point is the origin of life. Science does not understand all the exact details of how life arose on Earth. Nevertheless, whatever spiritual concepts from religion one may choose to believe, the essence of the story of life's beginning has actually been established beyond any reasonable scientific doubt. We know that the primeval seas contained a rich soup of chemicals whose interactions were catalyzed by lightning, heat, pressure, and other natural forces. Given eons to play out, gradually, by small steps, ever more complex molecules percolated, until eventually, after numberless combinations, some molecules came together into something like a simple living cell (with the crucial characteristic of being able to reproduce itself).[4] It took eons more before the next major step of cells coming together to form complex life-forms, followed then by evolution into the variety of life we see today, including us humans. This account represents a factual description of what we know must have occurred.

The emergence of life was a natural process driven by chemical action. Scientists debate whether this chemical origin of life was something entirely predictable or a rare freakish occurrence; a few even speculate that life on Earth was seeded from elsewhere, which of course merely transfers the question to how it arose in that other place. But in any case, there is no real debate that the answer to the question of life's beginning is in chemistry.

Bear with me as we look a bit closer at life's chemistry. At the core is the molecule DNA, a very long zipperlike chain of paired chemical components. Those pairs come in only four variants, and their sequence (a language whose alphabet has just four letters) encodes all the information for making and operating a living thing. In reproduction, the molecule unzips, and the components on each side work like

---

4. My daughter's grade school biology class was assigned to imagine and model the first organism. Most models were elaborate creatures with eyes, feelers, limbs, and so forth. Elizabeth's was closer to the truth—simply a water-filled balloon.

magnets to attract new mates to replace those with which they previously paired. The result is two new DNA molecules identical to the original one.[5]

The salient point is this built-in proclivity for the DNA molecule to copy itself. This is the one big fact. This is what has driven all life, its spread and its evolution, from the beginning. The reason all life became DNA-based, instead of using some other molecule, is that DNA was uniquely efficient at reproducing itself and thereby proliferating the life-forms that incorporated it. The only purpose—if you can call it that—is to make more and more copies. Evolution simply favors those organisms able to make the most copies of their DNA (that is, the most offspring). Nothing else matters.

I mean this literally. Of course we look with wonder at the marvelous variety of life on Earth, with all its amazing, elegant, and beautiful forms and adaptations, but never forget that this whole living world came about for just one reason. DNA strives to copy itself, and all of life is merely its vehicle for doing so. Every species exists only because it is good at replicating its DNA.[6] A chicken is just an egg's way to make another egg.

In this process, countless survival and reproductive strategies were tried—strength, size, sharp teeth, sharp eyes, camouflage, body armor, chemical weaponry, you name it. Eventually nature got around to trying intelligence which, combined with consciousness, was an adaptation that proved highly successful at DNA copying. So here we are.

An exploration of the meaning of consciousness will occupy a chapter entirely to itself. For our current purposes, let's just say that consciousness is a mysterious phenomenon that we take for granted but do not actually understand. Most living things function without it.

---

5. Or nearly identical. Occasional copying errors over time become a key source of life's variability.

6. Thus, it's wrong to see evolution as inexorably progressing toward "higher" life-forms. Again, reproductive success is the only kind that counts. In this light, one might say that ants are more successful than humans since their population numbers dwarf ours.

Bacteria, bugs, fish, and worms possess the gift of life, but no equipment for enjoying it. Higher animals (like cats) have consciousness to some degree, but not advanced and fully developed minds like ours. And, again, we humans evolved our exceptional minds as merely another of the fluky, unique adaptations that nature tried in our species as a new way to promote DNA copying.

So how does all this bear upon the meaning of life? The answer is that life is ultimately just a cosmic accident. The only purpose nature made us for is to proliferate DNA, which of course seems meaningless. Now, some might consider this picture bleak and dismaying. Yet we can instead see it as liberating, as gloriously empowering. If nature made us only to copy DNA, we are not obliged to buy into that as our own *raison d'être,* our reason for being, or to organize our lives in its service. We are not just hapless creatures of the DNA copying machine. Indeed, given lives without built-in meaning leaves us free, each of us, to make our own lives mean what we choose.

Of course, this is not applicable to germs or worms. It is our consciousness that makes the difference, giving us the capability to choose for ourselves how we are to live, and why. Our minds evolved only to help us avoid predators, find food, survive, and reproduce in order to keep the DNA chain letter going. That our minds can also be used to enjoy art, music, and literature; to love; to wonder; to dream; and to seek knowledge and wisdom, is merely an accidental side effect, but one that we are free to make the most of.

In other words, your life belongs to you, and it is entirely up to you what to make of it. It is a magnificent accidental gift, like finding a hundred-dollar bill on the sidewalk. It's now your money and you can spend it any way you like.

Most people, through most of history, could not afford the luxury of doing so. The struggle to survive has been the central concern of life, with little time left over to use one's mind in other ways. Many of us today, however, are exceptionally fortunate to be freed from a survival struggle and, as a result, are liberated to use our minds to the limits of their capability. This is really a third-level cosmic gift superimposed upon the other two: first, that we exist at all; second, consciousness; and third, this freedom to make the most of it.

Pondering all this, it seems absolutely incredible that I exist, and that I have a mind capable of such pondering. It seems so unlikely, the product of such a fragile chain of improbable circumstances.[7] It is like finding on the sidewalk not a hundred-dollar bill, but a zillion-dollar bill, a bill of almost infinite value. Now that's a heck of a gift!

Of course, there is a little catch to this great gift. You don't get to keep it. Indeed, you have it for only a very short time.[8]

This is the rub of the human condition. Life is a holocaust in slow motion. We are the only creatures who understand that we must someday die. It has been said, with grim truth, that the purpose of life is to get ready to be dead forever. All of our striving, our achieving, our relationships, our loving, parenting, creating, everything we do, is shaped by the knowledge that we are alive for only a limited time.[9]

It is hard to reckon mortality a blessing, yet it does compel one to savor life instead of taking it for granted and treating it carelessly. If you had an unlimited supply of chocolate, one bite would mean little

---

7. One can add that our whole life histories, too, are chains of improbabilities. I sometimes think about what a lifelong sequence of accidents brought me to the spot where I first stepped on the toe of the woman I'd marry. And, of course, everyone is the accidental product of which one sperm out of millions, at a particular nanosecond, happened to fertilize an egg; any other sperm would have produced a totally different person.

8. In youth we don't think much about mortality; life seems to stretch ahead practically to infinity. But, as one grows older, the distance to that horizon steadily shrinks. And once you realize that more than half your life is gone, each subsequent year seems far too short.

9. I believe that humankind stands poised to change this—not in my lifetime, but maybe in my child's. Aging and mortality are scientific problems that are potentially soluble, and science is working hard to solve them. The implications are so enormous as to be virtually beyond imagining. Death has, as stated, always been the key fact of the human condition; change that and we change everything. Analysis of this topic could fill a book itself, but is beyond the scope of these pages.

or nothing to you; but if you understood that you could have only one bite, and no more ever again, you would be sure to suck every possible drop of flavor out of that one bite. We get only one bite at life.

There was a nearly infinite abyss of time before your birth, and there will be another one after your death—all darkness—and sandwiched between these two black voids, bigger than any mind can fathom, there is a tiny spark of light, this fleeting eye blink of time, in which you are alive and conscious, an indescribably precious spark.

Throughout life each of us climbs a mountain of growth and learning, building an inner cathedral of knowledge and wisdom. And when we reach the top, we fall off a cliff—that edifice so painstakingly constructed crashes into dust. This is the tragedy of death. And yet the loss is not absolute; we can leave something of ourselves behind. While one's own climb must end, humanity's does not, and we are all part of that great climb, building man's cathedral to the sky. This book is written in that spirit so that some of the knowledge and understanding gained in my own life may live after me.

The meaning of life, the purpose of life, is to make the most of it, to suck every possible drop of flavor from your one bite. Once you are dead, it's over. All that will have mattered is how well you lived.

How to do this—how to live a good life—will be taken up shortly. But to prepare for that, we must first address some other fundamental ideas.

Reason, Science, and Human Values

Many people look to religion not only to explain the universe and life's meaning but also as a guide to right and wrong. They believe morality means following God's will and law, and that without God there can be no morality.

But such values need not come only from God. They can also come from our use of reason, grounded upon what we know to be the truths of human existence. And indeed, a system of values thus derived, with a foundation in indisputable reality, may even be deemed stronger than one grounded in religious ideas that rely on faith. We are on firmer footing with what we *know* than with what we merely *believe.*

Reason is of such importance that it merits explicit definition. Reason means objective evaluation of verifiable facts gathered by the senses, application of logic to those facts, and honest willingness to accept and face the conclusions thereby derived. Reason means embracing reality. It requires rejection of nonsensory, nonrational, or supernatural sources of knowledge and belief. An allied idea is that all phenomena have natural causes that can be explained (sometimes called "empiricism").[10]

---

10. Anything that actually occurs must be deemed within the realm of the natural. Thus, "supernatural" can only refer to imaginary phenomena outside of reality. Nothing "supernatural" can be real. (And, while human

In contrast to empiricism, religious or spiritual belief is grounded on faith. Some do try to reason their way into faith, yet the essence of faith is to believe because one makes a choice to believe. The believer may consider that choice rational, but the rationalization is post hoc; that is, the choice to believe comes first and then reasons are mustered to support it. The answer precedes the question. Certainly one cannot arrive at, say, Christian belief just through abstract, a priori reasoning. That is why religion insists on a mystical concept of faith rather than even suggesting that reason alone could lead one into belief.

Some say there are other valid sources of knowledge and belief besides reason, such as intuition or more mystical modes of thought. But what we call "intuition" is really just an unconscious form of reasoning. The mathematical savant who can multiply two big numbers in his head may not know how the answer comes to him, but somewhere in the workings of his brain there has to be an algorithm operating rationally to provide the answer; it cannot possibly come through a nonrational process. Likewise with intuition. It's certainly a complex phenomenon, seemingly pulling answers out of a mysterious "black box," yet somewhere in our brains the work must somehow be done to evaluate information and produce the answers.

But information, facts, and knowledge cannot enter our brains in the first place except from the outside real world through our senses. No person can legitimately claim to "know" anything by mystical, supernatural, or extrasensory means. Imagination is fertile. Our brains are quite capable of going off into the wild blue yonder all on their own, but why suppose such fancies have anything to do with the real world? Knowledge has to be gathered from reality; there is no other way to get it.

Of course, our senses are not perfect fact gatherers. They can mislead us. Eyewitness testimony in trials is notoriously unreliable. And famously, astronomer Percival Lowell saw canals on Mars mainly because he wanted to see them. Thus, our minds can actually get in the

---

interpretations of reality can be changeable, reality itself is not. Truth exists; our challenge is to understand it.)

way of our senses. Still, they give us our only window on reality, even if that window is sometimes clouded.

Because our senses are limited, facts can be elusive, and because human beings are not perfect reasoning machines, reason is admittedly a fallible guide. But it is nonetheless the best we have. There is no direct pipeline to truth.

The history of science is therefore a history of error. We sometimes laugh at how early scientists got things wrong. Aristotle certainly made some howling blunders, but he was not a fool; indeed, he virtually invented science from scratch, establishing the idea of gaining knowledge through direct observation of nature. This represented a huge intellectual advance. Many other people of genius followed him, often making mistakes, yet by painstaking effort pushing the ball forward. Isaac Newton once said that if he saw further, it was because he stood upon the shoulders of giants. And through this scientific method of digging out facts and applying our reason, the errors of past ages have been progressively overcome.

Some people regard science as just another viewpoint, not necessarily more valid than some alternative way of looking at things. Indeed, they point to past scientific mistakes and infer that scientific truth is transitory, that today's scientific understanding will change tomorrow, and that it can therefore be disregarded. But science is not just any old viewpoint; it is *the* method for knowing things, to which there is no rational alternative.

The essence of the scientific method is that answers must be falsifiable; that is, capable of being disproved if wrong. Science means continually subjecting answers to such testing and modifying them based on the results. Thus science, unlike nonscientific constructs such as astrology or religion, is a progressive process through which knowledge builds upon knowledge, advancing cumulatively by adding what is proven true and discarding what is proven untrue. If you think a scientific answer is wrong, the only valid way to counter it is with better science, not with nonscience. And the likelihood that we will know more tomorrow doesn't justify shutting one's eyes to what we know today.

The meaning of the word *know* is very important. To *know* something is not the same as supposition or merely thinking, believing, or guessing it's true. With any assertion of knowledge, belief, or understanding, one must always ask, "*how* do you know?" This is absolutely crucial. In science, the *how* is both clear and verifiable. In nonrational systems, it is neither. One can *choose to believe* (as in faith), but cannot *know*. Knowledge backed by proof stands stronger than mere belief. Such knowledge supports confidence. Nonprovable beliefs must admit doubt.

Logic is also integral to reason. We all know what logic means in a general sense. But it was Aristotle again who first delineated the principles of logic in a systematic and rigorous way. The most basic building block is the syllogism: "All men are mortal. John is a man. Therefore John is mortal." Logic is the method for understanding relationships among propositions; it is how we can correctly think about what is true and what is not.

Johann Kepler was a seventeenth-century astronomer obsessed with proving that planets travel in circles, consonant with his notion of beautiful heavenly perfection. Today we know planetary orbits are instead elliptical. Who discovered this? Johann Kepler. After meticulously gathering data trying to prove his cherished theory, he finally accepted that the facts actually disproved it and then he used them to work out the true laws of planetary motion. This is science. This is reason.

Charles Darwin likewise began by careful collection of a mass of facts. Then he applied logic to those facts, seeking a rational explanation for them. His resulting conclusions—evolution and natural selection—flew in the face of most people's fundamental beliefs. But Darwin did not flinch from what facts and logic told him; he did not flinch from the reality confronting him.

Darwin concluded his seminal book, *The Origin of Species*, writing, "There is grandeur in this view of life." By "this view" he meant the fact-based, reason-based picture that he set forth, as against the one supplied by religion. He was rejecting any idea that his scientific picture was somehow more prosaic and less majestic than that of religion. And there is grandeur indeed in the very fact that we humans, using the power of our reason, have managed to unravel nature's secrets, to penetrate her deep mysteries.

The epitome of this was Albert Einstein who, as a twenty-six-year-old patent clerk, asked himself what he'd see if he traveled along with a light beam. Through daring questions like this and the prodigious power of his human reason, Einstein came to grasp how our commonplace understandings of the nature of space and time were inaccurate, laying bare for us a deeper truth of the clockwork of creation.

Reason offers the only possible means for determining what is true and what is not. It was reason that lifted us from the Paleolithic caves to the mountaintop we occupy today. It is through reason and science that we have come to possess as much truth as we do. Our whole civilization is built on it. This has been the fountain for all humanity's achievements: the steam engine, electricity, computers, polio vaccine, did not come from mysticism and spirituality. For all our frequent recourse to them, it is instead reason that saves our skin when the chips are down and survival is at stake. Mysticism, spirituality, and non-rationality cannot do so because they do not enable us to deal with the hard factual realities that govern our existence. They are indulgences that can only be afforded because reason keeps us alive to so indulge.

Reason also gives us the prospect for control over our lives. The problems we face may be difficult and not always subject to rational solution, but if there is a solution then it is reason that enables us to find it. Religion puts us in the hands of a power beyond any possibility of being understood, let alone controlled. Reason puts in our own hands the power that allows us to be masters of our fate.

Yet in spite of everything, some people still profess distrust of reason. They see it as producing a terrible world beset by problems, and invoke the Holocaust as the ultimate example of reason gone amok. They say such things while sipping chardonnay in plush penthouses, oblivious to owing their very lives to the progress they so glibly denigrate. Yes, modernity entails problems; that's the price we pay for its vastly greater benefits. Who would trade modern living for a caveman's miserable lot? And if proper use of reason cannot show Nazism as wrong, what can?[11] The point again is that while reason is fallible and human beings use it imperfectly, reason still remains the best tool we've got. If we turn away from it, our problems can only multiply, and crimes like Hitler's can only be more likely, not less.

In the last analysis, the answer to anyone questioning reliance on reason is that the only alternative is unreason and irrationality. That being so, I choose reason.

In sum, all of one's beliefs, values, goals, desires, and actions must be grounded in the use of reason.[12] And it is reason that tells us what is good or bad, right or wrong. Those moral values come directly out of the facts of our existence as understood by reason.

First, this tells us to value human life above all else. That is, after all, the thing we struggle for; and every rational person understands the value of life to himself.[13] Thus, the first principle of any morality must be to promote human life; that which does so is good; and that which works against human life is not.[14] One might even deem this the very definition of morality. Following rules because they are rules is not what morality is about. The point is exemplified in Mark Twain's *The Adventures of Huckleberry Finn* when Huck decides to help a slave escape because his heart says it is right, even though, under the

---

11. If only Hitler could have read this book, perhaps he'd have been set straight. But seriously, reason wasn't to blame for Nazism—Nazis were. People will always find reasons for bad things they do. And certainly, throughout history, religion has likewise been used to justify horrific misdeeds.

12. Emotion, of course, also plays an inescapable role. We will talk about this later.

13. Some religious believers are so deeply convinced of a better life to come that they cheerfully relinquish this one; but most people, even if professing such a belief, are not so deeply convinced and, hence, cling to their earthly lives with great tenacity.

14. The above raises the issue of animal rights. This will be discussed later.

rules of his society, it is a crime that could send him to Hell. "I'll go to Hell, then," he declares. True morality means acting in ways that promote human welfare.

Some might object that humanity is unworthy of being placed on such a philosophical pedestal because it is so fault-ridden and guilty of so many evils. A simple response to such misanthropy is that if human life is not an end in itself, then what else could be? But, more broadly, the human species *is* worthy of our highest allegiance and love because, for all its faults, there is far more about mankind that is breathtakingly splendid. Kepler, Darwin, Einstein—such accomplishments moisten my eyes with human pride. Man's achievement is a theme that will recur later. Let it suffice to say here that my love for our species comes not from chauvinism but from, yes, reason. Human life is appropriately central to any moral system.

Another possible objection is that there are larger concerns than human life, such as the health of the planet. But ask yourself what the point would be of having the Earth in tip-top shape with nobody to enjoy it. Consciousness, with the capacity for suffering or happiness, is the only thing that gives meaning to *anything*. The reason to be concerned about the planet is so that humans can thrive. If there were no consciousness, why would it matter whether or not the universe even exists?

Further, observation of other people reveals that they have the same kind of consciousness, value their lives as greatly as we value our own, and hence, they are just as entitled to their lives as we are to ours. Corollary to this is not only the right of every person to live, but also to live as he chooses, without which the right to live would be meaningless. This implies *freedom*—or the right to live as one sees fit, without interference by others, provided one does not himself interfere with others. That proviso in turn calls forth a system of laws to govern our interactions. And this requires that every individual have a say in making the laws he must obey (i.e., democracy). Thus does reason lead us to recognize these natural and universal human rights.

Another basic concept of morality derived from reason is *justice*. Some people actually do not understand what justice means. They talk of "social justice" or "economic justice," as though any inequality of conditions of life among people is a form of injustice. This is actually contrary to reason. Justice instead means reward or penalty *as deserved*. Reason tells us that, while everyone is entitled to an equal opportunity to make his life, the person who does good should be rewarded while one who acts badly should not, and that every person differs in how much reward he deserves. Thus, justice, as discovered by reason, does not mean equality in what people get from life, but rather *inequality* due to the different rewards that different people deserve.

To be sure, we live in an imperfect world in which reward or penalty is often a function of luck or lack thereof. And certainly many people get neither an equal chance in life nor what in fairness they deserve. Yet of course this does not negate the principle of justice as an ideal toward which we should seek to approach as closely as possible. The best route is to foster a world in which each person is indeed free to attain the rewards to which his efforts justly entitle him. The equality to be sought is not a sameness of outcomes, but rather an equality of opportunities.[15]

Reason also dictates that you behave justly toward others, giving them what they deserve from you, and doing nothing undeserved to them. Justice means that you may not harm another without proper cause or take from him something to which you have no right.

Such reason-based morality is integral to membership in society and the essence of the *social contract* (a political idea that will receive greater attention later). If you value the benefits of rules that protect against bad behavior by others, then you must yourself abide by those rules. If you want others to respect your rights, you must respect theirs. If you wish to live in a community where amity and cooperation prevail, where people deal squarely with each other, you must yourself behave that way.

Because we recognize the reasonableness of this equation, we do

---

15. People also differ in their genetic endowments, and in using the word "equality," we must understand it as political rather than biological. We don't mean that all people are the same—instead, we mean *treating* them the same. Fairness does not require human sameness.

act justly toward others for the most part. It's like a convenience store's "add a penny, take a penny" tray. We treat each other decently as though putting decency in a bank, building up a credit balance of it, from which we ourselves may draw. It's not strictly self-serving. We understand that our treatment of Mary may have no actual bearing on how Jane will treat us. And there are some individuals with no compunction about taking but never giving. However, most people are not like that. Most people understand that society cannot function that way. So we internalize the concept of reciprocity and honor it even in our interactions with strangers whom we'll never see again.

I often drive a route where a certain turn is normally impossible unless another driver lets me cut in. Someone always does within seconds. It's a small sacrifice for him, yet why do it for a stranger? The implicit idea is that if he does it for me today, someone else will do it for him tomorrow. Every time this happens, it validates for me Anne Frank's positive view of humankind.

The foregoing may bring to mind "the golden rule," something we tend to associate with religion. The golden rule states that one should treat others as one would wish to be treated.[16] However, that's not a sure guide because other people may differ from you in how they wish to be treated. The golden rule is also flawed in that it provides no penalty for harmful behavior. In fact, both individuals and society are best served by a variant that's been called the "bronze rule," which is to follow the golden rule initially with someone, but if that person does not reciprocate, then treat him as he has treated you (or, in Ronald Reagan's words, "trust but verify"). This bronze rule is consonant with the idea of justice, as explained above, and serves communal interests by giving people incentives to behave cooperatively.[17] Otherwise, society cannot succeed.

---

16. This idea was also expressed by Confucius around 2,500 years ago.

17. The bronze rule is supported by modern game theory, as in the "prisoner's dilemma," wherein two partners in crime are interrogated separately. If both stay silent, both get six-month sentences. If only one talks, he goes free while the other gets ten years. If both talk, each gets two years. Though

* * *

I have thus far spoken only of reason as a source for distinguishing right from wrong. But it must be recognized that we don't get these values from abstract reasoning alone (or, for that matter, only from religion). In fact, these moral ideas are part of our natural makeup. They are built into us by evolution.

Some philosophers dispute that there is any such thing as human nature. But philosophizing can produce ideas at odds with everyday reality. While it's true that human behavior encompasses great variability, individuals are, nonetheless, genetically and physiologically very similar, they share the same evolutionary background, and looking at how people throughout the world and throughout history have behaved, it makes little sense to deny that some important characteristics are effectively universal. This was recognized by Aristotle, whose *Nichomachean Ethics* was not concerned with defining some abstract moral standard, but instead focused on the basic moral sense that most people exhibit most of the time, with the morality of our actions best judged by the effects they have upon real people.

It's quite obvious how nature programmed humanity with some basic tenets of morality such as the taboos against incest or murder. And our moralizing actually seems to be as much emotional as rational. (Steven Emmanuel, a professor of philosophy, once remarked to me that his students "shoot from the hip" in evaluating moral issues.) Clearly, moral notions are undoubtedly built into our essential human nature.

Since human beings evolved as social creatures, with our individual fates dependent upon the success of our band or tribe, both our behaviors and our moral codes are tailored accordingly. We actually do

---

both are better off if both stay mum, from a selfish standpoint betrayal seems a better strategy because neither can know the other won't talk. However, if the game continues through repeated iterations, the best strategy actually turns out to be tit-for-tat and betrayal only of a partner who has betrayed you before—i.e., the bronze rule.

tend to follow the bronze rule because that is what works and what has worked in promoting social cooperation and cohesion and thus survival.[18] And the fact that evolution and reason produce similar values cannot be deemed coincidental. Theoretically, one could imagine some set of ethics that promotes DNA replication while contravening the dictates of reason, but it seems more likely that nature and reason would be aligned. Since nature and reason do align, it's fair to say that, despite some people's efforts to intellectualize a lack of objective moral standards, at least some basic principles are, in fact, natural laws.

The result of all this—both human nature and our use of reason—is that most people actually *are* good most of the time. One can be cynical about human motivations, and there's no denying people often do terrible things, but "man's inhumanity to man" is the exception rather than the rule. Even if it's true that most of us are capable of acting like Nazis under certain conditions, such conditions are fortunately aberrational, and in normal circumstances most people don't act that way. The larger reality is that under normal conditions in our everyday lives we can readily observe that most people we encounter are peaceable, honest, decent, and kind.[19] This is another reason why I love our species and insist that its welfare must be the central concern of any moral system.

Only the broadest moral principles have been sketched out above. Further reflection will serve to flesh them out and reveal all their subtle nuances. We must use our reason to grapple with these further issues as they arise. Some may be complex and difficult and may not have

---

18. Such social cooperation is actually quite common in nature. It is seen in wolves hunting in packs, for example, and even in such lower creatures as ants and bees.

19. Indeed, this is a key operating assumption in my coin selling business; I send most shipments in advance of payment, often even to strangers, because nonpayment turns out to be quite rare. In fact, this is typical of how the world's business is conducted. Commerce could not flourish if most people weren't basically trustworthy. (Certainly eBay could not!)

clear answers. But if there are answers, they must be found and supported by the use of reason.

We began this chapter by positing that morality and values don't come just from religion. In fact, religion doesn't give us morality; it gets it from us. Before there was religion there was human nature and reason, and religion developed to embody the moral values that our nature and reason first built.[20] Thus, we don't need religion to be moral. If you doubt this, ask yourself what you'd do if there were no God. Would you rape, steal, and murder? Of course not. And that's because religion is not the true source of your morality. It comes from within you. Religion merely codifies it.[21]

The key points elucidated in this chapter were expressed with elegant precision in a few words in the Declaration of Independence: All men are created equal (but may not *be* equal), with the right to life, liberty, and the *pursuit* of happiness (though not necessarily its attainment). And these truths were held to be *self-evident*; that is, not handed down by God, but derived from reason.

---

20. Thomas Aquinas said that moral ideas come out of nature and are discovered by our reason, which is a gift from God.

21. And one can deem it a better form of morality to be good because you believe it's right than from fear of divine punishment. For these insights I am indebted to Michael Shermer's thought-provoking book, *The Science of Good and Evil.*

Living a Good Life

We have established the context for discussion of this issue: what a stupendous gift it is to be alive and conscious, but it's a gift we don't have for long. Every day, every moment, is infinitely precious. In seeing how best to use that gift we must look to reason and the fundamental moral ideas reason gives us. At the center is human life itself.

When all is said and done, the key question, if not the only question, is how much you have promoted life, how much human welfare, happiness, pleasure, love, and joy you've generated. And the most important person in that regard is you yourself. Your chief purpose in life is not to make others happy. *It is to make yourself happy.* But these two aims are not mutually exclusive. This is by no means a common idea, and requires serious explanation.

Epicureanism was a classical philosophy that held pleasure to be the proper goal of life. Another philosophy was *stoicism*, a word we use today to mean acceptance of hardship. To be more precise, the ideal of stoicism was to attain an inner serenity that would enable one to be happy in any circumstances. The pleasure sought by Epicureans, on the other hand, most importantly meant the pleasure of peace of mind. So the two ideas are not really in opposition. Sybaritic pleasure by itself cannot confer happiness without inner peace. And stoicism also means living in accord with one's nature. What that nature is, one must learn and accommodate. To deny and fight one's true nature is not a route to happiness or a good life. And for most people, a big part of their nature is to seek and relish happiness and pleasure.[22]

Now, there is much agonizing about what is seen as our modern culture of materialism, consumerism, and selfishness.[23] Drummed into us from an early age is the idea that we should share with others, that it's wrong to be selfish and to think only of oneself, perhaps even that it's wrong to put oneself ahead of others. Taking this to heart, some people strive to live what they consider good lives with such self-denial that they get scant pleasure or happiness for themselves. Some doctrines even call for mortifying the flesh and the self. There are ascetics who choose to live in caves on bare subsistence. And (to paraphrase H. L. Mencken) there are puritans whose greatest fear is that someone, somewhere, is having fun. All this does no one any good.

Others more plausibly insist that a good life is measured by how much you do for others, that if society has been good to you there is a moral duty to "give something back."[24] And Immanuel Kant maintained that morality means acting according to duty rather than doing what you like and that it's all about fighting what comes naturally.

This, too, may sound virtuous. But if we are to treat the idea with true seriousness, we must ask: why? *Why* must we share with strangers? Where does this obligation come from? Where do our duties come from? The issue is again the seeming conflict between the

---

22. The two are not, incidentally, the same. Pleasure entails short-term gratification—eating a cookie or having sex—while happiness is a long-term phenomenon. Happiness concerns not our feelings at a given moment but how we feel about our lives as a whole. Pleasure is transitory; happiness endures.

23. Actually, every human generation has seen itself this way—just as every generation always seems to think its children behave worse than children did before.

24. However, note that, in general, people rewarded by society have earned those rewards because they have already made a contribution—already "given something back."

claims of the self and of others—or the extent to which living a good life means doing for others as opposed to doing for oneself.

The moral concept of *obligation* is actually grounded in *reciprocity*, a two-way street and an unwritten contract; that is, duties and obligations toward others do not arise out of thin air but out of our relationships with them. We have obligations toward individuals—most obviously those who do things for us—but not to the mass of humanity, just on account of being one of them. You owe your existence only to your parents and not to any other human beings. You have a duty to take care of the children you sire but not others. You are obligated to pay a vendor for what you buy but not to part with cash otherwise. Your wealth, if you didn't steal it, was either earned or given to you by someone. To your benefactor you may be obligated, but you have no moral duty to any others.

Looking at it another way, a stranger has a right not to be harmed or interfered with by you, and you have a duty to honor that right. The reciprocity element here is your expectation that others will likewise respect your right to the same treatment. This again is the essence of living in society. But to decline *help* to someone is not a violation of his rights, and hence not a breach of any duty or obligation on your part.

Of course, none of this means you should never do anything for anyone except out of direct obligation. That something isn't required doesn't mean it's not desirable. Obviously we do a lot for other people out of love, loyalty, or friendship. This is a big part of our lives. And even when it comes to strangers, being charitable and generous *is* good and virtuous. But the point is that when we *do* perform such altruistic or charitable acts, *we do so not from duty, but from choice.* This is a crucial point worth repeating: not from duty but from choice. And it is indeed morally better to act altruistically from rational free choice than from a nonrational notion of obligation. While Kant was right in the limited sense that there is virtue in fulfilling rather than shirking the obligations we do have, surely there is more virtue when you do good even where it isn't duty-bound.

And so, why, when there is a real choice, do people act as good

Samaritans? Why did my toddler daughter jump up, abandon her ice cream cone, and run to retrieve a lost baby shoe for a complete stranger? Why did a woman in New York City literally run after me to return some money I had dropped?

Science may have something to say about this. If, as far as nature is concerned, our only purpose is to pass along DNA, you might expect us to be engineered to think only of our own individual interests. But it appears that nature may be more cunning and reckons that survival of the very similar DNA of our relatives and even tribe mates can have greater payback than survival of a single individual, so we are programmed to sacrifice ourselves for the family or group. Further, in the primitive hunter-gatherer mode of life, which dominated most of our history, collaboration and sharing among band members was essential. Social cooperation being crucial to collective survival, evolution naturally made us cooperative. That's not to say selfishness has been extinguished; selfishness and altruism constantly struggle within us. But our brains are wired to reward us with pleasurable feelings when we do good deeds.[25] We experience pride and a sense of righteousness when we act well, guilt and shame when we don't. Brain imaging studies have confirmed this. Socially cooperative behaviors actually do activate our pleasure centers. And a recent scientific experiment showed that helpfulness, like my baby shoe example, is in fact standard behavior for children as young as eighteen months.

But social cooperation is not just biology at work. Our reasoning minds are at work here too. Using reason, we understand that promotion of human life and happiness is a moral good, not only for ourselves, but for others as well. Unlike other beasts, we have the ability

---

25. This idea of natural selection by groups rather than individuals—with altruism having group survival value—is controversial among evolutionary biologists. But it's reasonable to think that both individual *and* group selection operated together. Though what makes individuals survive differs from what makes groups survive, optimizing the success of both presumably would require the right balance between altruism and selfishness among individuals.

to project ourselves into the minds of others, and so to suffer if we see our fellows suffer. Indeed, we can't help doing so.[26] Altruism expresses our fundamental humanity, our empathy and compassion, a recognition that we are all ultimately in the same boat, and, as the writer Susan Sontag put it, is an expression of our solidarity with the rest of humankind. Thus, helping another makes one feel good in a perfectly rational way.

Sharing and cooperation can be rational not just from an altruistic standpoint but also from the standpoint of pure self-interest. Sometimes we may expect to benefit from reciprocity, and often such behavior enhances one's social status. We all covet the approval of family and peers. In some human tribes, one's status is keyed to generosity in gift giving, and similar considerations loom large in the sharing of research results among scientists, for example.

The preceding discussion may lead us to ask whether there is really any such thing as a truly altruistic act, in the sense that the personal cost exceeds the reward, or whether people do seemingly selfless things only when the psychic payback, the feel-good factor, exceeds the cost. The latter can conceivably be possible even when someone gives his very life for others, calculating that to die is preferable to living under the burden of having refused to make that sacrifice.

That is an extreme example. But the point is that it's okay—indeed, probably unavoidable—to do good deeds for the sake of psychic and other rewards rather than in the name of true selflessness. When we understand this, we realize that there is not such a clear line between serving the self and serving others. Both the things we do to serve our own needs and desires, *and* our "selfless" acts are equally part of the tool kit we use for living a good life. My daughter experienced pleasure when she retrieved that stranger's lost shoe. And my wife derived great

---

26. There is evidence that feeling another's pain isn't just a matter of understanding it in an intellectual sense but is, rather, a literal feeling caused by the firing of "mirror neurons" that generate sensations akin to those produced by the painful event itself. (And a deficiency in such mirror neurons may be the source of autism.)

satisfaction when she was able to help a lost Mexican child at an airport. That good deed made her life more rewarding. She got pleasure from it just as she might get pleasure from eating a cookie.

There is a school of thought (Ayn Rand's *objectivism*) that holds (as I do) that a person's own happiness is the legitimate moral purpose of his life. Objectivism, however, casts this in opposition to a moral code of altruism, which legitimizes only acts done for the benefit of others. This sets self-realization in opposition to self-sacrifice. And objectivism argues that when one chooses a seemingly altruistic action, this actually reflects being brainwashed into the irrational idea that only selfless deeds are virtuous. I would contend that it is reasonable to believe that selfless deeds may be virtuous without necessarily believing that *only* selfless deeds are virtuous. The term "self-sacrifice" represents a misconception of what is really happening in an act of altruism; and there isn't an absolute antithesis between what is self-serving and what serves others. As we have seen, we get rational rewards from good deeds. It was not materially "self-sacrificing" for my wife to help that Mexican child; the psychic satisfaction she gained was genuine and legitimate, not irrational, and more than compensated for her time and trouble.

The perfect exemplar of this point is Ebenezer Scrooge who, in the end, derived joy and served his true self-interest by embracing a better balance between self-centeredness and consideration for others. This was not self-sacrifice. It was self-realization.

I wrote earlier that, ultimately, how good a life you live depends on how much happiness and pleasure you generate, and that your own happiness and pleasure come first. I hope that now my meaning is becoming more clear.

Many hold that at least part of living a good life is making the world better. But what, exactly, do we mean by "better"? Some folks actually think the planet would be better without people. Let us dismiss such antihuman notions and posit that a better world means one with more human satisfaction, enjoyment, comfort, fulfillment, and pleasure; and less pain and suffering.

Now, there is a streak of Calvinist guilt in some people that sees pleasure as bad; they believe that pain improves us and pleasure corrupts us. There are even some people, called "masochists," who actually take pleasure from pain. We should not deny them their peculiar form of pleasure. But for normal people, pain hurts and pleasure feels good.

Of course, pain is an inevitable part of life and experiencing pain *does* make us better people in many ways. We learn from pain. It helps us gain depth in our understanding of the human condition and greater appreciation of our own lives. That is all true, and we should not abolish all pain if that were possible. But meantime there is not any shortage or deficit of pain and suffering in the world; there is more than enough to satisfy any possible need we have for it—in fact, there is a huge oversupply. Given that stark reality, the human project is fundamentally all about combating and minimizing the pain and suffering we must endure while maximizing instead the joy and fulfillment we get from life.

There are six billion people on Earth. Imagine that we assign one pain point every time a toe is stubbed. More points are registered for proportionately greater suffering. Likewise, happiness points are assigned: one or two for eating a cookie, a great many more for falling in love, and so forth. At year-end, we deduct all the worldwide pain points from the happiness points to get a final score.

Ceteris paribus ("all else equal"), the higher the score, the better is the state of the world from the human standpoint.[27] And accordingly, if your activities increase the worldwide score, you have made the world better.

This idea is akin to the philosophy of *utilitarianism* expounded by Jeremy Bentham and John Stuart Mill. Bentham in fact tried to devise a system for allocating points and calculating human welfare numeri-

---

27. Some might quibble that if we increase the score by, for example, ruining the planet for future generations, we haven't made a better world. Of course that's true. Such cavils are covered by my "ceteris paribus." Obviously, all effects of our actions have to be taken into account; but if, after doing so, the score is higher, then the world is better.

cally. Such literal application of the idea is too fraught with difficulties to be useful. My thrust, instead, is not to advocate precise calculations, but rather to provide a way to conceptualize the state of the world from the human perspective to help us think about these issues.

The key point is that in this hypothetical worldwide reckoning of happiness versus pain, *your own happiness and pain count too.* This again shouldn't be seen as embodying nonvirtuous selfishness. You are, after all, just as human as anyone, just as entitled to enjoy life and avoid suffering. Your own personal happiness/pain score counts as much in the worldwide totals as does anyone else's. So, just as you make the world better by doing something for another, you equally make it better by doing for *yourself*, by getting more happiness and less pain in *your* life.

In fact, it isn't merely that you're just as worthy an object of your good deeds as anyone else. You actually owe a special duty to yourself. While you have no obligation to strangers, to say you have no obligation to yourself would of course be nonsensical. You are not responsible for strangers, but you certainly do bear primary responsibility for your own welfare. Further, if your goal is to raise the world's point score, then it makes sense to focus efforts where the payoff will be greatest. And of course, while your ability to increase someone else's happiness may be limited, your ability to enhance your own happiness is great. No one knows you better than you know yourself and no one knows better than you what buttons to push for your own happiness and pleasure. As Aldous Huxley said, "There's only one corner of the universe you can be certain of improving, and that's your own self." So you can best add to the global point score by working on your own happiness first and foremost.

This, again, is not mere selfishness. Indeed, nobody enjoys a sourpuss, and if you get sunshine into your own life, that sunshine will help light up the lives of others around you. In this way too, your own personal happiness really does make a better world.

While we have recognized that, absent reciprocity, you have no duty to do things for the benefit of others, you *are* obligated to avoid harming someone who hasn't harmed you. So while there is nothing inherently immoral in placing a priority on looking after your own interests, it is obviously problematic if you do that at someone else's expense, gaining your happiness through diminishing another's. That may admittedly raise the world's point score, if your gain exceeds his loss, and it's certainly ethically okay if he consents. But otherwise it's a dicey proposition. You don't have a right to harm someone for your own benefit even if you judge your benefit to outweigh the harm.[28] (And forgoing such action may generate altruism pleasure points for you, so the global score might rise after all.)

Nothing written here is a call for purely selfish hedonism. Once again, catering to your own needs and wants is not the only tool for happiness, as nature and reason give us rewards for aiding others. In fact, a good deed can be a "twofer," giving you pleasure while also helping someone else, thus doubly contributing to the world happiness score. Yet on the other hand, true self-sacrifice may not add to the score at all, and may even *subtract* from it, if you are boosting someone else's happiness at the cost of reducing your own.

In the final analysis, the key is to strike the right balance between self-oriented satisfaction and contributing to the welfare of others. Both augment your own happiness score and both make the world better.[29] The aim should be to balance the two so as to maximize the score *both* for the world and for you.

If you do that, you are living a good life.

---

28. Kant argued against utilitarianism by saying it can be wrong to achieve "the greatest good for the greatest number" by, say, killing innocent persons. This raises the issue of whether ends can justify means, to which we'll return. But this moral problem does not negate the *general* idea that actions promoting human life and happiness are good and actions undermining it are bad.

29. We will also see later that in the economic sphere, as Adam Smith famously explained, the broad public interest is actually best served by individuals each pursuing their own self-interest.

Happiness Is a Choice

The last chapter focused mainly on how doing for others relates to your happiness. Now we will look more closely at the other side of the ledger—serving your own personal needs.

There is evidence that happiness is at least partly a built-in personality trait, and that some people are made to be happy no matter what, while others are wired for unhappiness. People do seem to differ in their natural "set points" around which their moods fluctuate, and to which they tend to revert after the effect of some influence, positive or negative, wears off. Yet there is nevertheless an extent to which happiness is a choice. It is a matter of attitude, of how you see life, whether you view the glass as half full or half empty. While in part we are captives of brain functioning and personality factors beyond conscious control, there is always space for the operation of reason and will. We can persuade ourselves to override our programming and convince ourselves to see the glass as half full.

And even if we can't change our personalities—and many other things beyond our control—we still do have choices in how we actually live our lives. Pain may be inevitable, but pain and suffering are not the same thing. If we experience pain, we can choose either to embrace it, to wallow in it, to suffer, or we can choose to place our focus instead upon what is still good, positive, fulfilling, and rewarding in our lives, to seek out and immerse ourselves in the things that make us happier. Pain is a given, but suffering is a choice.

We've all heard the cliché that "if life hands you lemons, make lemonade." This may seem superciliously saccharine. Though I have tried to stress what a blessing it is to be alive, it cannot be denied that life does often give us lemons in the form of ordeals or trials. For all this book's upbeat talk, one can't ignore the misery endured by many people. Yet this does not negate the point, but rather makes it all the more compelling. The key thing is not the cards life deals us, but how we choose to play them.

Viktor Frankl was a happy, comfortable, and successful professional man when he was thrown a very big lemon. He lost his wife, family, vocation, home, everything, and was cast into the unspeakable nightmare of a Nazi concentration camp. This modern-day Job did not shake his fist at God over the injustice. Instead, he found within himself the way to deal with his situation and in fact triumph over it.

His book, *Man's Search for Meaning*, explains how. What Frankl discovered in the concentration camp was that the ones who survived were those who, instead of succumbing to despair, managed to envision a future for themselves and still saw meaning in their lives. They refused to be defined by what was happening to them. Thus, while some might deem optimism in the face of such horror to be grotesquely misplaced, Frankl found that, on the contrary, a positive attitude was not only valid but essential. In that pit of suffering and death, Frankl made the choice to affirm life and the meaning of his own life.

I have written that life has no ordained purpose and that this leaves each of us free to find his own way. In Viktor Frankl's words, "what matters is not the meaning of life in general but the specific meaning of a person's life at a given moment." In the concentration camp he found meaning by committing himself to responding to the demands of his situation and interacting humanly with his fellow prisoners.

The actor Christopher Reeve was another man hit with a lemon, a freak accident leaving him almost wholly paralyzed. At first, he couldn't see any reason to go on living. But he ultimately came to find rich meaning in his life: in the love he shared with his family, in working to mend his body, and as an advocate for others with the same problem.

This book has set the value of human life very high. This reflects the reality of how people value their own lives, even under the most daunting circumstances. Be very careful before judging that any human life is not worth living. My mother always used to say, "I'd never want to be eighty," yet now at eighty-five she still loves life. It's hardly surprising that people can cherish life even under conditions of difficulty, loss, and suffering that few of us could even imagine. This was true of Viktor Frankl and Christopher Reeve. It is true of most severely disabled people who in surveys rate their quality of life as good. In fact, patients on breathing machines are found to rate their quality of life higher than other disabled individuals.

Most of us, thank goodness, are not faced with ordeals of the magnitude that Frankl or Reeve confronted. Still, we must do what they did, and look within ourselves for meaning in our lives, even if it's merely to be a good artist, plumber, spouse, or parent. But of course the word "merely" is wrong. The meaningfulness of your life is not to be judged in relation to Frankl's, Reeve's, or Julius Caesar's. The only thing that matters is what life means to *you*. Whether it centers upon raising children, living according to one's values, using one's creative powers, exercising one's will to choose, or expressing love, these meanings are what we must each discover and act upon. This is self-realization. It is the key to being happy, even amid lemons.

One big drag on happiness is worry. Everybody worries. Our tendency to worry is in fact programmed by evolution. Nature doesn't give a hoot whether we are happy, it only cares that we survive and reproduce. Worrying is good for survival because the worrier will be attuned to threats and will try to duck them, always looking over his shoulder, whereas the carefree personality type may be oblivious to danger and fall victim to it. So evolution has made us natural worriers.

We retain that trait even though the threats to survival that early humans faced, like predators and starvation, have largely abated.

While people in some parts of the world still suffer much hardship and peril, and hence genuine worries, we in the advanced Western nations generally do not. In modern society, the direct causes of traditional human misery and worry have been removed. In comparison to our forebears, we live like kings, with plenteous food, comfort, safety, and entertainment. We inhabit a land of milk and honey.

So, no longer needing to worry about things like saber-toothed tigers or finding food, but still possessing worry genes, we transfer the worrying to lesser things. We worry about minor things and remote threats. We tend to imagine possible disasters and worry about them, even though most such possibilities will never come to pass. However, once you understand that a lot of your worrying occurs because nature originally wanted you to worry about saber-toothed tigers, and not because your worries are really that serious, it is possible to persuade yourself to worry less.

But there still is of course one very big thing that everybody worries about that is not just a potential threat but a certainty. We are all headed for the same destination, and it's not a land of milk and honey. How can one live happily under a death sentence?

Happiness *is* a choice. We have no choice about someday dying, but we do have a choice whether to worry about it.

Again, death is a defining feature of the human condition and, as such, merits some contemplation. It must ineffably influence how we live our lives. But we are not obligated to brood about it. You could spend your whole life gnashing your teeth that you won't live forever, and thereby lose not only that eternal future but effectively the present as well.[30]

The idea of future nonexistence *is* frightening in the highest degree. To contemplate this deeply is inimical to my happiness. So I make the choice not to go there. If I catch myself trying to get my mind around the concept, I literally force myself to stop. (I'm doing that now, as I write this.) Is this "denial"? No. I have reached an understanding of death. Having done that, I now choose to think about alternate topics.

---

30. Henry James's story "The Beast in the Jungle" concerns a man who spends his life in suspension waiting for a special, unique fate he feels certain will be his. It turns out that his unique fate was to waste his life waiting for it.

And look at it this way: your existence, your consciousness, and your ability to enjoy the conditions of life are all matters of cosmic fortuity. All this you've been given. Does it make any sense to gripe that you weren't given immortality as well? Life is a colossal gift, even if it's only temporary. Take the gift, seize it, use it, enjoy it, and don't waste it by brooding over what you cannot have.

Consider this as well: the certainty of death serves the salutary purpose of putting all our other troubles and worries in perspective. For example, suppose you are fretting about an upcoming exam. Now, even if you flunk the exam, the repercussions cannot be nearly as bad as dying. Yet here you are, worrying about the former but not the latter! Is that logical? If you insist on worrying about something, at least death is a big thing. But if you have made the choice to forgo worrying about that very big thing, then it hardly makes sense to be suffering instead over small stuff.

Furthermore, it is rational to refuse to brood about death precisely because it cannot be avoided. To think about being safe and healthy, how to *postpone* death, makes sense, because those things are within our control. Still, people often worry not only about mortality, but about many other things beyond their control. This serves no purpose except heartache. It is more rational and productive to focus on problems you can do something about.

It's true that luck plays a big role in life. But it's also a fact that optimists tend to have better luck than pessimists. It's really so, and it is because luck isn't entirely random. Positive thinking people make their luck. The best example I can think of is meeting my wife. It certainly was a stroke of luck to be in the same place at the same time. But it would not have occurred had I not dragged myself from a sickbed to attend a singles event. I did it because I believed that by sparing no effort I'd eventually find the right woman. I believed I'd get lucky—if I gave Lady Luck all possible help.

So again, it's not the cards you're dealt, it's how you play them. And it's also a fact that a positive attitude makes you a better player. One can't control all aspects of life, but by focusing on things you can control, you get a feeling of mastery and the impetus to be proactive, as in my personal example above. This sense of mastery makes you feel good about yourself, initiating a virtuous feedback loop. There is even evidence that mental attitude correlates positively with physical health. Negativity, in contrast, tends to have baleful effects on both mind and body and makes for a debilitating sense of disempowerment. The pessimist would not have made the effort of going to that singles event and would instead have remained in bed bemoaning his illness as well as his inability to meet that special someone.

One common thing we worry too much about is how we appear to others. This is yet again something nature programmed into us in order to enhance DNA copying. People with higher status tend to have more and better mating opportunities, so we are engineered to crave status. Women in particular are attracted by potential mates' status, and this is a key reason why men strive to increase their wealth. (Aristotle Onassis said that "if women didn't exist, all the money in the world would have no meaning.") But here again, we must be mindful whether this status fixation truly serves our own interests rather than DNA's. Lust for status is too deeply embedded in the human psyche to say we should just shrug it off. But we should at least understand what's really at play so that we can keep a proper perspective.

Status, by definition, concerns how others perceive us. Obviously, it does matter what our loved ones think of us as well as our friends, co-workers, or others with whom we have continuing connections; and, yes, potential mates. It is rational to care about how they see us. But *what strangers think of us does not matter.*

Imagine yourself at a crowded bus stop and you experience a wardrobe malfunction so your pants fall down. Embarrassing? Yes. But what does that mean if all the people watching are strangers? They may consider you a boob and laugh at you; may even remember the incident for decades. But whatever goes on in their minds, it has *absolutely no effect on you.* The actual impact upon you is no different than if there was no audience at all.

If this seems counterintuitive, ask yourself how, if at all, the impression of you in a stranger's mind affects you. And suppose you thought you were alone and unobserved at the bus stop, but actually some hidden stranger was watching. Does it make any difference whether you were truly unobserved or seen without your knowing it? In both cases the consequences for you are identical. The stranger's perception is irrelevant.

So, in programming you to worry about how any other person sees you, nature is playing a trick on you. It is making you think something matters when it really doesn't. And the choice is yours whether to slavishly go with the programming and worry about what everyone thinks of you or break free of that pointless programming and refuse to concern yourself with things that do not actually matter to you.

But the implications are far broader than worrying about how we look to strangers at a bus stop.

When I was young, I believed my life would be wasted if I did not make my mark on the world and become famous. It felt like the way to give my life meaning. And I actually got my fifteen minutes of fame,[31] in a small way at least, when a book I wrote about local politics was published. This proved a useful corrective. I had imagined that my book would apotheosize me, lift me onto some higher plane of existence. It didn't. (I still had trouble getting dates.) The experience caused me to reconsider how I was looking at my life and what I hoped to get out of it.

We all come to the same end. Death awaits famous people and commoners alike. We may remember Julius Caesar, but a fat lot of good it does *him*. He has turned to dust and gains no benefit from his enduring fame. Fame is ultimately meaningless for the same reason that what strangers at a bus stop think of you is meaningless: because it is all in the minds of people with whom you have no connection. As far as your own life is concerned, they might just as well be stone gargoyles.

Of course, even if one can analyze others' opinions of us into oblivion, fame and status are undeniably pleasurable to us because we

---

31. The artist Andy Warhol once said, "In the future everyone will be famous for fifteen minutes." Somehow, this inanity itself became famous.

are programmed to crave them. During his lifetime, Julius Caesar no doubt got satisfaction from his fame. But the point is to keep your eye on the ball. The bottom line, what really matters to you, is not what goes on in the minds of others, but in your *own mind*. The true aim is your happiness. Fame and status are just means for achieving it. They can add points to your lifetime happiness score, but because they rest on something ultimately meaningless (artifacts in the minds of strangers), they cannot be the foundation for your happiness. It is no surprise that many people who put the drive for status at the center of their lives find, when they achieve it, that it's hollow and that it has not made them happy. Do not envy them their status.

But understand, too, that if fame and status are somewhat hollow in and of themselves, *achievements*, which bring status, are not. Indeed, part of why we love status is because we see it as a *proxy* for achievement. We assume that high status comes from doing something to deserve it. And accomplishment is an authentic source of meaning for one's life. While I did get a crumb of fame and status from my political book, I derive more happiness from knowing that I wrote something that was good, that made a contribution to the literature on the subject, and that may have helped to educate and influence some people in a positive way. To achieve worthwhile things, and to derive satisfaction from doing so, is a sterling ingredient of happiness.

People gain particular satisfaction and find meaning through the exercise of their aptitudes, talents, and capabilities. What we enjoy most is what we do best. As psychologist Abraham Maslow wrote, "A musician must make music, an artist must paint, a poet must write." This he called self-actualization, or the process of becoming everything one is capable of becoming. We hear a lot about self-esteem as the foundation for achievement in life, but this puts the cart before the horse. Self-esteem comes from achievement, not vice versa. You feel good about yourself when you do things to feel good about.

And, of course, one cannot talk about happiness without bringing up love, which is really the best thing in life, both being loved and feeling love for another. Beyond question, a great many of us find meaning in our lives through love. This, too, is in part a matter of choice. We choose to bond with others, to marry, and what we will make of those bonds. Love is something you can give or withhold. The more of it you give, the more you get back, and the happier you will be.[32]

We also choose whether to have children and what kind of parents we are to become. Though I have stressed that we are not mere servants of nature's sole concern that we reproduce, nevertheless our greatest creative act is procreation. There is no more exalted way to find meaning in one's life than through launching another one. To our children we pass along far more than our genes. We also pass along who we are as people. Whether or not God made humanity, we each make our children. And if you are concerned with improving the world through adding to human happiness, your child is a person whose happiness you are not just augmenting, but entirely responsible for creating. That's a tremendous contribution to the global welfare score.

I also derive happiness from having made myself and my family financially secure; from playing around with coins and pride in my collection of them; from reading stimulating books; from music, art, savory food, and sunshine; and from observing the human pageant. I'm gaining satisfaction from working on this book. I derive happiness from my positive outlook upon what humanity has achieved and what mountains I believe we can yet surmount.

All these things are ingredients in the stew of meaning for one's life. And all represent a *choice*. That's what freedom is, to make choices for ourselves. I myself could choose to lament that I never achieved my youthful dreams of political or literary fame. I could choose to look at the world and focus on war, poverty, hunger, suffering; to look at humankind and see only stupidities and cruelties. I could choose to look at my own future and see death. The "half-empty glass" personality might embrace all those negative lines of thought. But I'm a positive-thinking optimist. *I choose happiness.*

---

32. A 2004 study suggested that a good marriage confers happiness equivalent to $100,000 of additional income.

Satisfaction

Deep thinkers sanctimoniously denounce the materialism of modern consumer society. Mostly, this is empty posturing, as one does not generally see these social critics living in caves and wearing animal skins. In fact, the desire to improve one's condition of life is altogether fundamental to human nature—and it drives virtually all human endeavor. Everything that anyone produces results from a desire to enhance his own life by reaping a benefit from his labors. Everything anybody buys is bought to add to the enjoyment of life. Were it not for this yearning of all people to make their lives better, happier, more comfortable, we would all still be living in caves and wearing animal skins, because that urge is the indispensable incentive motivating all the work, all the striving, all the innovation, all the risk taking, that has brought us up from the caves to the gleaming cities we now inhabit.

Recognizing this, the Declaration of Independence deemed the "pursuit of happiness" a fundamental human right. And it should be considered absolutely wonderful that so many people have attained such affluence that they can afford to indulge in so many of the kinds of purchases that social critics decry as materialist consumerism. Better this than poverty and squalor.

But a high proportion of spending by affluent people really is not so much aimed at materially improving their quality of life as it is about vanity, ego, and feeding self-perception of status. We have already discussed how nature programs us to crave status but that this is really a somewhat hollow pursuit. And while status can be a proxy for achievement, flaunting status disconnected from achievement is something else.

Rolex watches or the like are de rigueur for the wealthy. Are they better than ordinary watches? Well, yes, somewhat; but the difference in true useful value to the wearer of a Rolex is not remotely proportional to the huge difference in cost. In truth, a man does not buy a Rolex mainly for the sake of its quality; he buys it primarily to proclaim, "I am a man who can afford a Rolex." What he gets in return for his expenditure is the psychic satisfaction of feeling rich, and showing the world he's rich.[33]

Wine is another example. Certain bottles are very expensive. Most such wine is probably consumed not by true connoisseurs who can appreciate the quality difference but, rather, by people with less refined palates who buy it not so much to enjoy the wine as to enjoy telling themselves and the world, "Look at me, I'm drinking $100 wine!" And when telephone service was first provided (expensively of course) from airplanes, the first call I overheard was by a man who had absolutely nothing to say except "Hey, I'm calling from an airplane!" Thorstein Veblen coined the term "conspicuous consumption" to describe this.

This is how some people use their money in pursuit of happiness. Undoubtedly, ownership of a Rolex and drinking costly wine *does* confer some happiness. But a person who needs to validate his status by showy expenditure must not feel very confident and secure about himself. After all, if a man can afford a Rolex, he shouldn't need to actually buy one to feel good about his status. One fellow tells himself, "Look at me, I've got a Rolex"; the other guy tells himself, "I

---

33. There are actually even costlier watches for the super-rich. But Rolex's marketing has been enviable, making its watches expensive enough to possess that crucial cachet, while still being widely affordable.

could afford a Rolex, but I don't need to waste my money that way." Which is better?

Now, there is no harm in wasting money if one has so much that it does not make him noticeably poorer.[34] But that is not true for most people. Too many spend money up to the limit of their ability and beyond, often racking up hefty credit card debts (with their associated big interest burdens), buying today in hopes of somehow being able to pay it off tomorrow. And, consequently, for many people, money is a constant source of trouble, anxiety, and conflict (it is certainly a prime cause of marital discord). Whatever enjoyment and satisfaction they might otherwise get from the things they buy is canceled out by the financial insecurity and worry they also buy for themselves in the process.

The point was forcefully made by a Dickens character, sitting in debtor's prison. "Annual income twenty pounds," he said, "annual expenditure nineteen pounds . . . happiness! Income twenty pounds, expenditure twenty pounds and sixpence: misery!" (Dickens knew whereof he wrote. His father suffered in debtor's prison, and he, too, suffered in consequence.) We no longer have debtor's prison, but even today being in debt is no picnic. At the very least, it entails worry, worry, worry. It's not a formula for a happy life.

In *The Millionaire Next Door*, authors Thomas J. Stanley and William D. Danko contrast people who live prudently and build wealth against others who spend freely and don't. Of course, for most of us, no prodigies of saving will make us millionaires. And one may query the point of accumulating wealth if you're not spending and enjoying it. The point, in fact, is that the financial independence and security one thereby gains is itself an enormous source of satisfaction and happiness. Most Americans actually do earn enough that it's possible to achieve this while still enjoying a genuinely good lifestyle. The result is more true happiness and satisfaction than can conceivably be gained through lavish spending.

---

34. Though one could argue for harm in that the money wasted could instead have been donated to a worthy cause, its owner had no *obligation* to do that.

Perfectionism is also relevant here. Some people set very high standards for themselves. They must be the best and have the best. If Rolexes exist, an ordinary watch won't do. If first-class airline seats are available, they wouldn't be caught dead flying coach. Of course, perfection is very hard to achieve in this world, and for the perfectionist, the world is continually falling short. Such people live in a perpetual state of dissatisfaction.

Barry Schwartz, in *The Paradox of Choice*, distinguishes between "maximizers" who, on a purchase decision, for example, insist on ferreting out the best possible deal, and "satisficers" who end their search upon finding something merely good enough. One might think maximizers gain more happiness with their superior buys; yet the opposite can actually be true, when considering the downside of maximizers' agonizing over options and second-guessing even after deciding. For such people, having more choices can be a curse, not a blessing, if it means more to fret over. Thus, the "maximizing" mentality is often in fact self-defeating, and garners less real satisfaction than does "satisficing."

As all the foregoing implies, it is essential to be, in fact, *satisfied*—satisfied with what one has, in contrast to lusting after what one lacks. Here again, one's general outlook on life comes into play. Through my eyes, I am living in Candide's "best of all possible worlds." Voltaire put that phrase satirically in Candide's mouth, but I am highly mindful of how much progress there has been since his time, making the world incomparably better. We in America are especially blessed, not only with the highest of material well-being, but with liberty as well, something decidedly uncommon in the world's history. For me the glass is not just half full, it is full to brimming.

Given that, a Rolex would add nothing. But this is not the psychological matrix most people seem to inhabit. For too many, the half-empty glass mentality prevails. Their focus is not on all that they have, but, rather, on what they want to add to it. They are not satisfied, and, indeed, with that psychology, satisfaction is never really attainable because, no matter how much they achieve and acquire, there is always something more to gain. The glass never gets full, but always remains half empty. Thus, in polls over the last half century, during which average real-dollar incomes more than doubled, the percentage of Americans professing happiness has not budged.

In his 1840 book about this country, Alexis de Tocqueville queried "Why Americans are so often restless in the midst of their prosperity," and answered that in a society premised on equality, people are not so accepting of differing fortunes among them. This helps explain how we judge the quality of our lives. Americans don't compare themselves with Zambians or with people of past eras. Instead, their reference group is others like themselves. "Keeping up with the Joneses" is a powerful force.[35] A red-blooded American, eyeing his more affluent neighbor, sees no reason why he shouldn't be equal. In this light, what he possesses is not enough, even if it's a thousand times more than what a Zambian has.

Schwartz's book suggests we aren't grateful for our blessings because of the "adaptation" effect: quite simply, we get so acclimated to having them that we become oblivious to them. We also measure everything against expectations. That too explains why higher incomes don't increase the sense of happiness—as living standards rise, so do expectations; we live better, but merely at the level we now expect; so we don't feel any better. It's like a dog chasing its tail. Thus, Americans with affluence unparalleled in human experience do not perceive what a blessing this is.

All this also explains, at least in part, why Americans are such hard workers. We are driven to keep up with the Joneses. Undoubtedly this has contributed to America's remarkable economic advancement and high standard of living, which, of course, is ultimately bottomed on productive work. A contrast is often drawn with Europeans, who don't work as many hours and, therefore, produce less stellar economic per-

---

35. In other words, what matters most to people is their *relative* prosperity, not its absolute level. A study of Harvard students found that they'd prefer to earn $50,000 while their peers get $25,000 than to earn $100,000 if their peers are getting $200,000. The satisfaction of beating out the Joneses was apparently worth half their income!

formance. However, an alternate view is that the European attitude toward work reflects not a problem, but something positive, namely, a deliberate choice to take life a little easier, with more leisure time and vacations and less hard work, earlier retirement, and so on, sacrificing on money and material possessions yet gaining in true quality of life. It's worth thinking about.[36]

Another thing life teaches is that gratifying a desire rarely lives up to expectations. Something you don't yet have always seems more desirable than what you do have. As George Bernard Shaw said, "There are two great disappointments in life—not getting what you want and getting it." This is certainly true in coin collecting. An item you don't have, but want, may seem ever so cool. Acquiring it does provide a thrill. But that fades, and when the coin is in your collection, somehow it no longer seems quite as marvelous as when you didn't have it. The real thrill is the "the thrill of the hunt." That's why many collectors experience a letdown after achieving some goal, such as completing a series. Thus, the key thing is not to get all the coins you want, but instead to have coins to hunt for. A not-yet-complete collection gives more joy than a completed one!

Likewise with everything else one seeks in life, the key thing is not the destination but the journey, not the getting but the questing. It puts more spice in life to have something to look forward to than to actually get it. Hence, one secret for happiness is deferred gratification. Do not satisfy desires right away, but, instead, give yourself things to look forward to. There can be more pleasure in an hour of anticipating an

---

36. However, the European phenomenon may be less a function of personal preferences than of different economic incentives such as generous pension benefits. Meantime, Americans' work ethic partly reflects how profoundly they identify themselves with their jobs and find their lives' meaning in their work. This, too, is a valid and even admirable approach to life. But, in saying that Americans go a bit too far with it, perhaps the Europeans have a point. It's a cliché that no one on his deathbed says, "I wish I had spent more time at the office."

ice cream than in the five minutes of eating it. And certainly deferred gratification is better for happiness than immediate indulgence if the cost of the latter is financial distress. Dickens had it right. Living within one's means makes for happiness. Living beyond one's means is a recipe for misery.

It is true, as I've written, that the human tendency to always want more has been the crucial driver of all progress. We should not try to squelch it. But each person has the choice of how to live and must try to figure out whether an acquisitive psychology is really a route to happiness. For too many people there is a toxic tension between their wants and their means. Either they buy the Rolex, at a cost of financial anxiety, or else force themselves to forgo it and gnash their teeth to do so. In either case the Rolex, and the desire for it, represents not a healthy striving to improve one's life, but a curse that degrades its quality.

To me, the ordinary watch I wear is *good enough*. It does the job a watch is supposed to do. But I don't forget that it is an absolute marvel of engineering and manufacture. For most of history no such watches existed (and many people still cannot afford even an ordinary watch). So, you see, it is very important that when I say *good enough* about my watch, and so many other aspects of my family's very typical lifestyle—our house, our car, our food, and so on—my emphasis is very much on the *good*. Our lifestyle is not what any American today would call lavish, but we are very much living the *good life*. Our "good enough" lives are very good indeed. To spend one single second lamenting that my watch is not a Rolex would be simply absurd. And for anyone to be unhappy because he feels such a life is not good enough is tragic.

Economists say "Don't let the perfect be the enemy of the good." This means one mustn't reject a good solution to a problem just because there is some theoretically better one that (because of politics, for example) can't be implemented. This is a useful principle for the public sphere, but also for the personal as well. We have very good lives. Don't let an ideal of perfection be your enemy and undermine enjoyment of the good life you have.

The focus of this chapter has been on the getting of things. But, as a final point, acquiring stuff is not anyway what life is all about. Many of us are cynics who think society is pervasively materialistic. Yet, if stranded on a deserted island, wouldn't you miss human contact far more than possessions? Social concerns, not material ones, are what really dominate our lives. Our true focus is not on consumer goods, which we get so effortlessly, but rather on our interpersonal relations, so much more interesting to us and so laden with stimulating challenge. Indeed, much of the importance we attach to material possessions is in how we think they affect the way others relate to us. It's in those human relations, not materialism, that we find our real happiness.

Consciousness, Thought, and Personal Responsibility

We have already alluded to the puzzle that is consciousness. It is indeed one of the great ineffable mysteries, and it lies at the heart of what it means to be human. Science does not have a complete answer. The problem may be closer to the realm of philosophy, of metaphysics, than science.

Some people imagine there is a "ghost in the machine," that the *mind* and the *brain* are somehow distinct, that the mind is not necessarily rooted in the brain's physicality. But such spooky notions fly in the face of what reason tells us about reality. We know that our minds must arise out of what goes on within our brains; there really can be no other possible source. And this is confirmed by science, which, through advanced brain imaging techniques, has found that everything we do is associated with brain activity. Even thoughts and emotions are seen to be correlated to physical things happening in our brains; indeed, those brain events are little different when we perform actions than when we merely think about them.

We do understand pretty well how the brain works, how it stores information, and how it receives and processes signals. But the issue is how that physical reality of neuron function somehow gives rise to the metaphenomenon, overlaid on top of all the processing of signals, that we experience as consciousness, something that does not *seem* physical or material at all. Consciousness is the sense of self, the "me" that we all experience, caring about what happens to us, making decisions, feeling emotions, and the seamless continuum of this phenomenon over all the decades of life, with all our experiences constantly being referenced back against our coherent personal narratives made up of our past histories, beliefs, and modes of thought. We don't fully understand how this sense of self arises. Perhaps it can even be considered an illusion.

But a very good metaphor for the human mind is a computer running programs. Our brains are akin to the hardware, our thoughts the output of running software (of which we are generally not aware). The more I have studied and pondered consciousness, the more I am convinced that this is indeed a very useful way to conceptualize what our minds do.[37]

Computers, of course, are not conscious, and this raises the question of what is different about our brains. Conceivably, it is just a matter of complexity. No computer has ever yet approached the degree of complexity of the interconnections among our neurons, and perhaps if that could be reproduced in an artificial system, self-awareness might arise.[38] But in any case, we still don't know what it is about such complexity that causes consciousness.

The problem can be appreciated by looking at a different model people have often used to explain consciousness—that there is a sort of captain at the helm, inside our brains, running things, and that captain represents our "me-ness." But then one realizes that the putative

---

37. I use the word "metaphor" rather than "model" because, in reality, brains and computers work very differently—the brain actually has a far richer repertoire of methods for representing and processing information.

38. Some people question whether "artificial intelligence" is even possible. However, our minds are mysterious but not mystical. They arise through something happening among our neurons and their transmission of signals. There is no reason, in principle, why this could not be replicated artificially even though it is beyond our current capabilities. (And whether an artificial intelligence has "human rights" could one day become a genuine issue.)

captain himself requires a brain and consciousness, so this model ultimately explains nothing. Similarly, we might conceptualize eye function by imagining visual signals somehow projected onto a screen in the brain, viewed by a little person (the "me") who makes sense of them. But, of course, how does that little person see and process images? Is there another little person inside *his* brain? Again, this is a chicken-and-egg dead end.

You begin to grasp the difficulty.

Woody Allen's film *Everything You Always Wanted to Know about Sex* had a marvelous imaginary depiction of the brain's control room, but there didn't seem to be any connection between the technicians there, running all the body's systems, and the person's selfhood. The man himself was missing from the control room. (And that may have been a fair portrayal of reality, at least according to one theorist, Daniel Dennett, who has argued for a somewhat chaotic model of the mind, with no captain at the helm and a crowd of first mates fighting over the wheel.)

An interesting book, *Thought as a System*, by David Bohm, addresses the seemingly simple question, what is thought? As you may have now guessed, this is not really a simple question at all. What actually goes on in our brains when we think we are thinking?

Most of us conceive thought as a volitional process, subject to our will, with our minds in charge (in contrast to functions on "automatic pilot" like breathing and digestion). Again, as though there is a captain in your brain, consciously directing things, so that when your thoughts proceed from Point A to Point B it is because you have chosen to go down that path and had the option to do otherwise. But Bohm invokes, here too, the analogy of a computer running programs. We "think" because we have software in our brains for thinking, just as a computer can add numbers because it has arithmetic software telling it how to do that.

Of course, in a computer program no volition is involved. The computer has no choice about the path; it will always go from Point A to Point B if that's what its program directs. If asked to add two and two, it will always go through exactly the same steps and get four. This is like traveling along a railroad track, with no option to deviate from the set path.

How different is human thought? We imagine it as more like tramping in an open field, where we can go in any direction we like. Yet, if we are running the equivalent of programs, they are guiding our thought processes much like programs guide computer processing, which makes human thought really a lot more like traveling along a railroad track than in an open field. If we think our way from Point A to Point B, it is not so much volitional as it is the result of our programming. The outcome can be preordained so that when we think we are making judgments, choices, and decisions, what is really happening is more like what happens when you ask a computer to add two and two. It will always get four, because its program sends it along a preconfigured path to get there.

We know this is true from everyday experience. Certainly it seems many people's thoughts and beliefs are as though programmed. They tend to be predictable in their choices, their decisions, and the ways they react to situations. This is not to say we are machines, automatons doomed always to run along railroad tracks. The human mind is exceedingly complex, and every person is certainly capable of thinking his way out from the dictates of his programs. But that takes special effort. Most of our thinking does not involve such effort. Most people, most of the time, when they think they are thinking, do seem to be just running their programs, with preordained results.

Some of this software is built as we develop, a product of our learning and life experiences. But much is preinstalled as what we call "human nature." Some people hate this concept, preferring to imagine we are born as "blank slates," totally moldable by our environment or by social engineering. (This notion of human malleability, and hence perfectibility, has been a huge wellspring of political evil, as with the example of communism.) Science, however, has debunked the "blank slate" idea, finding that there really is a universal human nature with which we are all born, wired into our genes by evolution, and not amenable to tinkering. It's a crucial component of our thinking software.

Using this software is not necessarily bad. It certainly doesn't mean our thinking produces wrong answers. Four is of course the right answer when a computer adds two and two. For our species to survive, we had to evolve our software to produce right answers. And without it, our minds would probably be chaotic and would crash like a computer does when it goes on the fritz. Our software is what keeps us sane. So the point is not to reject programmed thought and its results but rather to know them for what they are. By doing so, we can superimpose another program, a metaprogram, over them; one that is more within our control—what we call "will"— allowing us to think more deeply, to think beyond the limitations of our programs.

The issue of free will has traditionally been a conundrum of religion. If Joe is faced with a choice between good and evil, doesn't an omniscient God *know* how Joe will choose? And isn't Joe's decision God's will? So does Joe really have a choice? Does he have free will?

But this issue also fundamentally arises, outside of religion, from our discussion above concerning the nature of thought. If a person's choices and decisions really result from the equivalent of running programs, as though traveling along fixed railroad tracks, can it be said that he is exercising free will? Can he be deemed morally responsible for the results?

Our society is more and more receptive to explanations of human behavior that abjure concepts of free will and personal responsibility in favor of seeing people as actuated by forces beyond their control. When we do wrong, guilt and shame are powerful and painful feelings, so naturally we cast about for some rationalization to squirm out from them and exonerate ourselves. "The devil made me do it" was the old excuse. Today's excuses are analogous. People grow fat because McDonald's seduced them into eating all those fries, or their violence was caused by violent TV shows. There was even a case of an attempted suicide blamed on a rock band's song. We run up against this again and again. People's bad behaviors are ascribed not to character deficiencies but rather to all sorts of "disorders," making them seem more like medical conditions than personal failings, or to things that happened to them in childhood. Anything to avoid the stark idea of personal responsibility.

This is all of a piece with nonjudgmentalism and moral relativism, something I will discuss later, which undermines the dichotomy between right and wrong. Pop psychology exalts feelings as some sort of irresistible force that must be respected regardless of where it leads. We don't want anyone to have to feel bad, so we create a culture of excuses, cop-outs, and victimhood to relieve ourselves of any need to feel guilty about our actions, behaviors, and choices.

This concept opposite to free will is *determinism*. It claims that everything we do can be attributed to causes, not just the inevitable output when we process certain inputs through our mental software, as already discussed, but also, in back of that, the genetic and environmental influences that molded the software in the first place.

The issue comes down to whether there really is a "self" in the mind, running the show and making decisions. While it's far from clear in the case of lower animals, humans have minds far more complex than what other animals possess, minds that equip us to make choices about our behavior by consciously weighing potential consequences. In doing this, language is a crucial tool, which other animals lack. Language gives us the means for sophisticated and complex evaluation. And in saying we do this "consciously," I mean that, even if we are running programs, there is nevertheless an awareness of the process that a computer or lower animal doesn't have. When a human thinks, even if he's really going along a railroad track, there is still a function of mind attending to it, monitoring it, and assessing it. Even if your thought response to something is reflexive, there is another part of your mind capable of recognizing that fact. Once more, it's the thing we call "will" that can exert some control. Computers and animals don't have recourse to will.

The result is that it certainly *seems* we have a self and free will. It feels to us as though we do. And it's reasonable for us to act accordingly. We are not prisoners of determinism the way animals are. We are different, and have minds capable of deciding how to behave. Even if something like a childhood history of abuse, for instance, can have a big impact on one's psyche and behavior, not all people with such a background follow the same trajectory. In the final analysis, the choice is yours whether to run your software or let it run you; to let your past dictate your future, or to cast off such a straitjacket and be the master of your life.

Even if mental processes are seen as beyond conscious control, society need not—and should not—care what people *think*. Instead, the only concern is what they *do*. And there is a big difference between thought and action. While people might not be able to control their thoughts, everyone must be deemed capable of controlling his actions.[39]

At the simplest level, personal responsibility means facing up to the fact that our actions have consequences. This necessity to confront reality is the essence of what is called *existentialism*. It tells us that we live truly only when we accept the challenges of existence and make free choices in response to them. Existentialism declares that to deny responsibility for our actions is an evasion of reality and violates our human duty to live authentically.

The difficulty is that causality may be complex. When something bad happens, there may be a whole chain of relevant circumstances, any one of which, if changed, would have meant a different outcome. That can make it all too easy for us to deflect responsibility from our own actions to some extraneous factor, allowing us to evade an uncomfortable feeling of guilt.

If a wet dish slips from my hand and breaks, I can tell myself it wasn't my fault. I dropped it not because I was a klutz, but because it was wet. Of course, this would obviously be a cop-out. I should have realized it was wet and handled it more attentively. It *was* my fault that it broke, even though other factors were at play too. This is often the case. When something bad happens, even though other factors were

---

39. Apart from real lunatics whose minds are so scrambled that they cannot be said to act as rational creatures at all.

involved, frequently the bad outcome could have been avoided if someone had been more on the ball or had acted better.

Accepting such responsibility for our conduct is part of facing the reality of the world. It is only by doing so, by grappling with truth, that genuine understanding and accomplishment can be achieved. And making a mistake is not generally such a terrible thing to accept. A baseball batter who hits .400 is reckoned exceptionally good even though he is failing 60 percent of the time. No one can bat 1.000 in life. We all make mistakes; it's normal and inevitable. "To err is human." To feel guilty for doing something wrong is also natural, but you needn't feel it makes you an unworthy person.

Yet vanity keeps many people from taking responsibility for their mistakes. They don't want to see themselves as imperfect, don't want others to see them as such, and don't want to experience guilt or shame. Of course, this is a refusal to accept reality. And the irony is that it makes the mistake worse and the fault greater when the person responsible denies it or tries to cover it up.[40] If instead you own up to your mistake, express contrition, and do everything you can to fix it, this assuages feelings of guilt, allowing you to legitimately feel better about yourself. You are indeed a better person than one who denies and covers up. In fact, while some people fear that others won't like and respect them if they're imperfect, in truth, a willingness to acknowledge your faults actually makes others like and respect you more. Thus, to accept personal responsibility truly better serves your own needs, your vanity, and your ego.[41]

Taking responsibility for our actions is the essence of participating

---

40. In politics it's said that the cover-up is worse than the crime. President Nixon lost his office for trying to conceal wrongdoing that, by itself, would not have been such a big deal.

41. The other side of the coin is excessive guilt—blaming yourself because something did not turn out for the best. But not everything does, and it's not always someone's fault. Some of us even feel guilty over our successes—believing them undeserved. But, whether guilt feelings are justified or not, nobody is perfect. Everyone messes up sometimes, and doing so doesn't make you unworthy.

in human society. In exchange for the protections and benefits of society, we all accept the need to control our actions and to restrain our impulses and appetites. If you see someone weaker than you with a candy bar you'd like, you restrain yourself from grabbing it. A more realistic example, perhaps, is the restraint that married people use on a daily basis when confronted with the powerful urges that accompany close contact with an attractive person of the opposite sex.[42]

This brings to mind Plato's metaphor of the human soul as a chariot pulled by the two horses, reason and emotion, which of course often pull in opposite directions. Having a matched pair of horses would make for a smoother ride, but we must wonder what sort of uninteresting creatures we'd actually be if, like *Star Trek*'s Mr. Spock, we lived without emotion. Obviously, emotion is essential to the richness of our inner lives. We would not want to give it up or even, really, to suppress it too much. What we want instead is to get the two horses of reason and emotion to work as a team.[43]

This means using our reason to put a brake on our emotions. Other animals don't have reason and can't control their behavior as humans can. This is a key difference between man and beast, by grace of which our civilization was built. Our rise would have been impossible without using the rational parts of our minds to control our behavior.

Admittedly, all this is to some extent an oversimplification. Mental compulsions motivating people can be powerful and resisting them may not be easy. But resisting them is what society requires, *what it must*

---

42. Jimmy Carter once famously confessed to committing "adultery in [his] heart"; that is, lusting for a woman not his wife. I do not believe that thoughts can be crimes. (Whether they can be sins I leave to religion.) Thoughts are, indeed, often beyond our control; and I would invoke the legal principle "no harm, no crime" (which is not applied nearly enough). No one is harmed by thoughts upon which no action is taken.

43. And we shouldn't think of them as irreconcilable. Many emotions are actually informed by reason—about our self-interest and needs, for example. Our loves can also be at least partly grounded in reason. That's true not only of love for people but also our love for such abstract ideas as justice and freedom, which can be quite emotional.

require. If people are deemed to have no control over their behavior, what would be the point of having laws concerning behavior? If society instead tolerates our acting on our impulses, thus excusing the harm to others, then it is all over and we are back to the law of the jungle.

In his book *Civilization and Its Discontents*, Sigmund Freud portrayed humans as universally motivated by primal forces of lust, anger, hatred, greed, and so on, that boil up from the unconscious. The key "discontent" of civilization is its requirement that we suppress these motivations, resist the actions toward which they propel us, and hence deny our true natures. This makes civilization an ill-fitting garment in which we cannot be completely comfortable. Yet Freud recognized that our conscious will is, after all, powerful enough to override our impulses so as to enable us to live in society. And we make that effort because the benefit of living in an ordered civilization vastly outweighs what we might gain by giving our base instincts free rein. We each suppress our own animal impulses in exchange for other people suppressing theirs so that we can all live in peace and harmony.

My wife and I disagreed about a local tragedy in which a man, under a lot of psychological stress, set fire to a building. Children died. My wife believed he was not culpable because he was beset by circumstances and forces within him that he could not control. While I felt sorry for the man, I also felt that no matter what may have been going on in his mind, lighting that match was not an involuntary act. He had the option of not doing it and, as a human being and a member of society, he was obligated to stop his impulse to light it.

We stop our impulses every day. Under normal circumstances it is not so hard. This arson was an extreme case and in such cases it is often difficult to exercise restraint. But it is precisely in such extreme cases—where life and death are at stake—that the requirement to restrain our impulses is all the more imperative. Society cannot exist otherwise.

In the final analysis, human freedom requires our free will. In a deterministic world, the whole idea of liberty is ultimately meaningless. It is through deploying our will in making decisions and choices about how we conduct ourselves that we live as free people.

Always Question

"Think for yourself" may sound trite. But, as we have seen, most people don't realize that when they think they are thinking, often their minds are actually just running along the railroad tracks laid down by the software that has grown up in their brains. However, once you do understand this, it is possible to jump the tracks and *really* think for yourself.

Socrates told us never to stop asking questions about accepted opinions. Be wary of conventional wisdom, the preconceptions and assumptions blithely shared by peers—or what social psychologists call "groupthink." Be skeptical of authority (university professors or public officials, for example). Such widely shared and seemingly authoritative opinion can be spectacularly wrong. Not so long ago in America, virtually all white people believed blacks mentally inferior. This was the conventional wisdom of the time. Anyone thinking differently was considered weird. And in Germany in the 1930s it would have been hard to find any non-Jew who didn't buy into the Nazi ideology. This was the very nation that had been the world's epicenter for civilization, education, culture, science, and philosophy! Yet the Germans succumbed to Nazi groupthink, shouted themselves hoarse for it, and goose-stepped straight into Hell.

Though extreme, this was by no means a unique case. Another was the atrocious Serbian crimes of the 1990s. One despaired of hearing any Serb voice, anywhere, denounce these deeds and hold Serbians in the wrong. Instead, nationalist groupthink was pervasive among them.

So do be careful about breathing in ideas that fill the air around you. When listening to professors or politicians or advocates spouting from moralistic high horses, remember what such voices in 1930s Germany or 1990s Serbia were spouting, and how right they sounded to their audiences. And don't swallow everything in this book either. Always question.

Parents are another source of authority from which we absorb ideas. It's true that rebellion against what parents represent is a common streak in human nature, and some researchers say parental influence is less important than we suppose, with peer influence being stronger. Nevertheless, our brain software owes a lot to parental programming. This is certainly true in the case of religion. Most people are deeply dyed with it as children and never stray far from the faiths of their fathers. Many of us accept a religion's truth largely because we've been told to do so and have never seriously questioned it.

One might think the trend is toward people being better educated, freer of social constraints, exposed to more diverse influences, and hence more independent-minded. But there is a countervailing factor. David Riesman wrote in *The Lonely Crowd* of a transition from the "inner directed" psychology, where one's guidance system is an internalized gyroscope, to "other directedness," with guidance by cues from peers, using radar instead of a gyroscope.[44] While people have always cared what others think of them, the modern other-directed personality makes this his lodestar, his central concern. The last thing such people want is to fall out of synch with their clan mates. This rise of other-directedness is growth food for groupthink.

Be cautious, too, about messages from popular media. None is unbiased and neutral. Behind what they choose to report and the way it is reported there is often a political agenda. The bias may or may not be conscious.

---

44. The ultimate exemplar of such conformism was Woody Allen's *Zelig*, a human chameleon who even took on the physical attributes of those around him.

It must also be remembered that everything popular media does is driven by the economics of the business, which means the need to attract an audience. Thus, they give us what they think people want and like, such as the absurd overcoverage of fundamentally trivial "news" sagas like the O. J. Simpson murder trial, at the expense of reportage about vastly more important but unfortunately duller subjects.

People enjoy listening to stories, and the media tailor their presentations accordingly, always striving for audience-attracting drama by emphasizing conflict and confrontation. They love "he said, she said" stories. They cover election campaigns as horse races, with total focus on who's ahead or behind, and with anything a candidate says seemingly important solely for how it may affect his chances of winning. "Narrative" is king. Subtlety and complexity tend to give way to simplicity. And once the media falls into the grip of a strong simple story line, other aspects of reality are crowded out.[45]

In 1998, responding to a terrorist attack, President Clinton ordered the bombing of al Qaeda training camps in Afghanistan and an alleged chemical weapons plant in Sudan. Then some stories popped up that the latter target was really just an innocent pharmaceutical factory. Administration officials denied this. But the notion that the US government had messed up and done something bad and was now trying to cover it up fitted perfectly with a widespread media mind-set of skepticism, even hostility, toward the government. Ever since the Watergate scandal, when a couple of reporters became cultural heroes for exposing Nixon administration wrongdoing and cover-up, that sort of adversarial muckraking posture toward government has been the model of choice for journalists. And so, en masse, the media latched onto the pharmaceutical plant story—to them, an attractive story line—of US wrongdoing and cover-up. Alleged facts that fitted this idea were eagerly emphasized. Rebuttals received short shrift. So

---

45. Look at presidential candidate Howard Dean's so-called "I have a scream" speech. It was really just a routine pep talk for campaign workers. But the press flogged the simplistic (and false) "scream" theme so relentlessly that it sank Dean's candidacy.

powerful was this media barrage that my own resulting impression (quite contrary to what I'd have wished to believe) was that, alas, America had indeed mistakenly bombed a pharmaceutical plant. And this has come to be considered historical fact.

Only years later did I happen to read a book[46] that examined this episode in considerable depth, making it clear that the whole "pharmaceutical plant" story was propagandistic disinformation concocted by the very enemies we had been targeting, and that, in reality, it *was* a chemical warfare plant that was bombed. The news media had subverted the truth and did this nation a shocking disservice. I was stunned to realize that even a sophisticated news junkie like me had been bamboozled by the media's misleading reportage. It drove home to me just how big the problem is. This wasn't a simple case of a factual mistake, which anyone can make. The US news media is such a huge, powerful, and authoritative institution that it might seem crazy to question it when, as often, it speaks with virtually one voice. But here was such a case, where the media's mind-set, its biases, and its internal culture, led it into horrible error.

Of course, sometimes governments and public officials do lie and cover up, and we therefore do need an independent news media to question government and hold it to account. The point is that one must never put blind faith in *any* human institution because people are always fallible. Never be afraid to think that perhaps the emperor has no clothes.

Beware, too, of attempts at persuasion grounded in emotion and feelings instead of facts and reasoned argument. We are living in an age when, lamentably, the former is gaining primacy over the latter, when emotional response is even deemed somehow to trump reasoned response. We are supposed to believe that everyone's feelings have to be respected, that one person's feelings about a subject are just as valid as anyone else's regardless of whether those feelings are derived from careful study or blind emotionalism. This nonjudgmentalist mind-set,

---

46. Daniel Benjamin and Steven Simon, *The Age of Sacred Terror: Radical Islam's War Against America*.

once more, amounts to turning our backs on reason, the one tool that has enabled us to confront reality and rise out of the slime.

Too often emotional response makes for facile and easy opinions that don't entail hard thinking. It is emotionally facile to be against war, for environmental protection, for social justice, against inequality, and so forth. Such stances are not necessarily all wrong, but many people buy into them reflexively, without confronting their difficulties and the hard choices they really require.

Take war. Now, I hate war, well and truly. The study of history is drenched with blood, and the vast majority of wars ever fought were launched for bad reasons, with bad results. This book stresses the value of every human life, and every life lost in war is a tragedy. For some, this makes opposition to war an absolute; they feel it must be moral to always favor peace over war. That sure *sounds* good. But the world is unfortunately not that simple. Pacifist absolutism denies that anything is ever worth fighting for. War is awful, yet we know from human experience that there are, alas, things even more awful. And while war exacts a human toll of suffering and death, sometimes peace does too, when it is a failure to deal with evil. There is thus a price to be paid for peace, which emotional pacifists don't always think about. Thus, simply being "for peace" doesn't come to grips with the truly difficult and challenging issues that human conflict confronts us with.

Pacifists say that "war never solves anything," and ask why we can't resolve disputes nonviolently. But while that is the preferred approach, it requires that all sides are willing to be reasonable and to compromise, and unfortunately, that ideal situation doesn't always obtain. America struggled with the problem of slavery for most of a century without solving it; war finally did solve it. Axis aggression in WWII obviously could not have been dealt with nonviolently; neither could North Korea's 1950 invasion of South Korea nor Iraq's 1990 invasion of Kuwait. In 1999 Serb atrocities in Kosovo could be halted only by war; its death toll was surely outweighed by the lives it saved.[47] And the 1994

---

47. We waged that war with no UN authorization; scant international help; no issue about weapons of mass destruction; no oil or other strategic

Rwanda genocide that resulted in eight hundred thousand deaths was finally ended not by diplomacy, mediation, negotiation, political action, or sweet reason, but by war; by using guns to kill the perpetrators who could not have been stopped by any other means.

Going to war is always a tough choice, but authentic morality consists in facing up to such tough choices rather than dodging them with facile pieties. Those who gave their lives in the Civil War to preserve this nation and end slavery were true moral heroes. So, too, were the Americans who fought in WWII and Korea and the Rwandans who took up arms against the genocidal forces. The same is true also of American troops in Afghanistan and Iraq making the highest sacrifice to give people in those afflicted lands the opportunity for free and decent lives. All those soldiers have been genuine heroes, making the kind of hard and painful moral choices that the issues of war and peace demand. It's a terrible reality that the human condition does sometimes require such heroism and sacrifice. The trouble with pacifism is that it would surrender the world to nonpacifists with no qualms about using violence to gain their ends. (For this reason Sam Harris, in *The End of Faith*, deems pacifism a "flagrantly immoral position.")

All else equal, no sane person favors war over peace. So be for peace, but recognize that all else is never equal and that both war and peace carry a price. One must face up to the hard realities to decide which price is greater.

Another highly emotive issue, which involves hard choices, is the environment. Sometimes environmentalists try to make it seem as though anyone opposing them actually wants our beautiful planet despoiled. Of course this is ridiculous. Nobody favors environmental degradation, and self-styled environmentalists have no monopoly on virtue, right thinking, and wisdom. Just like pacifists, all too often environmentalists tend to be absolutists unwilling to confront the costs of what they advocate.

---

interest; no threat to the United States, imminent or otherwise; and yet no outcry from the Left. (In contrast, in 2003 many pacifists were unwilling that any blood be shed to end Iraq's regime but were also unwilling to see the bloodshed keeping that regime in power.)

"Cost" is not a dirty word. Some object to cost-benefit analysis, deeming it impossible or even morally wrong to put a price tag on something like environmental quality, preserving species, or, for that matter, on a human life. Yet even people who say such things are probably not in the habit of thoroughly inspecting their autos before every drive, recognizing the opportunity cost of doing so and that there are more productive ways to use their time and resources. This too is cost-benefit analysis. It's an entirely natural practice we implicitly do all the time. The most effective method is to translate everything into dollars, a very handy universal standard, which enables us to compare different options on a basis of equivalency.

True, some things are hard to price. But that doesn't mean their value is infinite or that we can justify spending any amounts for them. Auctions reveal very precise valuations for even the most "priceless" treasures, and juries in wrongful death lawsuits must put dollar figures on human life. Society may reasonably judge worthwhile a program saving one life for every hundred thousand dollars spent, but not if the cost is a billion dollars per life saved—because we know we could use the billion dollars elsewhere to better effect. Likewise, scenic beauty, biodiversity, or air purity, may be worth $X to us but not $Y or $Z. Cost-benefit analysis is our tool for making such decisions.

When the Bush administration proposed changing the guidelines for arsenic content in drinking water there was a great hue and cry. It seemed so simple. Arsenic is toxic, so let's all be for less arsenic. But nobody wanted to tackle the real issue, which was the actual human consequence of allowing a little more arsenic set against the true societal cost of achieving an arsenic reduction. If the public health effect of the increased arsenic was relatively minuscule compared to a huge dollar cost of arsenic reduction, no one wanted to hear about it because it made the issue less satisfyingly clear.

Everything involves costs and trade-offs. Resources are finite. A billion dollars spent for a tiny and perhaps meaningless arsenic reduction means a billion not available for some other purpose that could well be much more worthwhile. If our resources were infinite, we could satisfy every need and wouldn't have to bother about cost-benefit analysis. But in the real world where resources are limited, whenever we expend them we have to be sure it makes sense in balancing costs against benefits. For example, it is often far costlier to get rid of the last 5 percent of a pollutant than it was to remove the first 50 percent. The latter may be a sound expenditure, but achieving unneeded purity by purging that last 5 percent may be a terrible misuse of resources. Emotional moralizing about saving our priceless environment contributes nothing to useful debate here.

Another instructive example: in Great Britain a deadly train wreck got a lot of publicity, prompting the government to spend heavily to upgrade track facilities to prevent a recurrence. Who could be against spending for rail safety? Well, a study pointed out that highway accidents take a vastly greater toll than railway accidents, and if the amount spent on rail safety went instead to traffic safety, many times more lives would be saved.

The point is that insistence on cost-benefit analysis and weighing trade-offs is not a pettifogging disregard for larger issues. It's instead a way to get a proper handle on such larger issues, which may indeed be matters of life and death.

And here's another case to ponder. Responding to environmentalist hysteria that the pesticide DDT might cause cancer and other problems, we banned it. In fact, the cancer danger was wildly overblown, and it's highly doubtful any lives were saved. But what's not in doubt is that banning DDT caused a population explosion of malaria-carrying mosquitoes and other harmful insects, producing a huge number of deaths in the third world, mostly children. Not a very advantageous trade-off.

So, even when the most emotive issues are at stake, you must still put on your green accountant's eyeshade and focus on what the facts and numbers tell you, not the facile simplistic answers that your emotions suggest. Always ask questions.

But even numbers often need to be looked at with Socratic skepticism. Benjamin Disraeli said that there are three kinds of lies: ordinary lies, damned lies, and statistics. Data can always be manipulated to show what you want it to show. For example, any comparison over time is highly sensitive to the starting point chosen. If you want to show high growth, pick a low starting year. If you want to show low growth or decline, pick a high year to start. And a great many of the statistical assertions floating around in the public sphere come from organizations that are not neutral, but have a definite bias, an agenda to serve, or an axe to grind.

Always take care to question what is really going on behind the data: who collected it, how was it interpreted, and for what purpose? One report showed that charter school students were doing worse on standardized tests than public school kids. This seemed a devastating indictment of charter schools. However, the report was sponsored by an organization of public school teachers, who felt threatened by charter schools. And then one had to remember that charter schools attract kids who are not doing well in public schools and start out far behind the average public school student. No surprise that their test scores were lower. But meantime, the data showed they were *improving* faster in charter schools.

The most common mistake about statistics is to confuse correlation with causation. Correlation means that two phenomena go together; that is, where you find one, you're more likely to find the other. That doesn't mean one causes the other. For instance, studies show that kids who watch a lot of TV violence grow up violent. The implication may appear to be that watching violent TV causes violence. But an alternate explanation is that violence-prone kids are attracted to TV violence and that it is their affinity for violence that causes the TV watching, not the other way around.

Furthermore, statistics quoted in public debate can be simply spurious. We may hear that large numbers of children are going to bed hungry, or are sexually abused, and so on. But we must ask how researchers arrive at these numbers. Often, they are more or less plucked from thin air by advocates promoting agendas. One such group in 1980 put America's homeless population at 2.2 million and, despite bearing no relation to reality, this number was publicized and repeated so often that many people still assume it is fact. And even where a statistic originally has some valid underpinnings, the story often gets distorted beyond recognition as it filters from one advocate to another. It's like the camp game of "telephone," where a whispered sentence is passed down a line of children. Invariably the message changes completely by the time it reaches the last child.

Evolution gave us a gift of intelligence far beyond that of any other species—enough to enable us to survive and thrive (for the sake of that all-important DNA replication)—but not any more than was needed. So most of us are still not totally intelligent and rational creatures. But, like so many things, intelligence is distributed along a bell-shaped curve, and while most people fall into the big bulge in the middle, there are happily those outliers at the vanguard of the curve whose intellects do jump that final hurdle. Those people are the drivers of human progress. If we didn't have them—if nobody was smarter than the average—our species would probably have done no more than the mere survival and replication that nature sought. We'd probably still be living in trees.[48]

This goes partway toward explaining how so many people could buy into ideas like Nazism and Serbian nationalism. These were software packages slipped into their minds and accepted without hard rational thought. We are often simply lazy about thinking, content to uncritically let the software run in our brains. But even intelligence and rationality, though perhaps necessary conditions for avoiding such error, are not sufficient conditions. Some otherwise very intelligent people supported Nazism, or at least seemed to. Smart people can often adopt postures they know are wrong for cynical reasons. But this does not complete the explanation either. The fact is that even highly intelligent and rational people can make big mistakes.

The lesson is not to mistrust reason—again, it's the best tool we have for understanding the world—but, rather, to *use* it, to *really* use it

---

48. Thus, human inequality is a natural fact and not something to be lamented. It's what gives us such rich lives, and not just materially. Where would we be without such very nonequal individuals as Mozart, Raphael, Flaubert, or Cervantes?

to question things, to analyze, and to refrain from accepting propositions just because a lot of seemingly intelligent and authoritative people promote them. Don't let other people install software in your mind.

One reason why groupthink happens, and people fall for manipulative emotionalist propaganda, is that it's easy to put ideas into someone's head if there are none inside to begin with. Many people are indeed empty headed as far as big ideas are concerned, and empty heads are too easily filled by demagogues. To properly see the world around you and determine ways to respond, it helps to have a framework of ideas for doing so, a matrix against which to evaluate other ideas. This is what this book seeks to provide, and why it keeps re-emphasizing the core values: live and let live, the primacy of the individual, fundamental human rights, and, yet to come, the social contract, limited government, and free-market economics.

At the other end of the spectrum from the empty head is the ideologue or true believer, whose responses are rigidly programmed. Some people become prisoners of their ideologies, developing a kind of tunnel vision, able to see the world in only one way. While having core principles is indeed desirable, one must also be open-minded, able to evaluate new ideas that challenge one's thinking, and adjust it in response to new facts. The world is always changing. When it does change, or when you learn something new, you should be prepared to change your mind.

Too many of us, though, are so wedded to our beliefs and ideologies that we're impervious to reason or even to reality. The political Right and Left in America know this and seem to have given up trying to gain converts by persuasion, recognizing the virtual impossibility of shaking people loose from their preconceptions. Instead, politics is really directed at reinforcing preconceptions, promoting not a dialogue but tandem monologues.

We build mental fortresses, walling off our deepest beliefs against all assaults. In fact, brain imaging has shown that an unwelcome challenge to our strongest biases is processed not by our rational minds, but rather provokes an unconscious and emotional response; rejecting it lights up our pleasure centers, and so does processing information that confirms our biases. Certainly this seems true regarding religious belief. The Book of Mormon, for example, centers upon ancient Jewish tribes traveling to America and building a mighty civilization that was destroyed in a huge war, leaving Indians as their descendants. Mormons are fazed neither by the total absence of archaeological evidence for these great kingdoms nor by DNA proof that Indians have no Semitic connection. Facts that contradict their dogmas effectively don't even exist for them as facts; they are stations along railroad tracks at which their mental program makes no stops.

Of course, one can never really approach matters of faith from the standpoint of reason alone. But recall our discussion of the meaning of the word "know." By what means do we know what we think we know is true? Our reason should at least make us step back and try to look objectively at why it is that we believe what we believe, especially when other people hold contrary beliefs with equal certitude and fervor. Somebody must be wrong; what makes you sure it isn't you?

As Thomas Kida's book title says, *Don't Believe Everything You Think*. In other words, always question, even yourself. After all, nobody can possibly be right about everything (not even me).

Meantime, the ideologue or zealot too easily goes in the other direction and becomes the extremist. Feeling certain he possesses absolute truth, he wants the world to bow before that truth and conform to it. He desires a salvation so imperative that no obstacle to its achievement is tolerated. Such obstacles can include, most prominently, human beings; and thus, through the ages, millions of lives have been immolated on the altars of extremist visions for utopia by true believers ranging from Torquemada to Lenin to Osama bin Laden.

If your path to paradise is a river of blood, please find another.

One mental software program, though, that you should definitely install is Occam's razor (also called the "principle of parsimony" and sometimes spelled "Ockham"). It tells us that in explaining any phenomenon, prefer the simplest, most obvious, most mundane answer. Most often this means the unexciting, dull answer and not the sexy and intriguing propositions that are more fun to believe. Thus, the purveyors of "urban legends," like crocodiles in the sewers, are more popular than the killjoys who debunk them. But, in any such situation, the boring answer has the key advantage of being more probably true.

Most Americans seem to believe that President Kennedy's assassination was a deep conspiracy involving key segments of the country's elite. The less interesting reality (confirmed by the actual evidence) is that Oswald alone killed him with a lucky shot. Many people also believe in UFO abduction tales, that aliens landed at Roswell, New Mexico, and that the government has been covering all this up. The idea that such an explosive secret could be kept by so many for so long defies common sense. Occam's razor tells us to embrace the more down-to-earth explanation for alien abduction stories: that their tellers are crackpots, lying, or delusional. There is absolutely no credible evidence that aliens ever visited Earth. But of course there is plenty of evidence for the existence of liars and loonies.

Yet in such cases it appears many people are not merely credulous and unable to apply Occam's razor, but are actually unwilling to do so. Something in us makes us *want* to believe. It's obvious that in the religious sphere, wholly apart from the particular doctrines for which faith is summoned, the very idea of faith itself has power. Such faith at least attaches to ideas that have power in their own right; but far less compelling notions are often magnets for belief too. There's always a ready audience for UFO stories, ghost tales, witchery, medical quacks, séances, and psychics. There is no charlatan, it seems, whose schtick is so preposterous that he doesn't attract followers. And how else can we explain undying interest in the "predictions" of Nostradamus, a sixteenth-century weirdo who wrote gibberish so unintelligible and vague that you can read into it anything you like.[49]

Believing in this kind of nonsense might make life more interesting. But I prefer to live in the real world.

---

49. I'm reminded of Yogi Berra's saying that it's tough to make predictions, especially about the future. And any "psychic" who actually could foresee the future would become very rich and powerful—and would not be found sitting behind a cheesy card table huckstering for small bills.

Relativism and Nonjudgmentalism

Jesus said, "Judge not, lest you be judged."

We are nowadays taught that people come in many different flavors, that one flavor is just as good as any other, that none is "better" or "more advanced," and that we should not negatively *judge* people who differ from us or "label" anyone; indeed, that even right and wrong, and good and evil, are relative concepts that depend on circumstances and perhaps have no real meaning. This is *moral relativism*.

Human beings do indeed come in many varieties, and, as this book consistently holds, all should be allowed to follow their own individual paths without unnecessary interference. Once more, live and let live. Recognize the other guy's right to do his own thing. This is *tolerance*.

Because of human variability—sexual behavior is a prime example—intolerance of differences means trying to fit square pegs into round holes. And while the word "diversity" has become a shibboleth, rarely do we actually ponder *why* diversity is a good thing. In fact, not only is it what makes our species interesting, but it is also what drives evolution, not just in biology, but in culture as well. If everyone were identical and we all thought alike, society would stagnate. Variability is what generates change and progress.

And tolerance, of course, goes hand in hand with freedom. If you want society to tolerate your own idiosyncrasies without stomping on your freedom, you have to be willing to extend the same tolerance and freedom to others. It's a two-way street. J. S. Mill deemed tolerance "the forbearance which flows from a conscientious sense of the importance to mankind of the equal freedom of all opinions."

However, there is a big difference between such tolerance and nonjudgmentalism. Making judgments is the essence of using one's reason and of the life of the mind. It is at the very core of intellectual activity—judging what is good and what is bad, what is right and what is wrong, and what is true and false. If we refuse to make such judgments, we condemn ourselves to intellectual sterility; we throw our brains out the window.

Robert Pirsig wrote a novel, *Zen and the Art of Motorcycle Maintenance*, which focused on the question, what is quality? That question was rightly deemed salient in philosophy. How and by what standards do we make our judgments? Are there any true standards, or are they merely subjective and arbitrary artifacts of culture? Can we truly judge that Michelangelo was a greater artist than, say, Damien Hirst?[50] This may indeed be a complicated problem if we tackle it seriously; but tackle it we must. Like Pirsig, we must eschew blithe assumptions and analyze the validity of the standards by which we evaluate quality. To hold, instead, that there can be no valid standards, that nothing is better than anything else, denies meaning to all of human culture, which is ultimately centered upon a striving for goodness, truth, and beauty.[51]

---

50. Hirst is an artist known for exhibiting preserved animal parts as art works—if you call that art. The question "What is art?" exemplifies the issue here. The "art" in contemporary art seems to be defined as whatever an "artist" says is "art." One "art" installation comprised a gallery with its door sealed shut against visitors (to make some political point). Of course, defining art in this way renders the word meaningless—and negates any possible application of standards.

51. As Charles Murray suggests in his book *Human Accomplishment*, to say "I know nothing about art, but know what I like" is a perfectly valid stance. Of course, different people respond differently to art, and some may

It is also fashionable to insist that issues do not have black-and-white answers and that everything is in shades of gray. Indeed, to say someone thinks in black and white is a put-down, whereas gray is the color of sophisticated deep thinking. Likewise, when it's said that there are two sides to every issue, it's often with the implication that each side is equally valid. Again, the idea is avoidance of judgment and that there is no such thing as right or wrong, good or evil, truth or falsity, black or white.[52]

This fetish of nonjudgmentalism and relativism also relates back to what was said earlier about the scientific method. Those who regard science as just another viewpoint, no more valid than any other, are led to deny that there are any universal standards to judge truth or falsity or logical validity. According to them, what seems to be true depends on your viewpoint; seeming truth is all colored by self-interest, politics, power relationships, and so on; and hence, it isn't possible to know that anything is really true. Of course, this allows you to believe whatever you feel like believing and to reject any fact you don't like. It's a recipe for intellectual anarchy and says that humanity's eternal quest for knowledge is a wasted effort.[53]

The nonjudgmentalist ethos may be traced back to the Roman playwright Terence, who said that "nothing human is foreign to me," which has since been extrapolated into a notion that everything human

---

actually prefer Hirst to Michelangelo. *De gustibus non disputandum est.* But the search for true universal standards must transcend such idiosyncratic individual response.

52. Perhaps some of us are still reeling from God's expulsion of humankind from paradise for tasting knowledge of good and evil. But others, unintimidated, bite the apple.

53. Deconstruction (a variety of "postmodernism") is an allied snare, a method to intellectualize away all real meaning. A text is examined not for its explicit messages but rather for the messages purportedly lying behind them. What this really means, in practice, is overprinting it with the observer's political preconceptions. Thus, a book like this one is analyzed in terms of the author's putative biases, psychology, social position, cultural milieu, and all that sort of thing—with scant cognizance of what he actually *says*.

is morally equivalent. This idea got a big push from the sexual revolution, and from the work of Alfred C. Kinsey, which revealed such variability in sex behavior that the idea of "normal" lost meaning. Consequently, most of us have embraced the very reasonable idea that, in sexuality at least, we can't always say that what's good for the goose is good for the gander. But too many have gone overboard in this direction, making the leap from tolerance to the idea that even *thinking* judgmentally is wrong, thereby extending nonjudgmentalism to *all* moral questions and effectively rejecting the very idea of morality itself.

This isn't at all what Jesus meant in saying, "Judge not, lest you be judged." He was actually targeting the self-righteous hypocrite who condemns his neighbor while overlooking his own failings. By no means was Jesus endorsing ethical neutrality, or an "anything goes" amorality. Part of the story, too, is a corollary we read into Jesus' statement: "judge not," so that you *won't* be judged yourself. If you can persuade everyone that judging people is wrong, then of course you too are exempted from judgment for your weaknesses or bad behavior. Indeed, if you are criticized, you can even turn tables, hurling the nasty word "judgmental" at your critic, as though judging wrong—not *doing* wrong—is the real crime.[54]

I recall a college student's essay about the 9/11 terrorist attacks. Here was a young woman thoroughly indoctrinated with the modern dogmas of nonjudgmentalism and moral relativism, taught that it is a sin to make judgments, that there is really no such thing as right or wrong, and that we cannot judge because what seems wrong for one person might be right for another. When she tried to form her response to men flying airplanes into buildings, it was a great internal struggle for her. But finally, she was able to overcome her deep-seated nonjudgmentalism and arrive reluctantly at a *judgment* that *evil* had been done.

This word "evil" seems to give some people particular trouble.

---

54. It is noteworthy that nonjudgmentalism and moral relativism are almost never concerned with denying the goodness of something; rather, they're always about denying the wrongness of something.

Part of it is that we have a hard time understanding evil; it frustrates and confuses us. The problem can seemingly be solved by declaring it nonexistent. Further, the word "evil" conveys an atavistic, ancient, and simplistic flavor that violates the dogma against black-and-white thinking. Moreover, it is seen as superstitiously implying that a malign force operates in the world to make bad things happen.[55]

Of course there is no such force. But, undeniably, there do exist human impulses and motivations that sometimes lead people to do harm. This is what the word "evil" actually means. It simply refers to wrongful actions; though it's a very strong word that should be reserved for very serious wrongs.

Still, some protest that any such judgment can only be subjective, never objective. And it's often said that people are neither good nor evil, but mixtures of both, and that all are capable of evil depending on circumstances.

Well, sure we are. Even if we are basically moral animals, and are good most of the time, human nature does certainly encompass non-moral conduct. Complicity in the Holocaust was widespread among Germans (and others) who, under normal circumstances, would have behaved with normal decency. Sadly, the Holocaust was not a case of inhuman behavior; it was human behavior (or at least within the natural human range of behaviors). But surely the fact that most people are capable of evil does not somehow render the concept meaningless. Here again, the word "evil" does have a clear objective meaning, applicable to a phenomenon all too real.

And there *are* standards for judging it. As we saw earlier, reason leads us to some universal ethical precepts, centered upon the value of human life, the promotion of happiness, the avoidance of suffering, the idea of justice, and the "bronze rule" for human interactions. Further, these basic imperatives are part of our evolutionary heritage as well and so, all in all, "objective" or not, it is fair to consider them nat-

---

55. Lance Morrow's book *Evil: An Investigation* repeatedly portrays it in this way, seeing evil as being somehow "in business for itself," as though it is like a toxic gas, "slithering upon the currents of air."

ural laws, rather than mere subjective artifacts of some individual's mind, or relativistic cultural constructs.[56]

This conclusion is not undermined by all the philosophizing, through the ages, over whether moral truths can really be derived through reason and logic. David Hume said that while one can prove that two plus two equals four, one cannot similarly prove the proposition "murder is wrong," and A. J. Ayer deemed it just an expression of subjective feeling and ultimately meaningless. Perhaps he'd have thought differently of the statement "murdering A. J. Ayer is wrong." The point is that this type of quest for philosophic rigor, while perhaps intellectually interesting, should not get in the way of common sense, which is, after all, an expression of our reason too. Philosophizing can sometimes be little more than a language game, producing answers that are completely divorced from human reality and, therefore, make no sense. Irrespective of any semantic conundrums concerning *words* about murder, the *act* of murder is not meaningless, and reason and logic can certainly tell us things about actions and their consequences.

Thus, even if one is squeamish about calling people evil, actions *can* be called evil. And even if everyone is capable of such actions, even supposing everyone occasionally commits them, there is a world of difference between such normality and, say, serial murder. Applying reason, we grasp that difference and can judge the serial killer evil in a sense that the ordinary person is not. What matters is not what we're capable of doing, but what we actually do. We *are* what we do; our actions and behavior define who we are. Normal people have consciences that produce feelings of guilt and shame when they do wrong, which generally serve to make them and their behavior more or less moral. While normal people may be capable of murder, most do not commit murder. Yet there are people who lack that moral regulator, and harm others with no compunction or remorse. Such individuals, and not just their actions, can fairly be termed evil. These aren't meaningless morally relativistic propositions.

---

56. Michael Shermer argues for a "provisionally true" morality, applicable to most people in most cultures most of the time.

Of course, one will always encounter gray zones where the moral lines are fuzzy and difficult to sort out. Some questions do have two (or more) sides with claims to validity and some answers do depend on circumstances. But subjectivity and difficulty of judging do not mean we must throw up our hands and say that one must never judge. To the contrary, we must, as thinking, rational, and moral beings, make the effort to resolve difficult issues. If a question is not black or white, that's no reason to refuse to make a judgment about the answer, about the right shade of gray; and it's no reason to deny that there are any standards for doing so. In fact, it's black-and-white that leaves no room for judgment, and it's precisely because black-and-white does not usually obtain that we must use reason to make judgments. We saw this in the last chapter when we discussed how war and peace and environmental protection are not the black-and-white issues many people think they are. We will see it again when we consider abortion.

To illustrate moral ambiguity, it's often said that "one man's terrorist is another man's freedom fighter." Certainly, evil often masquerades as virtue; and the whitest of intentions can produce the blackest of results. Possibly even Pol Pot believed he was working for human betterment. And investing evil with the appearance of righteousness makes it all the more dangerous. Hitler too saw himself as pursuing a righteous dream. Can we always tell when such dreams are evil? Once more, such difficulties do not mean we must admit defeat before even starting to make judgments. If good intent can mistakenly bring forth a bad outcome, failure to recognize evil before it's too late can also be a terrible mistake. Indeed, in today's world, where technology can empower a small evil impulse to produce huge evil results (9/11, for example), it becomes all the more imperative for us to grapple with such issues, rather than hiding from them in a bunker of denial. Evil is *not* a simple matter, while to deny its existence is itself the most simplistic of responses.

Judging ultimately means choosing; we are continually confronted with moral choices. Such is the essence of freedom. This cannot somehow be avoided through nonjudgmentalism, for that is merely making choices passively, by default. And we must struggle over these choices, not because the answers are compelled by some black-and-white morality, and not because they are thusly easy, but because they are hard. If that were not so, this whole discussion would be pointless. Furthermore, even if subjectivity is unavoidable, even if we may err and judge wrongly, at least we are engaging the intellect and striving toward an understanding of what is right and wrong.

A stance of nonjudgmentalism, on the other hand, is at odds with our fundamental humanness. For nonreasoning animals, making judgments is impossible and concepts of right and wrong really don't exist. For us humans, they *do* exist, because we are reasoning creatures. To deny that there is any such thing as right or wrong, good or evil, and to insist on seeing only gray neutrality, is moral abdication and intellectual self-castration.

The same is true of cultural relativism. It is an abdication of the intellect to buy into the notion that all human cultures stand equal and that none is better than any other.

We seem to be throwing away our own culture. This is the "dead white males" syndrome, a denigration and dismissal of the traditional icons of the Western canon as mere products of a patriarchal white European ethnocentrism from a remote benighted time. It's true, of course, that Shakespeare's plays, or a novel like *Middlemarch* (written, incidentally, by a woman), are steeped in the cultures of their authors' times. Yet these works contain universal truths of the human condition common to all cultures. Shakespeare and Eliot speak to our hearts across the ages with great broadness of spirit.

This is why their works have endured (and will outlast the narrow-minded spiritlessness of "dead white males" ideology). This is why the works of Shakespeare, Eliot, Homer, Dante, Milton, Hugo, Goethe, Tolstoy, and the like, are pillars of our culture. All have things to say to us worth hearing; things that make us better for having heard. And the importance accorded these works over the centuries means that they have become the bricks and mortar of which our contemporary culture was built.

Civilization did not begin yesterday. It is, on the contrary, a richly complex edifice, a product of everything that has gone before. Just as the richness of your own life is indispensably grounded in everything you experienced since your birth, all contributing to making you the person you are today, so too is the richness of our civilization built upon all past human experience. A stew's flavor comes from the sum of its ingredients. By all means let us include women, people of color, and modern voices that speak to us. But Shakespeare, Tolstoy, Goethe, and all the other "dead white European males" still remain key ingredients in our cultural stew; take them out, and you impoverish the flavor. Remove these pillars of our cultural inheritance, and what holds up the roof? Cultural relativists don't want our minds broadened, but narrowed.

Among differing human cultures, one can, should, and must judge their relative merits. Indeed, this has been a key inquiry for philosophers through the ages, starting with Plato, who concerned himself very much with the question of what makes for a good social order. It would be no great stretch to say that this issue of how to live properly is central to philosophy. And, in pursuing this question, we must compare human cultures, analyze their good and bad features, and make *judgments* about their relative merits; about how well they provide their members with the opportunity to live good and happy lives. We can learn from good features in different cultures and to avoid the bad features of others. And we must recognize that some do have bad features—bad in terms of holding back their people from enjoying their human potential.

Furthermore, let's not forget that bad cultures can harm more than just their own people. Nazi Germany was an evil culture that wreaked havoc on humanity far beyond its borders and so was Soviet Russia. Even today, the world is not free of dangerous cultures that threaten human values everywhere.

The political Left at one time mounted the ramparts for human rights and democratic ideals, but now has hunkered down into a cul-de-sac of cynicism. Cultural relativism is largely the work of intellectuals who despise their own civilization. Thus, they deem arrogant, imperialist, or dishonest the idea of spreading Western values. They say we should understand and respect other societies and be cautious about trying to change them. Caution and humility are always good; but this mind-set tends to see other cultures as unalterable, which actually denies a fundamental human reality of continuous striving for betterment. In fact, people can and do change, and so do cultures. Ironically, "social change" used to be a mantra of those on the Left; now cultural relativism has led them to ditch the idea, at least for other societies. Such an outlook, columnist David Brooks has written, makes people stop trying to fight evils, and pretty soon, to stop condemning them—a hardheartedness that flatters their moral vanity with an aura of sophistication.

Thus, cultural relativism often works out to be quite callous toward the actual human beings it purports to respect. Does anyone in the world have a genuine cultural preference for tyranny and repression? When we are told that some societies don't want democracy, free speech, or religion because these are "Western" values incompatible with their cultural traditions, the voices are never those of the people denied such rights. Oppressive systems are always rationalized by the elites who benefit, but never by the people held down under their heels. When it is said that cultural tradition in certain countries validates treating women as chattels, subjecting them to "circumcision" (genital mutilation), stoning them to death for having sex, or "honor killings" by their own families on mere suspicion, it never comes from the mouths of those women themselves. Likewise, in the old American South it was frequently said that blacks were happy with the "custom and tradition" of segregation, or even with slavery itself—but never said by blacks speaking freely.

Tolerance does not apply here. We must not tolerate societies that practice inhuman barbarism and threaten to spread it.

The Left understood this once, but its cultural self-loathing has destroyed its moral compass. Thus, these cynics now insist that democracy is unsuitable for some cultures and that some are not ready for it or capable of understanding it because they've never had it, don't really want it, and are bound to screw it up if they get it. All this was said about Afghanis before their first-ever election in 2004, yet they voted with huge enthusiasm and made a good choice. And it was said most relentlessly about Iraqis until the day that, facing down terrorist intimidation, millions of them literally risked death to vote. I will never forget the pictures of Iraqi women proudly holding up inked fingers, showing that, for the first time in their lives, their voices had been heard.

All people understand well enough what it means to participate in governance. And there isn't anyone who doesn't want to participate. Indeed, the thirst for democratic rights seems to be insatiable when people are given half a chance to express it. I believe there are fundamental human values, discoverable through reason, that are universal. They are the templates against which we must make our judgments.

Ultimately, nonjudgmentalism is a self-contradiction. It is, after all, a *judgment* to hold one lifestyle equal to another, Damien Hirst equal to Michelangelo, or Kalahari culture equal to America's. Of course, the nonjudgmentalist doesn't say that there are no differences, since the differences are obvious. What he effectively says, instead, is that the differences don't matter. And *that* is not only a judgment, but it's one both sweeping and highly dubious. If the standards for judging Michelangelo superior to Hirst entail subjectivity or other philosophical problems, more problematic by far is the idea that the differences between them don't matter. And more so still is a judgment that moral differences between one consequential action and another don't matter.

Indeed, such nonjudgmental judgments make no sense to us. We look at the Sistine Chapel and see beauty; we look at Auschwitz and see horror. To one we are attracted, while from the other we recoil. One we praise and the other we condemn. These are rational human responses. To try to turn off some switch in our minds and short circuit such judgments is to try to be other than human. We gain nothing and lose everything that gives life meaning.

And, truth be told, all rhetoric of nonjudgmentalism and moral relativism, including the derision of "black-and-white" thinking, is just a dishonest, bullying intellectual pose. Nobody, not even its loudest advocates, really practices nonjudgmentalism. *It is just a question of what to be judgmental about.* Politically correct nonjudgmentalists jump to make harsh black-and-white judgments when it comes to their own ideological sacred cows. Just try telling one of them that affirmative action is wrong and see how nonjudgmental he is about you.[57]

Indeed, American politics has become poisonous with harsh judgmentalism. For some, it is not enough just to disagree with the other side. Opponents are demonized and their motives impugned. One side sees its own stances as guided by the highest human ideals while condemning others as mean-spirited, motivated by crass self-interest, misled, misinformed, or manipulated. There is no recognition that those others might be moved by sincere ideals and might also be seeking the public good.[58]

Is this contradictory—condemning nonjudgmentalism and judgmentalism alike? Not at all. And here is the key point. Making judgments is what you must do for *yourself*. This is, again, the essence of one's freedom. Your personal life journey requires that you confront all issues, deciding for yourself what is good or bad, right or wrong. But recognize that those are *your* judgments, that others may judge differently, and they have a right to do so. You can argue strongly for what you believe, but forbear the other guy's argument and listen. He might just have some valid points. And making judgments for yourself certainly does not mean forcing those judgments down the other guy's throat. You may try to persuade him, but not to bludgeon him into submission.

---

57. I talked with a man who preached moral relativism and that evil is a meaningless concept. But when the Iraq war was mentioned, the word "evil" suddenly reentered his lexicon. It's funny how certain issues, like war, abortion, or the environment, turn professed moral relativists into absolutists.

58. And historian Richard Hofstadter wrote in 1964 of "The Paranoid Style in American Politics," characterized by overheated exaggeration and fantasizing sinister conspiracies. Its modern sufferers see a nation of CIA-corporate cabals, stolen elections, evil motives, looming dictatorships, and so on.

Thus, we may be passionate about our own beliefs while accepting the right of others to passionately follow their own differing convictions. You are entitled to think someone's way of life is wrong without insisting that he adopt yours. You can shout from the rooftops in denunciation of what you deem evil. It's okay to believe you possess absolute truth. But it's not okay to burn at the stake anyone believing differently.

This, again, is *tolerance*. It is agreeing to disagree. Our culture wars can be de-escalated from combat between enemies to disagreements among friends. Make your own moral judgments, but be tolerant. Live and let live.

The Mystery of Creation

One ancient cosmology holds that the world stands upon the back of a great celestial turtle. But, you may well ask, on what does that turtle stand? The answer: another turtle. Indeed, it's turtles all the way down.

Deistic religions hold that the world (or universe) was created by God. It has been argued, in support of this idea, that everything must have a cause, and that God was the "first cause" behind all creation. This supplies an answer for those who can see no other way to explain existence.

But it also begs the questions of where God came from and what caused the "first cause." There is no analytical difference from the turtle cosmology. One can believe it's turtles all the way down to infinity, with no bottom turtle, or that God created everything, but nothing ever created God. Either way, it's still fundamentally a mystery.

Yet religion does not claim to provide a rational answer to the mystery of creation; what it provides is a mystical answer. Whether it's turtles all the way down or a God that never had to be born, mystical conceptions are not amenable to proof or parsing by reason or logic. They are what they are. Accept them or reject them as you choose.

It would be nice if we could say that reason and science have the full answer. But they don't—not yet—not quite. Yet perhaps we are beginning to glimpse it.

* * *

We have already discussed the beginning of life and our own human origins, but evolution is so important that it deserves a few more words. The keys are in the phrases "descent with modification" and "natural selection." We all know that children don't exactly replicate their parents, that there are always changes and modifications to the basic blueprint. This is because parental genes get recombined and blended to produce a child, and are further subject to little errors in the copying known as mutations. This is also why no two creatures are identical and why some are better equipped to survive and reproduce, so that their genes proliferate while less successful variations fall by the wayside. This is natural selection. It is the process by which species change over time and evolve into different ones. It is how all life, including humans, evolved.

There is a common misunderstanding that evolution's being a "theory" means it may or may not be true. This simply mistakes the scientific meaning of "theory," which is a well-established set of principles explaining a phenomenon. When an idea has not been established by evidence, the word "hypothesis" is used. But evolution is not a mere hypothesis. While scientists do still argue over the details, the evidence confirming the basic idea of evolution by natural selection is incontrovertible.[59]

It's impossible to objectively study fossils and see no evolution, or a chimpanzee's anatomy and see no relation to Man. Whatever else one may believe about the nature and origin of the cosmos, evolution is a fact,[60] and is essential to understanding life on Earth and the

---

59. Another misconception is that something as complex as an eye could not have evolved in stages because an incomplete eye would be useless. In fact, eyes evolved from simple light-sensitive cells that acted as primitive motion detectors, obviously advantageous. And often, too, in evolution, structures originated with one use get jerry-rigged for another.

60. We can actually see it happening today—indeed, it's a big problem. Insects and germs are evolving defenses against our pesticides and antibiotics. It happens because those initially rare individuals somehow able to withstand our weapons are the ones that survive and proliferate—exactly as evolutionary biology would predict.

human condition. As the geneticist Theodosius Dobzhansky said, "Nothing in biology makes sense *except* in the light of evolution."

Some people bristle at the idea of being kin to monkeys. They suppose it somehow besmirches them.[61] In fact, we are related not only to apes but also to snakes, worms, slime molds, and every other living thing on Earth. This interconnectedness of all life is in no sense demeaning, but rather is beautiful and awe-inspiring. To repeat Darwin, "There is grandeur in this view of life." And furthermore, we may rightly take pride in how we have excelled our brutish origins.

Turning to the bigger picture, science also has a basic understanding of the universe's life story, all the way back to the tiniest fraction of a second after its birth. Admittedly, there are still some big things we don't yet understand, such as the unexplained "dark matter" that seems to comprise the bulk of creation, and the likewise unexplained "dark energy" that is apparently accelerating the universe's expansion. Nevertheless, given all that we do securely know, it must be considered a fact that our universe was born about 13.7 billion years ago in a "big bang."[62]

The problem, of course, is to understand how the big bang happened. This means understanding what the conditions were before it occurred—if the word "before" even has meaning here. This is a thorny issue if, in fact, time itself (as we experience it) *began* with the big bang. This points up the depth of the problem. In trying to get some handle on the fundamental mystery, we inevitably run up against

---

61. Many also rebel at the idea of "social Darwinism," that survival of the fittest is the law governing humanity. But, as I have argued elsewhere, the impersonal concerns of nature in creating us need not bind us in how we choose to live our lives. The biologist T. H. Huxley observed that human society is not condemned to play out survival of the fittest but can, instead, work on fitting more of us for survival.

62. The name "big bang" was actually coined by an opponent of the theory, astronomer Fred Hoyle, to mock it. He believed in a "steady state" universe that always existed. That concept has been disproven by all we have learned since Hoyle's day.

concepts that confound our mental processes. Infinitude of space and time seem to be concepts we can *almost* grasp. We can feel them tantalizingly just beyond our reach. But the idea of true nothingness is something else. When we try to imagine a place where there is no space and a time when there is no time, we are lost.

Furthermore, while our telescopes can see almost to the edge of our universe, and hence to the beginnings of time, we cannot see beyond that barrier,[63] cannot directly learn anything about whatever it was that birthed our universe. We can observe nothing of what lies outside our space-time. A complete understanding of subatomic physics would also help, but no microscope or collider is powerful enough to penetrate into that ultimate reality either.

Because of these conceptual and observational barriers, some deem it impossible for us to crack the final mystery. But we should be cautious in using an absolute word like "impossible." Certainly, much of what we have achieved today would have seemed equally impossible to scientists a few centuries ago. We have many more centuries—even millennia—ahead of us. We today will probably seem like cavemen to people a thousand or a million years from now.

And, as noted, perhaps we have already seen a glimmer of the answer. We wonder how the universe could arise out of nothingness, but "nothingness" (akin to the biblical "chaos" preceding creation) may actually be a complicated state of affairs. Even where there is no space or time, events may occur, call them "quantum fluctuations," perhaps particles popping in and out of existence (as they may well do in ordinary space-time), with minibangs continually occurring naturally, most stillborn, but one in a zillion whomping up into a big bang and a universe like ours.[64] It has even been suggested that perhaps the

---

63. We can see things up to about 13.7 billion light-years away, whose light has taken 13.7 billion years to get here; if there is anything farther out, its light could not yet have reached us.

64. Our universe seems to exist on the knife-edge between one born too dense, which would quickly collapse back upon itself, and one not dense enough, which would dissipate without ever forming stars. But, if the odds

"singularities" within black holes, where huge masses of matter are crushed down into very little or even zero space, causing a breakdown of the normal laws of physics, could be the genesis of big bangs and new universes launched into other dimensions.[65]

These are merely potential hypotheses, undeveloped stabs in the darkness, that are impossible to test by existing scientific methods. It's not unlikely that in the far future they will seem as quaint as the turtle cosmology seems now. But the point is this: notwithstanding the immensity of the mystery, notwithstanding the barriers to our solving it, the universe was certainly not the mystical creation of a mystical force. It is a product of reality. Its creation was the product of rational laws. As such, it is susceptible to being understood. The "quantum fluctuation" and "singularity" ideas have been mentioned not so much because they could be right as to show that a rational answer is at least conceivable.

We have really come quite far toward reaching it. What we know today is surely far closer to the truth than turtle cosmologies and their

---

seem steep against hitting the exact "sweet spot" between those two dooms, we don't have to beat those odds; we already have. Before your birth, the odds against creating a person exactly like you were astronomical; yet here you are.

There are other parameters of our universe that likewise seem preternaturally calculated to facilitate our existence. Change slightly, for example, the strength of gravity, and you get no planets. Perhaps there are myriad other universes, slightly different, where life cannot exist and there's nobody to know it. Since we do exist, it should be no surprise that we inhabit that rare universe where such is possible.

Also, one might ask how such a vast universe could have so tiny a cause as a quantum fluctuation. Yet size is a relative concept and, from the standpoint of creation, meaningless. The universe seems very large only in relation to us. Compared to an atom, we are very large. And compared to something else, if we could but imagine it, the universe might seem small.

65. If we analogize our own space-time to the surface of a sphere, a new universe birthed from a black hole on it can be envisioned as a new sphere, connected to ours only at the one point of the singularity. Such a budding process could create infinite universes.

like. I wish I could live long enough to see the end of this quest. I'd love to know the ultimate answer (if I could understand it). But the answer itself will be secondary to the immensity of our achievement in learning it.

Someday, I do believe, we shall stand upon that mountaintop from which we see *everything*.

Freedom from Fear

One of the big cases in my government career concerned the nearly completed Shoreham Nuclear Power Station on Long Island. There was intense opposition; local residents were very upset about what they saw as a safety threat. While not a single person had ever been killed by a nuclear power plant in the United States, no one could guarantee that the risk was zero, and this was unacceptable to the plant's opponents. Their hysteria resulted in Shoreham ultimately being scrapped, a $5 billion loss, much of which fell upon the utility's customers. They were willing to incur that cost to avoid what they felt was a danger.

We've discussed previously how lots of people worry too much (because nature programs us to be worriers). We also tend to worry about the wrong things, failing to see risks and dangers in a rational perspective.

Many Shoreham opponents, so concerned over nuclear generation of electricity, used natural gas for heating, a far more dangerous energy source. In fact, unlike nuclear power, gas brings a highly toxic substance right into people's homes. It can cause explosions, and it kills people year in and year out. But, in contrast to nuclear power, gas heat is something familiar that we have grown accustomed to living with. We don't even give it a thought. Moreover, some of those so frightened by nuclear power were overweight couch potatoes who drove without seat belts and smoked. These behaviors are dangers that kill *millions* of Americans.

In the case of Shoreham, there was an idea that insisting on zero risk was reasonable, that zero risk should be attainable, and that nothing less should be tolerated. Many people today do imagine they ought to be totally safeguarded from all dangers and are entitled to expect to live in cocoons of safety. They get upset at the least hint of risk. Anything that poses any danger is a scandal. Somebody (usually the government) should do something about it.

This is a misguided fantasy. No human activity is free of risk or danger. Indeed, no matter what we do, the mortality rate for humans is still going to be 100 percent. We should, of course, work to combat serious risks, but we have to grasp the difference between major and minor ones. Because life is full of risks, threats, and dangers, many of them huge and fundamental (such as heart failure, the commonest cause of death), to go to great lengths (and cost) to avoid some minuscule remote danger—like that of a nuclear power plant—is a misuse of effort and resources. It is akin to the proverbial rearranging of deck chairs on a sinking ship.

Taking sensible precautions against dangers is life enhancing. But excessive fearfulness is not; it degrades our quality of life. Constant fretting does not make for a sunny disposition. Stress is associated with all kinds of negative health effects. And being fearful doesn't really make us safer either; it can even do the opposite. One preteen boy lost in the wilderness actually hid from would-be rescuers because he'd been inculcated with a fear of kidnapping.

Popular media contribute greatly to our culture of fear. When children are snatched it's actually almost always by relatives, not strangers, but the news media make us phobic about such things. Scary stories sell newspapers and attract eyeballs to screens; hence, we see relentless and sensationalized coverage of kidnappings and other violent episodes. This leads many to imagine we live in a fundamentally violent society. But that's totally at odds with reality. Admittedly, domestic violence is a problem; but most of us go through our lives hardly ever actually experiencing or witnessing violence by strangers. Indeed, such episodes are newsworthy precisely because they are rare.[66]

Most health scares we encounter are overblown too. A recent warning concerned bacteria—a favorite bugbear of scaremongers—in unsterilized plastic water bottles. Yet bacteria is pervasive in our environment; we are awash in bacteria—our own bodies are bursting with it. We are told that unsanitized toothbrushes can harbor millions of bacteria, but overlook the *billions* of bacteria in the natural ecosystems in our mouths. Of course some rare germs are harmful, but the vast bulk of those we encounter (at least in everyday life) are not. We evolved to coexist with most bacteria, and do so very nicely. If you want to live bacteria-free, you'll need to find another planet.[67]

Some Americans are afraid to eat beef because a relatively few Britons contracted a rare brain disorder that *may* be related to mad cow disease (BSE), which is virtually nonexistent in the United States. You are far more likely to be electrocuted in your bathtub than to get brain disease from beef. Then, in typical sensationalist fashion, Britain's newspapers screamed that "the biggest food scare since BSE" concerned a toxin that accidentally got into some Worcestershire sauce. A study had shown that high doses of this toxin fed to rats daily for two years produced "pre-cancerous indications." To get an equivalent dose, an average man would have to imbibe about two hundred gallons of the tainted sauce—likewise daily for two years. (This might cause other health problems!)

Many people also worry about chemical residues on food, and pay extra for "organic" produce supposedly free of it; but, as far as scientific evidence is concerned, the health effect of such residues is so infinites-

---

66. And becoming rarer: since 1993 both violent crime and family violence in the United States have fallen by more than half.

67. Our germ phobia may actually be harmful—some researchers believe that limiting infants' exposure to germs inhibits full deployment of their immune systems, causing later health problems.

imal that to wash produce in fear of it is literally just wasting water.[68] Some people actually wash fruit with cigarettes in their mouths. Smokers lose *ten years of life* on average. Washing fruit is rearranging deck chairs.

Our phobia about chemicals like pesticides overlooks the fact that everything in the world, every substance, is a chemical. And it's wrong to suppose man-made chemicals are somehow in a class different from the "natural" kind. In fact, nature abounds with toxic carcinogens. Many plants produce natural pesticides just as toxic as man-made ones. But of course—just as we evolved to live with bacteria—our bodies have evolved to tolerate quite well the natural chemical toxins to which we have always been unavoidably exposed.

Many of the scare messages bombarding us are the work of advocates seeking attention, often ideologues with political agendas. This was certainly true of the movement opposing nuclear power. It is also true of many food scares. Some people are congenitally hostile to science and technology; they hate what they see as our hubristic "tampering" with nature. Nuclear power certainly pushes their buttons. Never mind that everything we've ever done to improve our lives since Paleolithic times has meant tampering with nature.

Genetically modified (GM) food is a perfect case in point. Modern Luddites viscerally loathe the idea of GM food; they demonize it as "Frankenfood," and invoke a "precautionary principle," which says we should shun anything new until we're 100 percent sure it's safe. That might sound prudent. But in the real world almost nothing is 100 percent certain, and to actually insist on this impossible standard would mean freezing all technological progress. A more sensible approach is to weigh potential risks against potential rewards.

---

68. And banning pesticides would, in fact, make people *less* healthy. How so? One good way to stay healthy is to eat fruits and vegetables. Without pesticides, they would be produced in smaller quantities and would cost more. People would consequently eat less of them.

And, of course, we've already noted how banning DDT has caused a huge death toll from insect-borne disease—yet another example of how excessive fear can actually make us less safe.

As for GM food, the truth is that practically everything we eat is a product of genetic modification, what in the past was called "selective breeding." Modern GM techniques are just more efficient and precise. So is GM food 100 percent safe? No; nothing ever is. But no objective scientific evaluation points to any dangers remotely commensurate with GM's overwhelming benefits.[69] We should not deny ourselves big benefits because of unreasonable fear of small dangers.

Incidentally, those who think modern tampering with nature has made food less safe could not be more mistaken. During the twentieth century the death rate from contaminated food fell *99 percent*.

In a decade or two, we will probably look back with bemusement at the GM food scare. It's a typical pattern for unfamiliar technologies. In the nineteenth century people worried that telegraph wires would affect the weather, and that trains would induce nervous disorders. Remember the big scare about power lines causing cancer? That fear, we have learned, was also totally misplaced, but not before we wasted many billions on repetitive studies. Then there was the scare about cell phones causing brain disease. Could be true—if you talk for a few billion minutes. And let's not forget the greatest poster child for technology scares: the Y2K computer problem. We were warned about the power grid collapsing, water not coming out of faucets, and airplanes falling from the sky. Some frantic people headed for the hills and built bunkers stocked with supplies. But what actually happened at Y2K zero hour? Nothing.

But, again, we often fail to see risks and dangers in a sensible perspective. Many have always been afraid of flying; and, after 9/11, a lot

---

69. For instance, trial use of GM rice in China by small farmers increased yields and reduced the need for pesticides by over 80 percent, which improved growers' incomes as well as their health (*The Economist*, April 30, 2005). But GM is useful not only in agriculture; it is being used to improve many other products in myriad ways beneficial to humankind. One small example is insulin (vital for diabetics), which is now being made far more efficiently than in the past by putting a human gene into a bacterium. Is this tampering with nature? Absolutely. That's how we live and thrive.

more folks thought they'd play it safe by avoiding air travel. Yet, while air crashes do occur, when you consider the hundreds of millions of people who fly safely, the risk of dying in a crash is extremely remote. Even factoring in the terrorist threat, the average passenger is still probably more likely to be hit by lightning than to die in an air crash.

In fact, the post-9/11 avoidance of air travel actually (surprise!) made people *less* safe. In lieu of flying, many opted for something that felt safer to them, but in reality is one of the most dangerous things we do: driving. In a typical year the US commercial aviation death toll is less than one hundred.[70] *But over forty thousand die annually in car crashes.* More driving instead of flying after 9/11 meant more highway deaths. It is even conceivable that, in this way, the 9/11 hijackers killed more people in cars than they killed in airplanes.

One explanation for skewed perceptions of road versus air safety is that we tend to be more fearful of risks that seem beyond our control. The idea of sitting in an airplane going down, with absolutely nothing you can do, is terrifying. Nuclear power seems scary in a similar way. In contrast, people imagine that behind the wheel of a car they have control. That's true up to a point, but many car crashes are the other guy's fault. And the bigger point remains that, mile for mile, auto travel is far more dangerous, and kills many more people, than air travel.[71]

This reality is highly useful in helping us develop a proper perspective on this whole subject of risk. Despite the notion of having some control while driving, most people do recognize the danger of car travel. Injury and death on the roads is, indeed, so common that most of us have witnessed it and know personally of victims. And yet, we continue to get into our cars every day and drive. Are we crazy?

---

70. For the three years between 2002 and 2004 combined, it was only 34.

71. Another factor distorting many people's risk evaluations is lack of an intuitive understanding of probability theory and big numbers, with "million" being a fuzzy concept. Thus, we don't grasp how truly tiny is the risk of dying in a plane crash or nuclear disaster, getting a rare disease, or many other things we worry over. (Similar misperceptions prompt people to waste time and money buying lottery tickets with astronomical odds against winning.)

Not at all. We also understand the benefits we get from auto travel. We accept the risks as a reasonable price to pay for the benefits.[72]

And there's something even more dangerous we routinely do: go into hospitals. The government estimates that *over one hundred thousand* Americans die annually in hospitals from infections unrelated to their original maladies. While, as mentioned, everyday germs in our environment are no threat, hospitals have become breeding grounds for some deadly bacteria. And at least as many people also die because of medical errors in hospitals. Yet nobody proposes shutting them down. We, as a society, judge that what hospitals do is still so beneficial that it's worth all the costs and risks. Hospitals kill a lot of people, but save more than they kill.

Most of the things we do in life involve such trade-offs. Nothing can ever be 100 percent safe. Just as we must balance costs against benefits, so too must risks and dangers be weighed against rewards. While we try to avoid taking big risks for small payoffs, we recognize the good sense of taking small risks for big benefits. Gas heat is dangerous, but we correctly see the danger as small in relation to its usefulness. GM foods provide enormous benefits at very small risk. Likewise nuclear energy—Long Islanders were foolish to junk a five-billion-dollar power plant due to a danger smaller, probably, than the risk of drowning in their own backyard swimming pools (which, of course, they didn't stop using).[73]

In evaluating all such issues and trade-offs, it is very helpful to keep in mind that annual auto death statistic. We accept that truly big risk, climbing into our cars every day to drive. We don't even fret over it. So what is the sense of torturing ourselves over the risks of GM food, tainted beef, nuclear power, or pesticide residues on fruit? Whenever you think about such risks, stop and ask yourself how they

---

72. Incidentally, there is some good news about the highway death rate. Per mile driven, it fell by 73 percent between 1966 and 2004, largely because cars have been made safer and seat belt use has risen.

73. It's been calculated that a family pool is a hundred times more dangerous to children than a gun in the home.

stack up against the risks of driving, with its known and certain forty thousand annual death toll.

The age of terrorism does present us with new fears. But let us not make the morbid error of imagining ourselves more threatened than in some earlier innocent time. Pain and death have been our eternal companions; yet if we do have new fears, we have at least been freed from many old ones. Childhood death, to name just one, used to be grimly common. But fears have never kept us from living our lives. Fear of children dying never stopped people from having children (indeed, it's partly why they had so many). Londoners did not abandon their city during the nightly WWII bombing raids. We fear car crashes, but we drive. And, after 9/11, we still fly; and it's right that we do. To live has always required the facing of dangers; has always required courage.

One of my daughter's sixth-grade classmates was not allowed on a field trip to a New York City museum because her parents feared a terrorist attack. Well, its probability was not zero, but neither is the probability of being hit by lightning or, more likely, by an automobile. That family's "precautionary principle" would keep them from ever setting foot outside their home. Oh, but wait: many fatal accidents occur in the home. Better not even get out of bed.

We can't live that way.

Keep to a proper weight. Get some exercise. Don't smoke. Don't abuse alcohol or other substances. Use condoms if not monogamous. See your doctor regularly and follow her advice. Drive defensively and use seat belts. Avoid walking alone through secluded crime-ridden areas after dark, and other such obvious risks. These precautions will take care of the big threats to health and safety, and, if you tend to them, all the rest is hardly worth worrying about. Do this, and enjoy your life in freedom from fear.

Love, Marriage, and Sex

Some think falling in love comes as a bolt from the blue. Perhaps it sometimes happens this way. The human psyche, after all, is extraordinarily complex, and who knows what it will do depending on circumstances. But the much more common experience of falling in love seems to be the product of several factors, not all of which are mysterious.

The first is readiness. The mind lays the groundwork even before the love object appears. One may not even be aware of this process of getting ready. Once again, our minds work much like computers running programs, and some programs run themselves without our cognizance. Certainly evolution, whose sole driver is genetic replication, has programmed us with a strong mating instinct. Likewise, our hormones have a big role to play in shoving us in that direction. In addition, we pick up a lot of cues from the general culture, our peers, and so on. So even if you don't think you're looking for love, your unconscious may have other ideas.

As to whom this love impetus will latch onto, physical attraction is certainly an indispensable factor. Of course, one is routinely attracted to numerous people without falling in love. What makes the difference is the interaction; the word "chemistry" commonly used is very apt because it is indeed rather like a chemical reaction between two substances. Usually when mixing chemicals nothing much happens. But mix the right ones and you get an explosion.

The process also has the character of a feedback loop. The pair push each other's buttons, doing and saying things that feed the attraction. This can take many forms; sometimes even indifference or rejection can actually feed it, making the love object seem even more desirable. But positive feedback works better. The fact is that, generally, we *want* to be in love, and given halfway reasonable material to work with, our psyches will try to make it happen.

I recall one second date I had with a woman who exclaimed that it had gone much better than she'd expected. "You must have had low expectations," I said. "No," she replied, "They were very high!" Saying things like that to each other, making gestures like that—pushing each other's buttons—rapidly escalated the warmth of feeling between us. (We'd have wound up married if I hadn't eventually pushed a wrong button that broke the feedback loop.)

The foregoing is a rational dissection of falling in love. Yet, to be sure, there is an irrational aspect too, unleashing powerful and primitive emotions. Research has revealed that the onset of romantic love activates parts of the brain, below conscious awareness, that produce and respond to dopamine, a chemical that also causes the kind of "rush" experienced from drugs like cocaine, winning at gambling, and so forth. Our susceptibility to such sensory rewards, indeed a craving for them, is what makes cocaine and gambling so bewitching. The effects of falling in love are closely related. The feelings thus triggered by such infatuation are more intense and quite distinct from those associated with mere everyday sexual attraction.

Of course, this sort of highly charged falling-in-love brain response is impermanent; over time it morphs into a longer-term bonding with the beloved, which is again quite different, lacking the raw force of intoxication, but more stable. For most people, such bonding provides psychic rewards of a different but not less valued kind.

So now you understand everything about love. (I hope you also understand about irony.) Okay, maybe love is a little more complicated. Or maybe it's the most complicated thing in the world.

In discussing "the good life," love was deemed an element of happiness and meaning. And, perhaps restating the obvious, love does rank right at the top of what makes for a rewarding life, both loving and being loved. Of course, this applies not just to romantic love, but to all forms; the love I share with my child is a great thing, and her love for her pets brings her joy too. But romantic love is something else and no analogy or metaphor can do it justice. The analysis above may make love sound prosaic; it doesn't express the poetry. But certainly, no theme has figured larger in all the world's poetry and other literature. This is not just because of the subject's inherently poetic character, but chiefly because there's no other topic humans find half so interesting.

Yet, while we are so attracted to love and romance, some liken it to the attraction of a moth to a flame. They fear getting burned. But a great prize is worth a risk; life's rewards go not to the timid, who hang back in fear, but to those with courage and boldness to face the risks of trying to seize them. In my own pursuit of romance (often inept or even clueless), I encountered more than my share of failure and rejection. Yes, it hurt; but those wounds felt like pinpricks as against my vision of what love could be. I saw nothing more important in life. That's what propelled me forward, to try again, and again, and again.

And you've surely heard Tennyson's line that it's better to have loved and lost than never to have loved at all. I've acknowledged that pain can actually enrich our lives; and love, while it can produce exaltation, can also give us the richest, most exquisite suffering. In a Simon and Garfunkel song, the narrator, eschewing love, declares himself a rock, an island: "a rock feels no pain, and an island never cries." He is missing something important of what it is to be human.

I lived with one woman for eleven years. I don't actually know if I was "in love" with her in the full romantic sense (it *is* so complicated), but we did have a nice loving relationship—for maybe a year or two—and, after that, our further life together, as we wrestled with our feelings and our situation, produced much pain for both of us. But

I would not go back and undo those years if I could. Being in the situation and grappling with it imbued my existence with intensity and meaning. Not just in retrospect, but even during the worst of it, I felt as though I was living high opera. And in the fire of that suffering I was annealed. I emerged from it a better, more mature, deeper, and wiser person. If I hadn't gone through that, I doubt I could have such a good marriage now (with someone else).

Grasp the nettle; embrace the risk. The rewards for success are great. And so, even, are the rewards of failure.

This book stresses the primacy of the individual and the individual's self-realization. But this does not mean promotion of aloneness. Now, it is a reality of life that we are isolated—while John Donne was metaphorically right that no man is an island, in the literal physical sense we are indeed islands—yet we are social animals; and a true flowering of individuality takes place only within the context of participation in society and interaction with other people.

Marriage is a paramount vehicle for such interaction, putting one's relationship with another person at the center of one's life. While we cannot run wires to interconnect minds as we can interconnect computers (nor do we really become "one flesh" as some marriage ceremonies proclaim), marriage, at its best, is about as close as we can get to that. Marriage is a bridge between islands, the ultimate antidote to human isolation.

And while romantic love is the starting point, what marriage is really all about is togetherness, companionship, comradeship, sharing experience, and building a history of shared experience that weaves a rich texture to your life. The passion part and the romantic part do not fill sixteen waking hours a day, 365 days a year. What does fill most of those hours, days, years, and ultimately decades, is the ordinary stuff of living. It is profoundly enriched by having a partner, by knowing that one is not facing life alone. Marriage is a safety net of love and support to fall back upon. It fulfills the universal human need, as Rabbi Harold Kushner says, to be loved, to be validated, to be wanted, to be cherished. Even if one actually draws upon such sustenance only from time to time, the key thing is just knowing it is there when needed; that whatever troubles the outside world may hold, you have a refuge, a sanctuary, a cheerleader, and an ally; and this sustaining knowledge is present in one's mind and psyche not just from time to time, but all the time. This is the real blessing of marriage.

To thusly share life is to build an edifice of such psychic satisfaction, brick by brick, like sedimental accretion. Life becomes a joint enterprise, more satisfying and rewarding than an individual project. This was part of why my wife and I decided to become parents; we knew that raising a child would be a joint project, which we believed would enhance and enrich the closeness and meaning of our marriage.

So, again, you see that the kind of romantic love that impels people into marriage is a very different thing from the kind of love that sustains it day to day and decade to decade. The former inevitably fades, though never to nothing if we're fortunate; and if we are fortunate, the latter builds upon its foundation and grows to greater height.

In any such relationship, you get out of it what you put in.[74] Just as there is no free lunch in the economic sphere, there is none in the emotional sphere, in the realm of relationships and marriage, either. A lot of marriages fail because people are looking for free lunches. They focus on what they're getting, or not getting, without regard to what they put in. If two people each seek happiness from the other, but neither is willing or able to give what the other needs, it isn't going to work, is it?

We love our computers. They crash now and then, sometimes refuse to do what we want, and give us all sorts of other headaches, but we wouldn't want to live without them. A spouse is very much like that. You can't expect your spouse to always do or be what you want. Indeed, you marry a human being, not a machine or tool, and human beings are even more complex and quirky than computers. You have to expect some problems, glitches, and conflicts. You have to be prepared to deal with them and ride them out. Often, marriage partners

---

74. Of course, this applies to all human relationships. To quote Yogi Berra again, "You can't expect people to show up for your funeral if you don't go to theirs."

are too selfish and perfectionist to accept this reality. They'd rather just wash their hands of a relationship that does not wholly conform to their preconceptions of what it should be like, even if such preconceptions and the idea of total satisfaction are completely unrealistic.

John Gray wrote a popular book proclaiming that men are from Mars, women are from Venus. Most of us (apart from some feminist extremists) seem to have gotten over the temporary insanity of trying to deny that there are innate differences between the sexes. While women are not inferior to men, they are not superior either, but they're certainly not the same.[75] Sometimes I think my wife is not just from a different planet, but from a different dimension. (She disagrees with much of this book!) But I wasn't looking for a wife who is like a man. I sought a woman, and women are not like men.

We have a good marriage because we are at ease with each other's differences, and that is a key point. Marry someone you can rub along with, as they are, without imagining that you can change your spouse to fit your specifications. Marriage should not be a procrustean bed.[76] That's a recipe for pain and failure. Marital partners need not be carbon copies, but should instead complement each other. Yet again, exercise tolerance. Live and let live with your life partner too. When your spouse has the freedom to find fulfillment in his or her own way, you have a happier partner and a better marriage.

---

75. Harvard president Lawrence Summers provoked politically correct hysteria by querying whether innate differences might help explain underrepresentation of women in science and engineering. Yet ample research confirms that male and female brains differ physiologically and operationally—Mars and Venus. On average, women have better communication skills while men have better visual-spatial skills. And male variability is greater—there are more men at both the high and low performance ends of the bell curve, while women cluster more in the middle (this was Summers's point). Some fight these realities as implying that women *can't* excel in science. But, of course, even if the male population has the mentioned advantages, it wouldn't mean that an *individual* woman can't be a whizbang scientist.

76. If you didn't fit Procrustes' bed, either you'd be stretched or else literally cut down to size.

Of course it's not that simple. It takes two to tango, and you can't control the other person's behavior. But you can control your own. You can at least do what *you're* supposed to do; and maybe that will influence what the other person does (another feedback loop).

What is the most important thing to be concerned about in a marriage? The marriage. That's an obvious answer, and yet, it often seems to get lost in the fog of other concerns. Life is like that; at any particular moment, you may have intense feelings about some particular thing that, in the long view, is really pretty insignificant. Most quarrels are like that. When people argue, the natural tendency is to ask oneself, "What can I say to win this argument?" Rarely do we ask ourselves, "What can I say that will help this relationship?"

Don't Sweat the Small Stuff is the title of another popular book, by Richard Carlson, and it's pretty good advice for life in general, but especially for relationships and marriage. The subtitle continues, *And It's All Small Stuff.* The latter part is a little tougher, but when we consider that we're all going to die someday, an awful lot of what happens in life can indeed be seen as small stuff. The rule of thumb I try to follow in marriage is to always say yes on small stuff, to say yes unless I have a really strong reason to say no. Of course, this is a hard rule to follow, and I'm not perfect, but nevertheless I think it is the standard to which it behooves a marriage partner to aspire. Again, you get out what you put in. To receive "yesses" from your spouse, you have to give "yesses."

These same basic notions apply to sex. Here, too, you get out of it what you put in. Sex with someone you don't care about may provide some thrill and gratification, but nothing like the psychic reward when it's mutual and loving. And, even just looking at the physical aspect, it's a reality of sex that while self-pleasuring is okay, it never produces the intensity that a partner's loving ministrations can provide (just as it's impossible to successfully tickle oneself). This is not just some odd quirk, but an integral fact of sexuality produced by evolution because nature, for obvious reasons, wants us to copulate, not masturbate. That's why going it alone is less fun.

Indeed, as with Christmas, it might even be said that it's more blessed to give than to receive—to focus at least as much on the pleasure you give as on what you're getting. Of course, this is not a prescription for altruistic self-denial. If both partners follow it, if each does focus on gratifying the other, then neither need be concerned over personal satisfaction, since they will both get it.

Understand too that in sex the physical part, the orgasm, is not the critical thing. Our most important sex organ is the brain. What happens there matters far more than what goes on below the waist. And what most gratifies the mind in sex is the human interrelation. This, too, is why it's best when shared with a loving partner. Again, one can produce a solitaire orgasm, but that leaves out an awfully big part of the sexual experience, its embodiment of intimacy with another person (which, of course, is why we resort to fantasizing when working solo). A kiss is pleasurable not so much on account of the physical sensations as because of the person at the other end of it. A woman's breast is exciting to a man not because of its physical attributes per se, but rather, mainly because her exposing it to him implies her desire to be intimate with him (or her intimate submission to him),[77] which is the thing his psyche craves more than the orgasm. And many women (not all—there are no universals in sexual preferences) like the feeling of submitting.

Furthermore, even as far as the physical aspect is concerned, there is a lot more to sex than just the genital sensations. It also triggers the release of mood-altering hormones and brain chemicals. This potent cocktail of physical and chemical *plus* emotional factors is what makes sex so important in human relations. It is a powerful bonding glue. (That's why arranged marriages have so often been successful. Even if the partners had no emotional ties before, repeated sex together tends to create them.)

All this is why, in human society, sex is such a big deal. And yet, one actually hears peculiarly often from young people the phrase "no

---

77. Thus, rape is usually not so much about the sexual act as about the rapist's expression of how he seeks to define his relation to the victim.

big deal" applied to sex, usually invoked toward parents and elders who may be censorious about it. "No big deal" dismisses such concerns. The teenager blows them off by asserting that sex with a boyfriend or girlfriend is "no big deal."

This is tragic. Sex is one of the sublime things in life; it *should* be a big deal! To treat it as a routine commodity, to regard the sex act as little distinct from brushing one's teeth, is akin to saying that Beethoven's Fifth Symphony is no big deal, that Michelangelo's *David* is no big deal, that *Hamlet* is no big deal.[78]

But, alas, for many people today, this is true of sex because it is so freely available and so freely indulged in. That which is rare is precious and highly valued; something commonplace is not precious or highly valued. Notably in the youth culture of "hook-ups," where dating, courtship, and romance have become obsolete, sex is a debased currency of little value. Not only is sex divorced from love, it is divorced from any real semblance of human relationship. Call me an old fuddy-duddy, but I insist this isn't progress.[79]

In contrast, my own experience was very atypical, but all the better for driving home the point. In my early adulthood I was quite inhibited in relationships. This meant that sex, though I craved it, was not at all freely available to me. And, when I finally did find the key to unlock the door, the treasure within seemed precious indeed. The idea that sex is something very special was so deeply imprinted that it has remained with me ever since. And I consider this a gift that I am lucky to possess. Being able to share this precious thing with a life partner who feels the same way has enhanced the happiness of our marriage. For both of us, it is a big deal.

Thus, I wince whenever I hear some young person blithely deem sex "no big deal." That means it will be no big deal too when, and if, a real love comes along. How sad!

---

78. Some voices actually argue for "demystifying" sex or even love itself. What a thoroughly horrible notion! Shall we make all of life prosaic?

79. Yet there is good news. By no means are "hook-ups" ubiquitous among younger Americans. And sexual promiscuity actually appears to be declining.

Not everyone, of course, has the blessing of a loving long-term partner providing sexual fulfillment, and those who don't cannot be told to just accept celibacy. People do need sex. But the choices are not limited simply to monogamy, celibacy, or promiscuity. A balance can be struck between the impetus to express and experience sexuality, on the one hand, and, on the other, the desirability of preserving its specialness. This means avoidance of the kind of promiscuity that debases sex and denudes it of meaning by divorcing it from human connection, which is what happens when the sex act is just simply an act, and the person on the other end is a mere instrumentality.

What this points toward is the goal of situating sex in the context of finding and developing an intimate relationship. This process calls forth the whole range of human feelings, in which sexuality plays a proper role. It is almost necessarily a journey of false starts and abortive trials (witness my own tortuous history), and that's okay; sex can have meaning even in a relationship that doesn't ultimately work out. So, if you don't have the ideal of a loving partner to share sex, then at least let the expression of sexual feeling be part of the quest to connect emotionally with another person and build toward a loving intimacy. Fully realized human beings have a great yearning for this; it's central to our lives. Keeping sex in this context keeps it, rightly, a big deal.

Political Vocabulary

The previous chapters have looked mainly inward, to the self, and to personal issues. Those that follow will look outward, to larger societal issues of politics and economics. Your first reaction may be "Snore!" But by "politics" I don't mean candidates and campaigns; and economics (traditionally, "the dismal science") doesn't mean just stuff like banking and finance. These subjects are far bigger. They concern how the world works and how people fit into it.

Before going further, it seems desirable to address what some political words mean. Getting the language straight should help us get the ideas straight. But unfortunately, political vocabulary is a source of much confusion and often serves to muddy rather than clarify debate. Indeed, the misuse of words seems endemic to the political realm. This is illustrated by the fictional political slogans such as "War is Peace," in George Orwell's *Nineteen Eighty-Four*. And when the North Korean regime talks about its "freedom and democracy," the words are disemboweled of meaning. If you've ever wondered how you could think without language, you can see what's at stake here. One can't begin to think properly about political issues without properly understanding the language.

Most of us understand what *democracy* really does mean: rule by the people. This was literal in classical ancient democracies, with citizens all gathering together to make decisions. Because this is impractical in a big country, we elect officials to represent us in decision-making. This is called a *republic*. But the key feature is that government is still answerable to the people, and so, we still rightly use the word "democracy." A regime like North Korea's may see itself as "democratic" in that it supposedly makes decisions on behalf of the populace, but if the people have no say, that's a sham, as are "elections" with no genuine choices. What's missing is any accountability of the regime to its subjects.

That accountability is what gives any government its *legitimacy*, its right to make laws and decisions and to enforce them. Legitimacy is a crucial political concept. Our government has the powers it does because we have agreed to give it those powers, through voting; and ultimate power always remains with the people, through their ability to change the government by voting. In contrast, regimes that cannot trace their powers to the free choice of their people (as in North Korea, China, and Iran) have no legitimacy—and no more moral right to govern and expect obedience than a robber has to take your money at gunpoint. And indeed, it is only through force that such regimes hold power.

Sovereignty is a related concept. A sovereign was, in classical terms, a ruler. A sovereign government has the power to rule and a sovereign nation is one empowered to rule itself. But sovereignty cannot sensibly be divorced from the idea of legitimacy. While we must respect the sovereignty of an independent nation, that should not extend to its regime if that regime lacks legitimacy. Nations have rights in international law, but illegitimate regimes should not—just as the law does not recognize a gunman's right to rob you.

The classical political division is between "Left" and "Right." Historically this derives from the seating arrangement in the national legislature during the French Revolution, with the radicals sitting on the left side and conservatives on the right. Radicals (the Left) wanted change and to overthrow the status quo (which means the way things are); conservatives (the Right), as the word implies, were keener to keep things as they had been.

In the nineteenth and twentieth centuries, *socialism* was the signature creed of the Left. Socialism called for radical change—including government ownership and operation of industries, supposedly on behalf of the people. *Communism* was an extension of the socialist idea; it was rooted in the writings of Karl Marx, a nineteenth-century German thinker. He denounced *capitalism*, the prevailing economic system, wherein a large business is financed by raising capital (the money needed to build the factory, pay the workers, and so forth) from investors, who then own the business and its profits. Marx considered it unjust "exploitation" for owners to get all the profits from labor, giving workers only enough to live on.[80] Communism's remedy was to eliminate the capitalist owners, with workers themselves instead "owning" businesses. Under communism, all people were to be part of a "collective," for which they worked and which would take care of their needs.

This, in theory, was the organizing principle of the Soviet Union and other communist states. They wore the sheep's clothing of equality and social justice, but the wolfish reality was that people became serfs of an all-powerful state, with no rights at all—as with *Star Trek*'s "Borg." Use of the word "collective" in both cases was no coincidence. Like the Borg, communism crushed the individuality out of people to make them cogs in a machine.

Another nineteenth-century political thread, centered in Great Britain, was "liberalism." Liberals were heirs of the Enlightenment.[81]

---

80. Marx thought that workers were powerless and that their wages would, therefore, be pushed down by owners to bare subsistence levels. This proved untrue (in the West), in part due to workers organizing into labor unions, in part due to government interventions, but also, in major part, because technology greatly increased productivity and skills gave workers economic power. The result was a huge affluent middle class, which Marx never foresaw.

81. The Enlightenment was an eighteenth-century European philosophical movement that emphasized reason, learning, and a quest for verifiable empirical truth in contrast to the revelations of religion.

They believed in maximizing liberty, and hence in democratic and limited government, free trade, and no government meddling in the economy. The buzzword was *laissez-faire*, meaning "let them do as they please," a phrase which still remains a fixture of political debate—often used derisively, as though the idea is nonsensical on its face.

The 1920s and 1930s saw the rise of *fascism* in Italy and somewhat similar Nazism in Germany. Because both fought communists (considered the extreme Left), fascism and Nazism got tagged as "Rightist" movements. This is where the confusion really begins, because there was nothing conventionally rightist or conservative about fascism (a label which includes Nazism). To the contrary, these movements were quite radical, with Leftist economic programs involving a large role for the state; indeed, "Nazi" was short for "National Socialist." Fascists and Nazis battled communists not out of ideological enmity so much as in competition for power.

These three "isms" can be lumped together as *totalitarian*, which, as the word implies, means they totally monopolized power and control in their societies, tolerating no opposition of or deviation from their ideologies. Totalitarianism represents an attempt to mold humanity. Rather than accepting people as they are, totalitarians strove to reengineer the species. Nazis attempted to weed out the supposedly less fit, and communists tried to abolish economic motivations.

The misleading idea that fascism is "right wing" and somehow the opposite of communism has gotten stuck in our vocabulary; and the Left loves to slap the label "fascist" indiscriminately on anyone it disagrees with.[82] By such rhetorical jiujitsu, the Left paints conservatism ("right wing") as only a step removed from fascism.

Modern American politics effectively began with the Great

---

82. The Left does try to differentiate by labeling fascism "corporatist," with the state allying itself with industry instead of swallowing it, as under socialism or communism. It is true that fascism did allow industry to remain in private hands, but this only showed it to be less thoroughly totalitarian than communism. It certainly does not mean that governmental efforts to promote industry are "fascist."

Depression of the 1930s and the response of Franklin Roosevelt's Democratic administration to the crisis. Roosevelt vastly expanded government's role in the economy and social welfare. This conception of activist government became the ideology of the Democratic Party, took on the label *liberalism*, and was the dominant political ethos in midcentury America. The word "liberal" had a nice, positive sound, conjuring up images of broad-minded humanitarianism, and liberals do indeed see themselves in that way, as caring about the less fortunate and seeking to mobilize government to improve things. However, they have little in common with the classical European liberals whose name they took and who would be aghast at the bossy activist state promoted by their American namesakes.[83]

The word *reactionary* is a pejorative term for those on the right who react with opposition to the Left's agenda. In America, the "reaction" against liberalism (on the Left) got serious with the 1964 Goldwater Republican presidential campaign. Since that movement was in opposition to Left-liberalism, it took on the tag "conservative." But, while its adherents did tend to be socially conservative, their political agenda was not conservative at all, but quite radical, in the sense of wanting to change the existing liberal status quo.

Whereas liberalism generally means placing human welfare at the center and a willingness to compromise on freedom in order to advance welfare, conservatives generally put freedom first, believing that greater freedom is the best route to maximizing human welfare. While liberals typically look to government to solve societal problems, conservatives (to paraphrase Ronald Reagan) regard government as more of a problem than a solution. Conservatives see the free market as the virtuous engine for improving humanity's lot; liberals see it as morally suspect, needing government supervision and regulation. And conservatives, disliking big bossy government, tended to hate communism more intensely than did liberals.

But, since the 1960s heyday of a clear liberal-versus-conservative

---

83. The word "liberal" still retains its original meaning in Europe; but, hereafter, this book will use it in its American sense.

divide, the political landscape has evolved and become messier. For a time, as disillusionment with liberalism's failings set in, conservatism seemed to be winning, and the word "liberal" came to be virtually a cuss word in American politics. Few politicians today accept that label. Most people on the left have sought to rebrand themselves as "progressive," once more trying to conjure up happy connotations of enlightened thought.[84]

And meantime, American conservatism has mutated into a multi-headed creature. Some still stress the respect for liberty and individualism that was the heart of Goldwaterism. But the movement has been spoiled by success—"conservatives" put in charge of big government have succumbed to the same sorts of impulses to exploit it (and perpetuate their power) that shaped liberalism. Even under President Reagan, whose detractors made great rhetorical hay condemning supposed government program "cuts," the government was still actually expanding. In fact, columnist Michael Kinsley calculated that, in recent decades, government spending has increased more during Republican than during Democratic administrations.

Another brand of modern "conservatism" is grounded in religious fundamentalism, and is all too comfortable with government bossiness on behalf of a social agenda. There are other tendencies too, such as opposition to free trade and a xenophobic isolationism, that old Goldwaterites can hardly recognize as "conservatism." And then there is the *neoconservative*, which Irving Kristol defined as a liberal who got mugged by reality. Most prominently, "neocons" put great store on human rights and democracy and seek to aggressively spread these values throughout the world. Their militant foreign policy can be seen as the modern-day incarnation of the old conservative anticommunism (and is opposed, somewhat reflexively it seems, by the Leftist "progressive" heirs of 1960s liberalism). Yet neocons also often want government action to promote their notions of moral virtue.

So, to sum up, the one thing that's clear about the Left-Right political divide today is that it's clear as mud. But it is still a fair general-

---

84. No one wants to be thought "regressive" (or, indeed, "illiberal").

ization that "Left" means governmental activism and intervention with a putatively social welfare slant. Another fair generalization, sad to say, is that "Left" today means negativity toward American society and policy, whatever it may be, anywhere. The Left has come to regard America as quintessentially un-Left. And as to the political "Right," perhaps it's best to define it in relation to the Left: the Right is simply whatever the Left is not.

Last to be mentioned is *libertarianism*, which carries forward from classical nineteenth-century "laissez-faire" liberalism. The libertarian wants government limited to its core function of providing an environment in which every individual is free to travel his own path to happiness. Thus, libertarians envision government not as the boss of society, telling people what to do, but rather as its janitor, whose job it is to keep the wheels turning while staying out of people's way. This means that government should be responsible for maintaining order, defending the country, providing a currency, enforcing contracts, and little else.

In the modern world, where the state looms as a behemoth, libertarianism might be dismissed as romantic naiveté. Or, alternatively, given that overweening role the state has come to acquire, libertarianism might be seen as the only possible principled human response.

The Social Contract

"**M**an is born free, but he is everywhere in chains." So began Jean-Jacques Rousseau's 1761 book, *The Social Contract*. Not long afterward commenced the smashing of those chains with America's declaration that all men are created equal, with natural rights, and that securing these rights is the purpose of government, deriving its just powers from the consent of the governed.

These were radical ideas in a world ruled by kings who claimed to govern by divine right; that is, with God-given authority. In truth, they ruled neither by God nor by consent, but rather by naked force, their subjects having no say about it. On July 4, 1776, we declared our separation not just from Britain but from this whole ancient model of governance.

That old system of rulers and subjects was backwards, perverting the reason why "governments are instituted among men," which was to protect people's rights, not suppress them. John Locke had said this in 1690. Yet, virtually from its beginnings, government had been hijacked by men seeking power and self-aggrandizement, to rule over others by force.[85] In 1776, the time had come, at last, to start seizing it back.

---

85. When an ancient city-state was faced with some emergency, perhaps an attack by another city, citizens would settle upon some "big man" to take charge. Having gotten a taste of power, and liking it, he would often try to keep it, using an army loyal to him to fend off any challenges. This is basically how kingship developed.

The idea of the Declaration of Independence is that of the *social contract*. Thomas Hobbes famously wrote of life in a "state of nature" being "solitary, poor, nasty, brutish and short." The point was to approach political theory by imagining a time before government or law, when individual rights did not yet exist, might made right, and everyone was at the mercy of everyone else—the "war of all against all." Not a pretty picture.[86] Now suppose those people got together to discuss their predicament and devise a solution. The answer was for each person to give up his own recourse to "might makes right" in exchange for others giving up theirs. You were no longer free to bash your neighbor with a club and grab his food, but now he couldn't do it to you. Everyone was better off because there were fewer bashed heads, and they could now spend more time and energy gathering food and less on defending themselves and nursing their wounds. Most people would recognize this as a good thing—giving up some freedom and agreeing to follow the rules in exchange for having rights protected by law.

This is the social contract. Just like any contract, it is an agreement among people, with give and take, entered into voluntarily. Of course, Hobbes's "state of nature" never really existed, with even the most primitive societies functioning according to a kind of social contract. An informal one might work in a small tribe where everyone knows each other, but, for a larger and more complex society, we need government to manage it and enforce the rules. The object is, again, to protect people from the passions, depredations, and violence of others. Hobbes himself was actually something of a pessimist about human nature, believing that to achieve the desired safety requires despotically tough government. However, most people, though having self-serving impulses, are not murderous thieves at war with each other, but are, once again, fairly socially cooperative; and freedom to steal and kill is not something most of us even want. This also means that,

---

86. William Golding's *Lord of the Flies* envisioned a Hobbesian "state of nature" with a planeload of boys stranded on an island. The bullies and the violent soon gained ascendancy.

contrary to Hobbes's view, government does not have to be tyrannical to fulfill its protective function.

But the real point is that government, whether strong or weak, is empowered by *consent*, not any divine right. This was the key idea embodied in the Declaration of Independence (and later, the US Constitution). The authors aimed at a government serving its proper function of protecting people's security and rights, acting indeed as their servant, not their master.

If people are to control government, rather than vice versa, there has to be a means for doing so. This is democracy—the mechanism by which consent of the governed is realized. And everyone must accept everyone else's democratic rights. You cannot expect the protection of the rule of law, restraining what others can do, unless those others have a say in making those rules, just as you yourself want a say. Such democratic tolerance, allowing political space for minorities—and a "live and let live" ethos—is essential.

All of this is consistent with the fundamental values embedded in human nature and supported by reason. These universals, again, encompass the right of every person to live as he chooses, without unjust interference by others, and to have a say in the rules to which he submits. This, again, is the essence of the social contract.

Though in America's early days people generally did hold to the Founding Fathers' conception of government as servant rather than master, that idea has largely gotten lost over time, and today, citizens generally have reverted to seeing government in the ancient way, as their ruler.[87] This is perhaps understandable, given how huge government has become, how remote from people, and how bossy; with laws, rules, and regulations that we must obey, filling miles of shelf space. But still, the foundation at the bottom of it all is the social contract.

---

87. Polls regularly show that shocking numbers of Americans have a kind of "divine right" conception of government, with no notion that it should actually be answerable to them, and that, if we held a referendum on the Bill of Rights, some of it might well be voted down.

This is not to say that it is, or ever was, a literal reality. The point is, again, not whether anyone ever conducted the negotiation imagined by Hobbes and Rousseau and actually agreed to set up a society according to such principles. And, of course, no one today is asked to sign an agreement not to bash his neighbor in exchange for membership in society. The point, rather, is that this concept nevertheless *implicitly* and necessarily does lie at the heart of our participation in society. We obey its laws not merely from fear of punishment, but mainly because we understand that, in return for doing so, we receive the protection of the law. And we tolerate government's impositions because we value its benefits more.

This is the bedrock of all political theory and politics. It is indeed the prism through which all political issues must be viewed; because everything government does, every law it makes, every program it undertakes, ultimately involves precisely the trade-offs embodied in the social contract: we trade some of our liberty to get in exchange the benefits of society.

It is all about liberty. The authors of the Declaration of Independence believed every person is equally entitled to every bit as much happiness as one would wish for oneself; and, because each person is unique and must be deemed the best judge of his own advantage, the way to give everyone that equal chance at happiness is to foster maximum freedom with which to seek it. Thus, the individual, his rights, and his fulfillment are the lodestars of politics.

To reiterate, in the social contract, each person does give up some freedoms he would enjoy in a state of nature, where there are no constraints. But, in turn, he reckons to get back more than he gives up. He has more true freedom living in a society assured of peace than in a state of nature, where he's at the mercy of anyone stronger. Thus, the social contract is not about loss of freedom, it is instead about leveraging and maximizing freedom.

So when we calibrate the precise trade-offs we make in the social contract and in politics, the objective is to do so in such a way as to maximize our freedom. If we give up too little, we will not gain the greater freedom that comes from security; if we give up too much (as in a totalitarian state), we might get security but no freedom. Somewhere between those extremes lies the happy median where the trade-off is most advantageous and freedom is maximized.

This is, once more, the goal of all politics. This is the theme music behind the discussions of government and politics to come.

Individualism and Society

The previous chapter referred to the primacy of the individual as central to a positive vision of society. This merits a little more attention. Some people actually lament the advance of individualism.[88] They see it as a bad thing, inimical to societal cohesion and welfare, as though society and its members are somehow natural enemies.

Differing cultures have varied attitudes about individualism. Some Eastern traditions exalt ideas of submission to a deity or to fate, acceptance of one's lot, subordination of the individual to family or collective interests, and even a sort of passivity. But the European or Western tradition, rooted in ancient Greek thought and augmented by Christianity, sees life as being most fully lived through positive rational action, as opposed to resignation or passivity. In the Eastern conception, nothing that happens in one person's mind can matter much; to Westerners, it matters a lot.

The latter seems more consonant with the reality of human nature. We are, at the most basic organic level, individuals. Our place in

---

88. The word "individuality" refers to the fact of differences among people. "Individualism" concerns behaviors and attitudes. The word is used with very specific meanings by certain philosophic doctrines, but it will be used here merely in the general sense of people giving expression to their individuality.

society is not analogous to that of the cells comprising our bodies, which have no meaningful existence apart from their role in the larger organism. Neither are we like computers hooked up to others forming a network. For such computers, as well as for cells, participation in the larger whole is nonconscious and nonvolitional, whereas we humans have our own motivations, thoughts, and feelings—a sense of self. All these mental phenomena make us self-centered in the literal sense. Everything we do is a response to, and a product of, what happens in our individual minds. Even our most social actions are the products of our individual minds. Thus, individualism is not something to which we can say yes or no, it is a fundamental fact of human existence.[89]

None of this would mean much if people were essentially all the same, like bees in a hive. They too are individuals in a narrow sense, but what's good for any one bee is equally good for another. Give them identical stimuli and they respond identically. People, of course, are not like that; they have differing characters, affinities, talents, wants, and desires. One-size-fits-all doesn't work for humans. Thus, again, individualism for us is not an option but a fact. And a desire to give expression to one's individuality seems virtually universal in the human character. We cherish our individual "specialness." We rebel at any idea that we're cookie-cutter products; and much though we do conform ourselves to social norms, because we want to fit in with our peers, we don't want to *melt* in with them. The word "conformist" is not a compliment but a put-down.

Further, because we do have individual consciousness, feelings, and motivations, what happens to us matters to us, and we naturally want to do something about it. This is why philosophies of passivity or annihilation of the self are ultimately ill fitting; it is basic to human nature to instead be proactive in working to enhance our conditions of life. This is, again, the Greek ideal of living through rational action. And for most of our history, we had to work very hard at doing just that in order to survive at all. Life was a tough challenge. Acceptance, res-

---

89. This is what Margaret Thatcher meant in saying, "There is no such thing as society"—human beings must properly be considered as individuals.

ignation, or passivity were characteristics spelling doom for our ancestors and, hence, were weeded out of our genetic makeup by evolution.

And individualism is not in some way at odds with the interests or welfare of society. We participate in it as part of our striving to make the best lives we can. Society is the creation of individuals all rationally desiring its benefits and therefore willingly promoting its success. Moreover, society is better served by such proactive individualists, motivated to improve their own lives and move things forward, than by passive or submissive souls who don't believe in their own power. We don't want a society of drones. Most of our advancement in knowledge, science, and technology, such a boon for society, is the work of people who believed in themselves and followed individualistic visions. Such individuality also makes for a more vibrant, interesting, and stimulating culture, in contrast to one of bland gray uniformity. And in economic life, the free market's "invisible hand" makes self-serving individual action advance the common good too (something we'll revisit).

We must also never forget that society is not the end, but the means. Humans don't exist to serve society—it's the other way around. That is why we value society. It ultimately makes no sense to talk in terms of sacrificing individual interests for society's sake. If we must deny ourselves to serve society, instead of *it* serving *us*, then why even have it?

But that's not how it is. Society actually thrives in symbiosis with individual self-realization, not only in the materialistic ways already noted, but also because we are social creatures who are nourished and rewarded by our connections with others. Thus, participation in society and family life is a crucial part of our lives and happiness; indeed, the realization of individuality gains much of its value when it occurs within the context of membership in society and the family. Robinson Crusoe was free to be as individualistic as he pleased, but, being removed from society, that was of scant value to him. Society's paramount importance is that it provides us with the environment in which our individuality can flourish and be enjoyed. That, not any duty for self-sacrifice, is why society compels our allegiance and support, and that's why it's wrong to think in terms of subordinating ourselves to society.

Yet the idea of sacrificing individuals to larger social interests retains a strange allure. That was the basis of totalitarian systems. Likewise, leftist political theories regard people as basically just selfish; hence, these ideologies focus on schemes to coerce individuals into cooperating for the common good. It's ironic that their advocates see such nostrums as somehow promoting human values when they are bottomed on such a negative view of humanity. And it's an incorrect one. As emphasized before, our longtime history of struggling to survive required not only looking out for ourselves but also cooperation, and thus, cooperativeness and social consciousness became deeply embedded in human nature. We get rewards from social cooperation. We don't need to be frog-marched into it. And though people do help each other naturally, they also naturally resent compulsion, so trying to impose social cooperation by force is counterproductive. It does not enhance social cohesion, but destroys it. Coercion—not individualism—sets man and society at odds.

This was seen in the collectivism of Soviet Russia and Maoist China, both of which aimed to enforce at gunpoint the ultimate in social cooperation, and thereby actually produced more of an "every man for himself" mentality and far less true social consciousness than in the individualistic West with its supposed culture of selfishness. In contrast to the West, public-spiritedness, personal social activism, community and neighborhood organizations, volunteerism, and charity were all virtually nonexistent in populations under communism.

Some, like Aldo Leopold, have even argued not just for subordinating individual concerns to society but for a "holism" in which the relevant collective is actually all of creation. This rejects the "atomism" of thinking in terms of individual value and rights, holding instead that people have meaning only as parts of a greater whole and not in themselves. This might sound very broad-minded. But we must ask, what is the value or virtue really being served? The biosphere—

the god this philosophy worships—exists, but is not alive,[90] has no consciousness or sentience, no thoughts, feelings, or desires. In this sense, "holism" is akin to worshipping a wooden idol—and sacrificing living beings to it.

It is only *individuals* that experience pain, joy, suffering, or love. Some animals also do (we'll return to that), but the inanimate, insensate biosphere does not. Of course, we must keep the biosphere healthy, as we cannot thrive otherwise. But, just as in the case of society, service to it is not the meaning and mission of human life. Holism has actually been labeled "environmental fascism"—the analog of political fascism, where the interests of the state supersede those of the individual (begging the question of what value the state then serves). And, just as fascism will sacrifice individuals to advance state interests, if we actually did similarly subordinate ourselves to the service of the biosphere, then it would be fine to kill people if that were necessary to protect some endangered species of weed. Would Aldo Leopold willingly have thrown himself on that pyre?

But in the last analysis, it is nonsensical and tautological to see individuals only as serving some greater collective or entity, since the only meaningful ultimate purpose to promoting such a collective—whether the state, the biosphere, or society—is for the sake of enabling sentient individuals to flourish. As suggested before, what does it matter if the universe even exists if there's no one to enjoy it?

We must also reject any idea that an individual has *value* only insofar as he serves some greater good. Again, that's tautological—putting the cart before the horse—because the greater good can be worth serving only if it somehow promotes the welfare of individuals. A person's value is to himself; we all value our own lives, and that's a bedrock human right. Thus, the value of each and every human life is axiomatic, inherent, and not contingent on anything outside that life—that is, "unalienable," meaning it cannot be taken away. Society has no

---

90. The "Gaia" idea of the planet as a living organism is a nice metaphor but certainly not a literal reality.

right to judge the value of individuals[91]—or their lack of value. We have been down that road, and we know where it leads.

For most of our time on Earth, individualism was suppressed—by political, social, and economic structures, and by generally unforgiving conditions of life that required people to behave within narrow confines in order to get by. Only in modern times have all these constraints upon individualism been loosened for much of humanity. Only now can people be all they can be, and attain true self-realization. Only in our era have such human rights at last won a place under the sun.

The day of the individual has dawned. Sing hallelujah!

---

91. Criminal justice is a special case, discussed later.

Government Is the Problem

It seems natural to see some societal problem, or some injustice, and think, "Government should do something." Such is, indeed, the liberal or progressive mind-set, epitomized by a line in a speech to Congress by President Clinton, "Government must do more." Many of us are highly desirous to see good done, and view government as the most obvious and powerful tool for achieving it.

But as already noted, another president, Ronald Reagan, cautioned that "government is not the solution to our problems, government *is* the problem." Government has been described as a collection of very smart people that does very dumb things. It is indeed the powerful force envisioned by liberals; but it is a very blunt tool, wielded as though by a half-blind man with clumsy hands. The rational person ducks for cover.

Government does an awful lot, and I won't try to tell you it's all awful. We obviously need government to enforce the social contract and, in the economy, to do what the market cannot, mainly superintending the rules of the game. There are some problems only government is equipped to deal with, and no one can deny it does some good things.[92]

---

92. My entire professional career was with a government agency, staffed by very dedicated people who maintained a high standard of excellence in serving the public. However, my proudest achievement was putting the kibosh on a proposal for supposed environmental improvement (burying power lines) that would have wasted billions with dubious benefit.

This book needn't detail them because we get more than enough messages trumpeting and advocating for what government does. Hence, most of us develop the "government must do more" mentality. We don't think enough about the other side of the coin. However, there are, in fact, important reasons to mistrust government action and to doubt its efficacy.

First, of course, there is the familiar point that government does not operate with the profit-and-loss discipline of private businesses. For a business, performance is everything. If it doesn't satisfy its customers, competitors will eat its lunch, and it will fail. Government has no competitors, doesn't have to perform, and cannot go out of business. In fact, while a business thrives only by performance, government actually thrives on failure. If a government effort fails to achieve desired results, what is the typical consequence? Not to shut it down, but to expand it and spend more money on it (or add yet another government program).

Further, it is usually very hard to measure the success or failure of anything government does. Take a straightforward example: poverty reduction. In the 1960s, President Johnson declared a "War on Poverty." You might think we could just measure poverty before and after to see whether it decreased. But, in the first place, defining and measuring something like "poverty" is very complicated and subject to much debate. More important, poverty is affected by a huge host of factors besides government programs. An economy of three hundred million people is exceedingly complex, and innumerable disparate influences are always at work. Even the weather, for instance, has an impact: a cold winter may aggravate poverty by raising heating bills, reducing opportunities for outdoor work, and so on. To know whether a government program reduces poverty, you would have to strip out of the data all such extraneous factors. Of course, that is impossible. Thus, we can rarely know whether any government initiative really does the job. And without that information, it's hard to hold government accountable.

Not just information, but how it's processed and digested, is crucial. Government does, again, employ an army of smart people. In the human brain, an army of individual neurons coordinates to produce intelligence; but that doesn't seem to happen with government's "neurons." The US government, despite possessing so many pieces of the puzzle, just couldn't see 9/11 coming, thereby failing us in its most basic mission. It failed again even when many in government actually did see Hurricane Katrina coming. Too often government is like a gigantic creature with no brain at all.

Adding to the problem is the fact that government so often works, not by direct action, but rather, by telling people what to do. Here accountability is even more attenuated because government doesn't really have to concern itself with the costs and other consequences. Want cleaner air? Require factories to change production methods to reduce pollution. That might sound good, but what if the cost to a factory is vastly disproportionate to the air quality improvement? Let them pay, you may say; but, as ever, there is no free lunch. If we force the factory to waste money on ineffectual or inefficient pollution abatement, this is a cost to society as a whole. It may show up in the prices the factory must charge for its products to stay in business, or, if it can't, the costs will show up as a loss of jobs. The air may be a little cleaner but, on the whole, society is worse off.

After years of hearings, the Environmental Protection Agency (EPA) put out a detailed thirty-five-page set of rules requiring equipment on industrial smokestacks to filter out benzene. One Amoco plant emitting a lot of benzene spent $31 million to comply. The only trouble was that most of its benzene wasn't coming from its smokestacks, but from its loading dock. That could have been rectified far more cheaply; but the government rule instead required fixing the wrong thing, at great cost, with minimal public benefit.

Government tends to be very poor at making judgments of this kind. As the Amoco example shows, the world is very complicated, and government can never have enough information or intelligence to grapple with it effectually. Thus, too often, its dictates produce costs disproportionate to benefits. And government has to be responsive to voters, who themselves are not very good at balancing trade-offs, as they generally possess even less information and often go by emotional response rather than by objective analysis.

Recall the example from Britain. A train wreck got the public worked up about rail safety, so a responsive government threw a lot of money in that direction, though many more lives could have been saved by spending instead on traffic safety. But the train wreck was splashed across the front pages, unlike the routine car crashes that collectively cause vastly more casualties. So rail safety got the attention, and the money.

In lawmaking, the most important law of all is the *law of unintended consequences.* This law says that, whatever may be the good intentions behind a government program or legislation, the actual results may be very different (and often bad) because society and the economy are so complex that it is impossible to foresee how any scheme will work in practice. And a crucial factor here is that people all have their own motivations and will always look for ways to gain advantage, exploit loopholes, and subvert the government's aims to their own ends. Nobody in government is ever so smart that this can be avoided. We're all familiar with how the old welfare system, nobly conceived to help poor families, actually helped to destroy them by penalizing work, marriage, and responsibility, while encouraging social pathologies and a lamentable culture of dependency. Somehow, no one foresaw any of this when the programs were created.

The history of campaign finance reform is also instructive. In the wake of the Watergate scandals of the 1970s, laws were passed regulating political fundraising and spending to stop perceived abuses. But politicians quickly figured out ways to get around these laws. The problem, in fact, grew worse and so malodorous that a new push for reform gathered steam in the 1990s, culminating in the McCain-Feingold law. But hardly was the ink on it dry before the political class once more figured out how to rejigger their activities to get around it, and nothing at all really changed.

EPA rules require cleaning up any toxic waste on industrial land before it can be reused. That, too, sounds fine and dandy. But then the law of unintended consequences kicks in. The required cleanup usually costs more than the land is worth, so the owner's answer is simply to walk away from the site and start fresh elsewhere. The rules' intent was to clean up a dirty site; the real-world result is, instead, two dirty sites.

Both of the above EPA examples are taken from Philip Howard's book, *The Death of Common Sense*, a compelling indictment of how government laws and rules too often make things worse instead of better. Part of the problem is the ideal that everything should be certain and uniform, leaving nothing to arbitrary individual judgment. The idea is virtuous in the abstract, but those pesky unintended consequences subvert it. When government tells people not *what* they must accomplish, but *how* they must do it, this does indeed throttle the use of judgment and common sense, replacing them with overbearing and often mindless rigidity. Following rules takes precedence over solving problems or doing what is right, as in the Amoco example; rather than simply telling the company to reduce benzene emissions, government rules specified precisely what equipment to install—equipment which in Amoco's case made no practical sense.

The Occupational Safety and Health Administration (OSHA) is another government poster boy for this. Again, the intent seems admirable. But OSHA's real thrust, in practice, is not requiring businesses to operate safely, but rather to slavishly implement highly specific, detailed, nit-picking rules covering every facet of their operations —and to maintain mountains of paperwork documenting every detail of that compliance. Genuine safety concerns get lost in this bureaucratic morass. OSHA dictates how many inches apart the rungs on ladders must be. It fined one company because it failed to warn its employees not to eat the toner in its copier machines. The government spends billions enforcing such idiotic regulations, and businesses waste untold billions more complying with them. It's a huge drag on our economy, making few of us safer or healthier, but surely making all of us poorer.

Inflexibility like the EPA's and OSHA's is all too common in laws and rules, and their enforcement. Congress, in a fit of thoughtlessness, passed a law calling for deportation of aliens who had committed crimes. And so, federal officers rounded up great numbers of people to deport. It didn't matter if the crime was trivial, decades old, and had already been punished; didn't matter if the person had been in this country for many years, paid taxes, and was a responsible member of the community; didn't matter if he had a wife and children who were US citizens. Deport him, the law said, and so out he went.[93]

There is also a tendency to imagine that if something is *desirable* it ought to be *required*. Thus, we have reams of rules specifying all sorts of persnickety details to make every daycare center a model facility. Yet again, good intent. Result? Meeting all these requirements is very costly; so legal daycare centers must charge high rates that many parents can't afford. Those parents put their kids in cheaper illegal day care, where all the government's high-minded rules are disregarded, so instead of ensuring high-quality child care, the rules actually ensure low-quality care for many children. Similarly, housing codes contain myriad nobly conceived rules for required niceties in apartments—making it impossible to offer simple cheap housing that the poorest can afford. Result? Homelessness.

Because government programs do so often backfire, this creates a demand for yet more programs trying to undo the harm. Billions are spent annually on "affordable housing" schemes, yet a key reason why housing is not affordable in the first place is government action, such as mentioned above. One government response is rent control. The ostensible aim is lower rents—but it actually pushes rents up by creating a disincentive for developers to build and maintain apartments, artificially crimping the housing supply. So we need *another* government scheme to rectify *that*.

---

93. Such inflexibility also characterizes various "zero tolerance" policies, which often mean zero common sense. Thus, a schoolgirl was suspended under a no-drugs rule for having cold medicine; a little boy disciplined, under a no-guns rule, because of a toy gun one inch long; and a teenager arrested and charged with a felony for writing a story about zombies invading a school. A local girl ran afoul of a school rule banning "gang colors" despite a different intended symbolism for her necklace's colors—red, white, and blue!

And of course, while the government with one hand doles out subsidies to tobacco growers, with the other it spends money to discourage smoking. But such government action at cross-purposes is entirely predictable. Government doesn't have to take sides between the tobacco lobby and antismoking crusaders. With your tax dollars, it can cheerfully placate both.

Much government intervention and regulation of business is driven by the idea that the public needs protection against shoddy or unsafe products and other abuses. But what are consumers typically "protected" against, in practice? The benefits of competition and innovation. Why? Because those most intensely concerned with the workings of government regulation are the very companies being regulated, and they exert pressure to ensure that they are "regulated" in ways that suit them and maintain their comfortable status quo.

I saw this firsthand in one of my earliest cases as a Public Service Commission lawyer. We went after a small moving company for breaking the rules. Its crime? Prices *too low*. Who were we protecting? Certainly not consumers. We were actually protecting the other moving companies against competition from this upstart daring to charge less! This is sadly all too typical of government regulation in the real world.

Yet don't consumers need some government protections? Look at the Food and Drug Administration (FDA), requiring drug companies to prove medicines are safe and effective. Who could be against that? Not long ago, the FDA proudly announced its approval of a drug that would save fourteen thousand lives a year. But the approval process had taken a decade. Had there been no FDA, the drug could have been available ten years sooner, presumably saving one hundred and forty thousand lives. Who was really protected by the FDA's approval process? One answer is actually the FDA itself—no bureaucrat wants responsibility for approving something that might conceivably, somehow, harm someone, but no bureaucrat ever gets blame for those who die because a drug's approval is delayed.

No doubt, absent the FDA, bad products would hurt some people. But more are probably harmed by the FDA's keeping good things off the market. This is a consequence not only of the approval procedure's long duration but also the fact that it costs hundreds of millions of dollars per drug. That not only makes drugs less affordable for consumers, it also makes drug companies reluctant even to research anything without a big potential market. So, if you have a rare disease, forget it.

And query whether we really need government telling us we can't try a drug that might not be safe, but could be beneficial. Isn't that the kind of personal decision individuals should have the right to make for themselves? Let them know the facts and risks, but let them decide. If a medicine is harmful or ineffective, the market will expose that soon enough anyway. (Competitors will publicize it with alacrity.) The free market is likely to be a far more efficient regulatory mechanism than any government bureaucracy.[94]

But there is a tendency to assume people in government are more nobly motivated than those in the private sector; that government's minions work for the public good, whereas those in the business world seek only profit. This is why "privatization" is used as a scare word. Yet there is actually scant truth in the generalization. We have discovered a big problem with the FDA—once it has approved a drug, there is great (and humanly natural) unwillingness to look further and risk finding out that it has erred. So it isn't just businesspeople who can have motivations at odds with the public interest. It's a universal phenomenon that equally affects government.[95]

Another factor is the elevation of process over action. Now,

---

94. The idea that government should protect us from every conceivable harm flows from some misguided notions discussed earlier—that such total safety is not only attainable but an entitlement and that people shouldn't really be held to account for the consequences of their decisions. So what's next? Shall we have a federal agency monitor the Internet to protect us against misleading, incorrect, or harmful information?

95. We will discuss later how business is unfairly demonized. While business—just like government—*can* traduce the public good, it also has key motivations that are consistent with societal interests.

processes and procedures are necessary to ensure that decisions are made properly and fairly and with due regard for affected people's rights. But following procedures often seems to become an end in itself, with modern government like an impotent giant in a straitjacket of process. Howard's book mentions the discovery in Chicago of a water leak plainly threatening imminent disaster. It could have been fixed right away for seventy-five thousand dollars. Instead, the government official in charge started the convoluted process of soliciting contractor bids for the job. But long before bidding could be completed, the water broke through, flooding the city, with over a billion dollars in damage.

Bidding procedures exist as a safeguard against corrupt contracting. Government is indeed very good when it comes to following procedures. But it also needs to safeguard against floods. Taking timely and responsible action like that is something government is rather less good at. Being tangled in procedures kept the government from doing anything with the information that some young Middle Eastern nationals were in flight schools without interest in landing skills.

But the main reason to distrust government action is simply that government is political. That may seem like stating the obvious, but its ramifications are worth exploring.

To begin with, voting is actually a clumsy tool for making public choices. In shopping for food you can select among countless different products in a host of stores or restaurants, so those businesses have to be highly responsive to customer preferences. But voting occurs only at long intervals, and options are very limited, usually being just an either/or choice. If we chose food like that, we might get to vote only once a year on the menu—and everyone would have to eat what the majority picks.[96]

---

96. This analogy comes from John Stossel's excellent book *Give Me a Break*, a devastating analysis of why government fixes for problems almost always fail and why the free market does a hugely better job at improving people's lives.

Of course, in politics, appearance often trumps reality. When there is a problem, the best thing for an officeholder to do is to solve it; but usually this is hard to do, and the second best option is to *appear* to be doing something to solve it, which of course is a lot easier; never mind if it's inefficient, ineffectual, or even counterproductive.

But the most important point is that all government action affects private interests. The very essence of politics is the clash of competing interests in society; government is the arena in which those battles play out. The American Founding Fathers understood this quite well; our governmental structure, with its checks and balances, was expressly designed to deal with the clash of interests. Debtors versus creditors is a good example. Debtors want generous bankruptcy laws; creditors want strictness. The intent for government is to ensure that each side gets a fair shake at advancing its agenda, but with neither able to run roughshod over the other.

The system usually works well in such cases, where one aggressive interest battles another. But that is not always the situation. All too often, a well-defined aggressive interest is pitted against a diffuse and silent one. Indeed, *most* government actions affect *most* people very little, while affecting *some* people, maybe *very few* people, a great deal. Those latter interests, who are greatly affected, will of course mobilize mightily to influence the outcome, while everyone else stays asleep.

Look at the federal farm subsidy program, which costs taxpayers scores of billions yet makes no sense from the standpoint of the interests of the nation as a whole. It robs the poor to give to the rich. It is a waste of money that we'd be better off without. It even hurts the poor in other countries, because they can't compete against subsidized American farmers. And this, furthermore, undermines wider international trade negotiations with potentially huge costs for the whole world's economy.

How can such a bad program be enacted, perpetuated, and become politically impossible to kill? Farmers who benefit are only a tiny minority among the nation's voters, but the program is hugely important to *them*, so naturally they organize to fight very hard for it in the halls of Congress. And Congress listens to those who scream loudly—and contribute heavily to campaigns.

Meanwhile, though most taxpayers are harmed by the program, no one group suffers in anything like the same degree that farmers benefit, so there is no well-organized, well-financed opposition to the farm program lobbying legislators and contributing to their campaigns. Most people are just not hurt enough by it to get riled up—most don't even realize how they are hurt.

In fact, the program is sold to the public as helping the "family farm," which many people romanticize. Yet it is the large agribusinesses, not the little family farms, that do the heavy-duty lobbying, contributing, and political string-pulling in Washington, so they make sure that whatever may be the fine intent to help small farms, the money really goes to the big ones—actually making it harder for small farms to survive. The simplistic lie is promoted by a huge special interest propaganda army, while the more complex truth is a virtual orphan.

This is the key to understanding political reality. Most government action has only a diffused impact on the nation as a whole, but a big impact on special segments. Those so affected will fight hard for the outcome they want; others will not be roused to fight at all. And the importance of this can hardly be overstated because the stakes are typically huge. Government spends *trillions* of dollars. The whole game is to influence whose pockets that money goes into.

The chief means for exerting such influence is itself money. Now, if you tell a public official, "I will give you ten thousand dollars to support the Crumbley-Snoot bill," that is bribery, and forbidden. But if you contribute to his reelection campaign, and he understands perfectly well your interest is the Crumbley-Snoot bill, which he then supports, this is not considered bribery. Do you see the difference? No? Well, neither do most people. This was the problem the previously mentioned McCain-Feingold law was at least partly intended to address. Its abject failure testifies to how deeply the money game is embedded in American government and politics.

Politicians need that money because of the high cost of campaigns, chiefly television advertising. Big contributors do not normally give money out of disinterested belief in what a politician stands for, but rather because they expect some payback (it's called "pay to play"). They don't want to waste money on losers, which generally means they back incumbent officeholders and not challengers. Not only are incumbent legislators thusly well funded, they also have a lot of power to ingratiate themselves with voters, so it takes almost freakish circumstances for a congressman to be unseated. This effective lack of electoral competition undermines American democracy.[97]

So, again, big farm businesses contribute liberally to political campaigns in order to keep their gravy train rolling. And they get quite a bang for their buck. They may give tens of millions to politicians; but the payback for them, via the federal farm program, is tens of *billions*. And, again, there are no campaign contributions coming from opponents of farm subsidies.

The farm program is merely one example of what is really a systemic problem of big government. There is just too much money at stake. It isn't even just government spending. Everything government does has huge financial impacts, every government mandate, every regulation, every clause and comma of the tax code. Businesses also try to enlist government to pass laws (like tariffs or import quotas) that hobble their competitors—in sum, anything to put money in their pockets. The old term for all this was "rent seeking." And when a special interest can thusly use a political contribution to buy a government subsidy or an obscure change in the tax code that is worth many

---

97. It is aggravated by "gerrymandering," the drawing of legislative district boundaries for political advantage. A Republican gerrymander, for instance, would concentrate Democrats into a few districts they win overwhelmingly, while everywhere else Republicans win. Not only does this mean noncompetitive elections, but where it is almost certain which party will win, a candidate need not worry about the whole electorate; instead, he will cater only to activists of his own party who control the nomination. This exacerbates partisan divisiveness and ideological posturing.

times more than the contribution itself, this has a gigantic distortive effect on the legislative process. The true national interest hardly stands a chance.[98]

Moreover, private interests are not the only problem. America's biggest industry is actually government itself, employing more people than any other, and the labor unions representing government employees (including teachers) are the largest and most powerful politically. They too, of course, have a huge stake in government decisions. As do the bureaucrats whose paychecks, power, and perks are dependent on political outcomes. These potent forces mobilize their muscle to serve their own interests—too often, again, regardless of public needs.

In fact, special interest politics has become so pervasive that almost all of us are sucked into the game. We each get our own little piece of the booty: some government subsidy, grant, program, or tax credit. Forgotten is John F. Kennedy's exhortation to "ask not what your country can do for you." Instead, today's politics is mainly about who gets what, rather than what's good for us all. Writer Sebastian Mallaby calls this "transactional" politics—parties and candidates see buying off interest groups as the way to win elections and power, and their main agenda in power is to placate those interest groups, a "me-me mindset" that corrupts and discredits most workings of government.

---

98. Trying to solve this by limiting campaign spending (as in McCain-Feingold) runs up against freedom of speech, which means making one's voice heard on political issues and in elections. Even moneyed interests have that right.

A better solution would be to give citizens a 100 percent tax credit for political contributions (with some limit). In effect, contributions would be paid for by government (it already does subsidize some campaigns through a different system). The tax-credit scheme's virtue is that it would generate a flood of citizen contributions, rendering irrelevant all the special-interest money. This would free elected officials to say no to special interests seeking to milk the government cow (as in the farm program). And, since such milking costs taxpayers vastly more than is spent on all political campaigns, the tax-credit scheme would actually save us many billions. Our politics would be far less corrupt and the national interest would be far better served.

All these reasons should make us cringe when we hear someone like Bill Clinton solemnly intone, "Government must do more." If more needs doing, maybe we ourselves, as individuals, should take more responsibility, instead of running to Daddy Government.

And given their enthusiasm for big active government, it is a great irony that American liberals are so often appalled by what government actually *does.* They are the ones quickest to denounce its actions and policies; theirs are the loudest voices protesting the evils of campaign finance, corporate welfare, the military-industrial complex, government trampling of civil liberties and privacy rights, and endlessly so forth. And government does repeatedly trample the human values liberals profess to cherish. Yet weirdly undaunted is their faith. For all the wrongs they see governments commit, still they continue to idealize government as a vehicle for righting wrongs, like battered wives who, through bruised lips, still profess undying love for their batterers. Truly a triumph of hope over experience!

Russian peasants used to say, "If only the Czar knew." If he only knew the misdeeds of his officials, "the good Czar" would fix everything. We're still suckers for a variant of this myth—that if only we elected good selfless people, our problems could be fixed. But in the real world, so much power and money are part and parcel of big government that they are inevitably magnets for sharp-elbowed connivers very different from the virtuous and disinterested public servants we wish for. The good Czar—big but benevolent government—is a fantasy.

The sort of dysfunction afflicting government actually applies to all social action. The law of unintended consequences is a powerful force. After a lifetime of activism in social causes, Professor Derrick Bell, in his book *Ethical Ambition*, ruefully acknowledged that such efforts have proven costly in failure and counterproductive even when their goals were seemingly achieved. Amazed at how the best of intentions can go awry, with actions aimed at helping some people unexpectedly harming others, he accordingly urged humility upon would-be social reformers.

Does all this mean nothing good can ever be accomplished and we should just give up? If so, I wouldn't have bothered writing this book. No; what it does mean is that grandiose schemes of social engineering tend to be misconceived and ultimately reduce overall human welfare rather than enhancing it. Yet we *can* make the world better—fundamentally, by making it more free. That, in the end, is the key. To give people more freedom, more choices, more opportunities to pursue and realize their dreams, produces better lives, both spiritually and materially; it supplies the means by which people can achieve this goal (as will be discussed more fully later).

We can do this. Progress doesn't happen by itself, propelled by some ineluctable natural force; it happens solely because of human action to make it happen. And we have, in fact, made it happen, through our efforts in science, technology, business, in political action to expand freedom, and, yes, even sometimes in well-intentioned social action. It's people who improve the world. One ordinary woman, Rosa Parks, with one quietly courageous act, helped to liberate people and enhance human dignity. By dint of our efforts, the world has indeed gotten better and better, with ever more of us living ever better lives.

That progress can continue toward a very bright future for our species if we keep doing what we've been doing right. More individual action—more freedom—not more government control.

The Forced March to Paradise

We have seen that government action is simply not a very good way to achieve good things, because so many factors militate toward ineffectuality, failure, or even counterproductiveness in everything government does. But there is another overriding concern.

At the heart of American liberalism, or progressivism, lies *coercion*. Progressives may talk a lot about civil liberties, yet they seek to achieve their aims by force and by limiting freedom. They want government telling people what to do and making choices for them.[99]

This is manifest in the growth of regulation, government making explicit rules that people must follow. Now, of course, we need laws to protect us from harm by others. But regulating citizens' lives and telling them how to live is something else. The idea of the social contract, again, is to shield people from depredations in order to provide them as much freedom as possible to make their own decisions, to do as they please, and to live as they choose. That's why people sign up as members of society—not to be bossed around.

Obviously, we have strayed pretty far from that idea when the

---

[99]. For some, it seems, the concept of "civil liberties" begins and ends with freedom of speech and thought. Those are important, but human rights are vastly broader than that.

pages of federal rules and regulations, if laid end to end, would stretch halfway to the moon.[100]

It bears reiterating that this is all bottomed on the idea that people are essentially selfish and immoral, and hence, will only behave in ways that serve society if forced into it. That's the key assumption of liberalism or progressivism. It overlooks how deeply a basic moral sense and social cooperativeness are built into human nature. We don't need to be coerced into goodness, and such compulsion tends to work badly, anyway, because it undermines people's love for the society that represses them. I don't want to overstate the case because this is not a universal rule. Sometimes regulating people can be justified and efficacious.[101] The point, instead, is that it's fundamentally wrongheaded to think people are bad and can be made good by cracking the whip. Totalitarianism was the ultimate expression of that idea. Of course that's no way to build a truly humane society. Freedom and social virtue are not opposing values; they are consonant.

Progressives also like to talk about standing up for the little guy and fighting for the common man. Yet, on any issue involving, on the one hand, individual initiative and choice, and, on the other, top-down decision making by a know-it-all elite, progressives usually go for the latter. They battle against allowing school choice to give those poorly served by bad schools some way to escape the trap. They oppose any Social Security plan that would give people some ownership and control of money they put into the system. Indeed, on that issue they literally argue that individuals shouldn't trust themselves to make their own decisions and shouldn't want ownership rights in their pension contributions. Progressives may chant "Power to the people!" But their program is really "Power to the bureaucrats!"

---

100. Actually, I made that up. I don't know how far they'd stretch—but it's pretty darn far!

101. In fact, I'll even cite one example that did work out pretty well: the 1964 Civil Rights Act banning racial discrimination. However, it worked not so much because people knuckled under but, rather, because most people accepted with goodwill the law's moral thrust. In other words, it worked not by forcing bad people to be good, but because most people *are* good.

And this empowerment of bureaucrats undermines democratic control. Elected officials who do something unpopular can be voted out, but bureaucracies are more insulated from such accountability (it's hard to fire government workers even for not showing up). Government by bureaucrats is closer to oligarchy than democracy.

Such removal of decision making from citizens also happens when judges substitute their own views in place of legislation. The liberal do-gooder impulse, and the penchant for imposing their nostrums undemocratically, is seen when judges of their ilk decide that, just because they happen to consider an idea good and right, the Constitution must somehow *require* it. Judges have ordered state and federal government to spend billions to carry out policies they favor. And look at the *Roe v. Wade* abortion decision. The Founding Fathers would have been gobsmacked to learn that the Constitution they wrote addresses abortion at all. We can debate (and will address later) whether abortion rights are good or bad, but the Supreme Court has taken that debate out of the hands of elected legislatures subject to popular will. Citizens can no longer be heard on this subject—and many others—through the democratic process. Women may have a "right to choose," but voters don't.[102]

But the biggest thrust of the liberal coercive impulse is taxation. Certainly, we must all pay some taxes or else we could have no government; this too is part of the social contract, the membership dues of society. However, the progressive goes further and wants to force others to pay for his do-gooder impulses. How often we hear that some scheme or other could be funded if we merely increase taxes on the richest one percent, or five percent, or whatever. The assumptions are that the "rich" can afford it, don't really need the money, there are better uses for it, and others are somehow more entitled to it.

And of course there is a double agenda: not only the aim of

---

102. This is, indeed, why the issue became so poisonous in American politics. Europeans have avoided this by legalizing abortion not via judicial diktat but through open democratic majority rule, the results of which the minority were willing to accept.

funding programs thought to be worthwhile in themselves, but also to redistribute wealth to make society more equal.

If you judge that your neighbor's garden has more flowers than anybody really needs and that it's okay to just take some, we all know that's stealing and that your rationalization cuts no ice. When government does the equivalent, some call it social justice. Robin Hood supposedly took from the rich to give to the poor; but forcibly taking anything from its rightful owner is still stealing. And no matter how you pretty it up, theft and justice are antithetical concepts.

Some may respond by focusing on that word "rightful," arguing that no one has a right to be rich while others want. Now, if someone acquires wealth wrongfully, such as by fraud, the law should properly rectify that. But otherwise, all wealth is ultimately generated by productive effort that contributes to society, and thus is held rightfully and justly. And the right to keep and enjoy what one earns is among the most fundamental human rights and a key principle of genuine justice. (It's what "pursuit of happiness" means.) One who earns wealth has a greater right to decide what happens to it than does anyone else.

Yet still, undaunted, progressives want to arrogate to themselves that disposition of wealth, indeed, even to decide how much wealth it's okay for one to keep. What gives them that right? Moral superiority? High-minded objectives?

This raises the classic dilemma of whether ends can justify means. If your objective is good, does that justify doing some bad things if necessary to get there? Most would consider acceptable a small wrong to achieve a great good, to sacrifice one life, for example, if that will save many; we recognize that such balancing must depend on circumstances.[103] But this is a slippery slope. People can be poor (or cynical) judges of the magnitudes of wrongs, and if you justify one small wrong for the sake of a worthy end, pretty soon you may excuse another and another, until you are neck deep in wrongs. Human experience is blotted with great horrors that were justified as means to

---

103. A classic example of the dilemma is whether it was right to use the atomic bomb on Japan in 1945. This question continues to be hotly debated.

ends. Lenin, Stalin, Mao, all sacrificed many millions as the means to reach the anticipated paradise of communism (a dubious end).[104] They were clearly evil, but such moral clarity is rare. When faced with issues of this kind, when tempted to let ends justify means, we must at least understand that we are indeed on a slippery slope. And we must remember it whenever anyone proposes that government dragoon people into the service of what is imagined to be a good cause (as Lenin, Stalin, and Mao all did).

Even if you believe, contrary to all experience, that some do-gooder government scheme will beat the law of unintended consequences, the point is still that everyone is forced to pay, giving individuals no choice in the matter. I contribute to Doctors Without Borders because I deem it a worthy cause, but I don't seek to impose my charitable preference on others by forcing them to contribute through taxes.

Recall the earlier discussion of one's duty to others. While it is good to help another out of free choice, you have no moral duty or obligation to help strangers or give them part of what you've earned. This applies even more forcefully to government programs, taking money from some people to spend it on others; this way we cannot even evaluate for ourselves how much duty we owe others, because the decision is taken out of our hands by government. Individual charity is a virtuous and loving expression of human solidarity; government forcibly taking from one to give to another is none of those things. We should support good causes out of free moral choice. People don't enter society to have those choices made for them by an anointed elite imagining that its own ideas of benevolence and wisdom are superior.

The libertarian says that if Program X is really such a good and worthy idea, then why can't it be funded through voluntary contributions? But if people must instead be forced to contribute (through taxes) because otherwise they would not choose to give their money, then maybe it is not really such a worthy program.

---

104. Leftist intellectuals have always seemed willfully attracted to projects for achieving utopia through human sacrifice. The results have uniformly been dystopia.

In democratic theory, admittedly, a program is funded through taxes because a voting majority supports it. Thus, it represents a societal decision, which we might hold should be honored as long as everyone had a voice in reaching it. Of course, as we have seen, a lot of government spending actually reflects something different, being at the behest of special interests who game the system. But even if we set that reality aside and assume that a government program really does reflect the considered will of a majority, the question still remains, is it right for the majority to force the minority to contribute? If the majority really does want the program, why can't the majority instead fund it voluntarily rather than using government to extract contributions from the unwilling?[105]

And political majorities do not, in general, work their will by taxing primarily *themselves*.[106] On the contrary, the implicit political equation is that "Program X would be good but I don't want to pay for it out of my own pocket. Instead, it should be a government project, which means someone else should pay for it." People want government—in other words, other people—to pay for things they want done but do not want to pay for.

The healthcare issue is a paradigm of this. For all its complexities, twists, and turns, the ongoing healthcare debate in America comes down to this: most people believe there should be lots of healthcare for everyone, with universal medical insurance that covers every kind of treatment and prescription drug,[107] but nobody wants to pay the costs.

---

105. It is worth reiterating that one of the key functions of our government is the protection of minority rights from abuses of power by the majority. This is why we have a Bill of Rights that specifies things government may not do. And, of course, this is totally in keeping with the idea that our Constitution is grounded upon the social contract—with individuals relinquishing some freedom in order to receive protection from the depredations of others—including those of a political majority.

106. This is, in fact, guaranteed by graduated income tax rates that collect a majority of revenue dollars from a distinct minority of voters.

107. We have a societal consensus to assure everyone a minimally decent living standard, though not the affluent lifestyle of middle-class wage

Indeed, not only do people not want to pay for the generous health benefits they so compassionately believe should somehow be provided to others, *they don't even want to pay the costs for their own healthcare*! That's, in fact, how we see health insurance—as a system to relieve us of paying the full costs of our medical care.

So this whole political ruckus is about how to somehow get somebody else to pay; how to square the circle of paying for something that everybody wants but nobody wants to have to personally pay for. Thus, we get proposals for a "single-payer" system (a nice euphemism for what used to be called "socialized medicine"). The "single-payer" would, of course, be government, that is, taxpayers.

People do tend to imagine that if government pays for something, it is *as if* nobody is paying—or at least not them. Of course, we realize that there is no free lunch and that taxes are related to what government spends.[108] But whenever some specific government program is at issue, the idea is to have someone else pay. Isn't that what government is for? To do the things we can't or won't do as individuals? People probably do understand that we as a nation must somehow ultimately pay for all the healthcare we consume, but they don't feel this applies to them specifically. Health costs are a kind of hot potato game, and whoever is holding it when the music stops must pay; and no one figures to be that loser. Heck of a way to run a society.

But, to close the loop, it is all bottomed on coercion—government requiring people to pay taxes. Those who support government programs upon the implicit notion that this means other people will have to pay are accomplices to the coercion of their fellow citizens, the picking of their pockets. Heck of a way to run a society.

---

earners. But we haven't come to grips with applying this concept to healthcare and deciding just what level of care society ought to guarantee.

108. However, the US government usually spends more than it collects in taxes. That gap (the "deficit") is closed by borrowing. A big deficit is graphic evidence that what we want from government outstrips what we are willing to pay for through taxes. It ultimately means that we are passing the bills along (compounded by interest costs) to our children.

The Era of Big Government

The same President Clinton who once said, "Government must do more" later said, "The era of big government is over." History will likely judge that in fact it had hardly begun. Only a few years after Clinton's pronouncement, we could already say that "the era of big government" was back with a vengeance.

The great battle of the last century was against totalitarian fascism and communism, or big government in its most extreme form. But while those ideologies were defeated, the idea that government should have a major role in the economy and in people's lives still reigns supreme.

In America, there is little direct government control of business by way of ownership. But we do have ever-more-pervasive regulation of business, with detailed government requirements, mandates, prohibitions, and oversight. (Recall OSHA and its rules for ladder rungs, for example.) And government increasingly butts into our personal lives as well. This is the "nanny state," a paternalistic government overseeing us much the way a parent supervises a child. "Wear your seat belt" is good advice, but must it be a law?[109] Will "wear your mittens" be next?

---

109. One common answer is that, if you're injured because you didn't buckle up, society bears some of the costs. But why should it? Why shouldn't people who make dangerous choices be responsible themselves for all resulting costs?

Government, through taxing and spending, also dictates where much of our national income goes. Freedom to spend our own money is really the most meaningful liberty we have because it is the prime vehicle for "the pursuit of happiness." And, of course, when the government taxes you, it takes away some of that freedom.

Under the extreme statism of the Soviet Union, government control was close to 100 percent. In America, at the turn of the century, federal, state, and local government accounts for about 40 percent of the national economy. "Tax freedom day" is when the average citizen has earned enough to pay all his taxes for the year, after which he can begin working for himself instead of government. It falls sometime in May.

Moreover, the dollars directly paid in taxes are not the system's only cost. The titanic complexity of tax laws, regulations, and forms forces individuals and businesses to expend untold billions of dollars on accountants, lawyers, and paperwork, which subtracts from the economy's productivity and from our standard of living. Furthermore, much economic activity and decision making is driven by the often perverse incentives of tax considerations; most notably affected is the incentive for productive effort. Our "progressive" tax structure has rates that rise with income, based on the assumption that higher earners can afford more. This means that the lion's share is paid by the wealthiest (serving a redistributionist ethic). But it also means that the more you earn, the more you pay—and this is actually aggravated by tax deductions because they reduce the government's take and, hence, have to be made up by setting tax *rates* on income after deductions that are much higher. The result is that for every extra dollar many people earn, nearly half goes to government. And that makes them think twice about whether it's really worth it to earn some more overtime pay, take entrepreneurial risks, or otherwise exert themselves. This puts a damper on economic activity, to the nation's detriment.[110]

---

110. On the other hand, cutting tax rates stimulates economic activity. That means more income to be taxed, at least partly offsetting the government's revenue loss. (Some "supply side" economists have argued that it can conceivably *more* than offset the revenue loss.) Certainly, simplifying the tax

So it's clear that, even in democratic free-market nations, the state looms large, its role in the economy being close to half of what it was under Soviet communism. And it is quite noteworthy that, even in America—after President Reagan's sizable tax cuts and much decried supposed "cutbacks" in federal programs, followed by the likewise loudly decried "Gingrich Revolution," which sought to roll back the state in the 1990s, and then George W. Bush's tax cuts—the government's share of the economy continues to creep upward. Even in Great Britain, after Margaret Thatcher, whose very name has come to stand for curbing the state (and whose determined efforts also were loudly decried from the Left), there has been no substantive retreat by the state. All these massive political efforts to pare back government, over decades, accompanied by huge controversy and recrimination, at most succeeded in holding the line, temporarily, more or less. They were mere pauses in the long-term trend of inexorable state expansion.

It seems that a one-way ratchet operates with regard to government programs, spending, and economic presence. They expand readily but resist any contraction. It is all too easy to add to the state's role—with more programs, more spending, and more regulation. The "government must do more" mantra is very seductive. People always want more. And while there's no free lunch, and the nation as a whole must somehow, someday pay for it all, an individual beneficiary of a particular government program *does* get a free lunch. And so, more government spending, more government programs, handing out more government goodies, is a vote-winning formula for politicians. As George Bernard Shaw said, "A government that robs Peter to pay Paul can always depend upon the support of Paul."

The term "pork barrel" refers to government spending at the behest of a particular politician to curry favor with a specific voter group. The officeholder can go back to his constituents, and seek reelection, saying, "Look what I've done for you." Not only is he

---

code to eliminate deductions and thereby bring down the marginal *rate* of taxation on added income would be an economic stimulus.

trying to *bribe* voters—but to bribe them *with their own money!* And it works![111]

So the path of least resistance, politically, always favors more, more, more. And once a program is started, any effort to cut it back is pretty much hopeless. Now, some interest groups have a stake in its continuation—not only business interests and other beneficiaries, but also bureaucrats who run the program and who get paychecks and power out of it. Remember, yet again, the ramifications of a narrow but intense interest versus the broad public interest.[112] Those who benefit work fiercely for a program's continuation, propagandizing the public and wrapping themselves in claimed virtue. Any who voice opposition are painted as heartless villains. (Look at Newt Gingrich—not only hounded out of politics for daring to talk seriously about curbing the state, his name now lives on as bogeyman to frighten voters.)

In America (and other advanced nations), demographics are aggravating the relentless push toward "more, more, more." As life spans lengthen and baby boomers retire, spending on entitlement programs for older people seems set to explode. The Congressional Budget Office has estimated that the costs of Social Security, Medicare, and Medicaid will grow from 8 percent of national output in 2005 to 14 percent in 2030 and a whopping 21 percent in 2075. This would require some wrenching political decisions to either slash promised benefits or raise taxes dramatically (which would devastate the economy). Today's polarized politics presages brutal battles as that train wreck looms, stymieing any serious efforts to head it off. An

---

111. Pork barrel politics is so pervasive that, even when it came to something as urgent as protecting America's ports against terrorism, a sizable share of the funding went to inland states like Oklahoma, Kentucky, and New Hampshire, diluting efforts focused on the really critical targets.

112. Another example: mohair got a subsidy because during WWII it was needed for military uniforms. That need is ancient history, yet the subsidy lives on because Congress won't say no to the mohair industry.

optimist can only hope that the voting public will somehow wake up and shake up the system.[113]

In the meantime, nannyism blossoms apace too. With government having gotten into a parental mode, there is hardly any check on the moral improvement projects do-gooders can advocate. Where the old conservatism preached getting government off people's backs and out of their lives, a new strain sees government as a handy tool for fixing morality deficits. Do we really need the federal government making solemn adjudications of whether the salty language of soldiers in a war movie, or an actress's bare skin, is suitable for us to view?

And while the main thrust of the "progressive" big government ethos—ubiquitous cradle-to-grave subsidies, underwriting childcare, pensions, education, food stamps, welfare hand-outs, job protections, healthcare, goodies for business of course, and so much else—all sounds high-minded and well-intentioned to promote societal values, we have discussed specific ways in which society is actually disserved. But beyond that, the big government machine conditions us to become a nation of selfish special pleaders, entangled in a web of pervasive entitlements, and so deeply invested in the status quo that we fiercely resist anything that smacks of reform or change. The system, in the words of David Brooks, "has bred a stultifying conservatism, a fear of dynamic flexibility, a greater concern for guarding what exists than for creating what doesn't." The nanny state makes its citizens timid children, trapped in a suffocatingly cozy parental nest, from which we cannot extricate ourselves and spread our wings. This is why liberalism or progressivism, and the statist colossus it erects, for all their trumpeting of human concern, are ultimately so antihuman.

And it is in the nature of government to be bossy, to tell people what they must do and may not do. The more government we have and

---

113. Then again, the words "if present trends continue" often introduce dubious conclusions. The world is always changing and future expectations tend to be confounded by developments no one foresaw. It has also been said that if something cannot continue, it won't.

the bigger it is, the more laws, regulations, and edicts we have to obey. Quite simply, we have less and less freedom. And this applies to political freedom, too. We have already seen how the state's huge economic role, with so much money at stake, corrupts the political process; with both major parties deeply compromised by the political money game, the significance of citizens' voting is marginalized, and democracy is undermined.

Friedrich von Hayek, in *The Road to Serfdom*, and Milton Friedman, in *Capitalism and Freedom*, argued that political liberty cannot endure without economic freedom and is ultimately incompatible with a controlling state. This is due to the state's concentration and centralization of power, while, in contrast, a free-market system separates economic and political power so that one offsets and puts a check upon the other. The wider the range of matters given to government control, the more issues are decided politically rather than by private action, the greater is the enforcement of conformity, and the less diverse and free is society. So far, Hayek and Friedman have not been proven wrong. So far, not only have statist economies always failed, but none has succeeded in combining economic statism with preserving political liberty. The Soviet Union, again, was the prime exemplar, with 100 percent state control and zero percent political freedom.

I keep mentioning Soviet communism because it provides such a case study of what not to do. The Soviets tried economic planning, to make the economy follow a blueprint devised by government bureaucrats. They thought this would produce better results than just leaving the economy on its own. Of course that was wrong. We have already noted the difficulties hobbling government when it tries its hand in the economy: overwhelming complexity, lack of performance incentives, impossibility of measuring results, "rent seeking," and the law of unintended consequences. What Soviet economic planning and government control produced was bleak gray poverty. They would indeed have been better off with no planning and no controls; in other words, with laissez-faire.

A modern experiment along such lines actually took place in

postwar West Germany when Ludwig Erhard overnight swept away all government economic controls and regulation. Many thought he was mad. But the result came to be called the German "economic miracle," rapidly boosting the country from devastation to widespread prosperity and high living standards.

Similarly, Hong Kong—despite twenty times India's population density and barren of significant natural resources—vaulted, in less than a century, from poverty to an average income actually *exceeding* that of its colonial master, Great Britain. Can you guess how this was achieved? The British governed Hong Kong, but chose to leave its economy essentially ungoverned—laissez-faire—and the results are clear for all to see.

Yet ideological distrust of the free market and belief in the need for assertive government economic intervention are so deeply ingrained in much of the intelligentsia that, despite their dramatic success, Hong Kong's and Erhard's examples have not been imitated. The British, even while overseeing the smashing bonanza of laissez-faire in Hong Kong, went the other way in their own country, smothering themselves in socialism, regulation, and nationalization of industries—which, in the 1970s, earned the moniker "British Disease." Margaret Thatcher did manage to undo some of the damage and put Britain back on a more prosperous path. But, meanwhile, Germany forgot the lessons of Erhard, ultimately backtracked into a heavily regulated economy, and fell into high unemployment and stagnation.

Much governmental economic regulation is of course conceived to protect people from exploitation and deprivation. Germany, and "dirigiste" France, are prime examples, with their cherished "European social model." But if one compares their economic anemia against, say, China, which threw off that kind of straitjacket and unleashed explosive economic growth, it becomes obvious that whatever may be the arguable virtues of regulating business activity for the sake of social objectives, they are simply overwhelmed by the societal benefits of the leaping incomes and spread of wealth that a freer economy generates. Trying to protect the poor can actually protect poverty.

Why the free market is able to do so much better than government will get further attention. But the point here is that big, intrusive, meddling government does not help the economy work better; instead, it gums up the works. The bigger the state's presence in the economy, the less productive it is likely to be, and the less well-off society will be.

All of this may sound alarmist. After all, we certainly do have very big government already, and the sky has not fallen. Living standards have actually continued to rise despite government growth. But how far can we travel this road before getting into quicksand and before government suffocates the free-market golden-egg-laying goose and our freedom with it? Perhaps we can live with the state controlling 40%, or 45%, or even 50% of the national economy—if we could feel sure it will stop there and not go on growing to 55%, and 60%, and 70%—but nobody seems to know how to stop this voracious beast. Few even seem to want to.

Those who do, once more, are called libertarians. They want government limited to its true core functions so as to leave the greatest scope for personal freedom and initiative, and, thereby, make life better for everyone. Most intellectuals, saturated with the idea of a big activist state, give short shrift to libertarianism, if it's taken seriously at all. One common objection to libertarianism is the fear that if the state were really pared back, that would leave a vacuum, which other societal forces, such as religion, would move to fill. Those who think this way trust government more than people. Let's not forget that, in contrast to churches and the like, government has unique powers to make laws everyone must obey, to seize possessions through taxation, and to use its monopoly on violence to enforce its will. A church can do nothing of the sort. Religion, and all nongovernmental entities, operate strictly through voluntary participation. Expanding their role would be no threat, and might well make for greater social consciousness among citizens who are drawn to participate in them. But even if you detest the idea of a bigger societal role for churches or other private organizations, at least you'd still be free to have nothing to do with them, since they cannot boss you around as government can.

Of course, our reality is not retreat by the state, but inexorable expansion, crowding out those private voluntary social institutions, whose importance is inevitably reduced. Local nongovernmental social welfare and charitable networks and initiatives, for example, had more vitality in past eras, before government moved aggressively to supplant them. Again, handing these roles to government—remote, less accountable, political, impersonal, inflexible, and bossy—does not enhance societal consciousness and cohesion or welfare, but undermines them.[114]

It's well established that having a sense of control in one's life, as opposed to feelings of helplessness and dependency, confers multifold benefits, both psychological and physiological. We are happier and healthier when we see ourselves in the driver's seat. Even small infants have been shown to respond positively when given something in their surroundings they can control. Such, of course, is the essence of freedom. And this, too, is why a government that diminishes freedom and choice, a paternalistic and controlling nanny state (no matter how benevolent the intention), does not serve true human values and actually subverts them.

We are also seeing a growth of what may be termed "soft paternalism," with government not necessarily dictating people's choices but, instead, trying to nudge them. Antismoking advertising is an example. People do often make bad choices and the idea is for government to help them overcome their baser tendencies and lack of self-discipline. But such challenges can be seen instead, *The Economist* suggests (quoting J. S. Mill), as opportunities for people to exercise their humanity. After all, the children of a softly paternalistic state have no reason to grow up.

Meantime, government mostly works not by giving suggestions,

---

114. Tocqueville saw voluntary associations and civic participation as key factors in America's social dynamism. More recently, Robert Putnam's book *Bowling Alone* has documented the decline of this phenomenon. Many factors are responsible, but the expanding role of government is surely among them.

but orders. Sometimes it may know what's best for us; but maybe not. Remember that annoying law of unintended consequences. Henry David Thoreau once remarked, "If I knew for a certainty that a man was coming to my house with the conscious design of doing me good, I should run for my life."

It's said that if you put a frog in boiling water, he'll jump out; but if you put him in cold water and slowly heat it, he will that way be boiled. It's probably not really true about frogs, but it could be true about citizens who, of course, would never agree to suddenly give *all* their incomes to government, letting it control everything—but who could perhaps be cooked that way in small steps.

So why hasn't it happened already? Milton Friedman has answered that the forces seeking to subordinate people to a supposedly greater good are countered by one of the most powerful and creative forces there is—the drive of individuals to promote their interests and live by their own values. This encompasses not just material concerns, but the whole range of values people hold dear. Enabling those values to be pursued is the key strength of a free society. Let us put our faith in that.

But What about the Truly Needy?

So, then, are most government programs and spending misconceived? But what, you might ask, about the truly needy people helped by government? What about the really disadvantaged, the disabled, the unemployed, the elderly dependent on what they get from government, the poor children in programs like Head Start? Should we heartlessly do nothing for society's less fortunate?

This is a fair question.

Human welfare is a social good—for all of us. The strong helping the weak makes a society better for everyone in it. The rich man sleeps better if there are fewer poor to nag his conscience. Indeed, this is fundamental to human nature; we experience empathy and compassion, we feel the hurts of our fellows, and salving those hurts enhances our own lives.

We have practiced this ethic from our beginnings. There is plenty of evidence that even the earliest humans, amid the harshness of their existence, took care of their sick, injured, and infirm. Today, the wail of an ambulance siren—people rushing to the aid of strangers—is a loud reminder of the fundamental goodness of a society organized according to such principles. Hearing it makes me glad to be human.

And if we truly do want a society as good as it can possibly be, for everyone in it, we must take a critical look at the big picture and how government fits into it.

To begin with, helping the needy is really only a small part of what government does. Most government benefits and subsidies flow to people who are not in that category. (Look at Social Security and Medicare—yes, poor seniors benefit, but the great majority of beneficiaries are not at all poor.) It is a fact of political life that the really disadvantaged are not politically strong or activist, indeed are disadvantaged in competing for a place at the government feeding trough. They don't make big campaign contributions and they don't hire well-connected lobbyists. The bulk of government largesse goes to those who do. It goes to the politically crucial middle class and the better off. And much goes to businesses too; for example, the massive farm subsidies we've discussed and other forms of "corporate welfare." For all the lofty lip flapping about caring for the needy that fills public discourse, the reality is that the needy are at the bottom of the political pecking order and get only crumbs. (And in any budget cutting, they take the hit.)

So, eliminating all government transfers of income and wealth would affect not just the needy but actually most of the population. Nearly everybody would lose his or her particular free lunch. That's why it will never happen. But, if hypothetically it did, *most* people would actually wind up far better off.

Obviously, taxes would plummet; and we would gain more in tax reductions than we lose in government goodies. Note that government largesse is not a straight transfer of wealth from Peter to Paul. The government itself is a huge operation that costs a lot of money to run. For every dollar it spends, it has to collect rather more than a dollar in taxes to fund the bureaucracy that administers the spending. Further, when government runs a deficit, the interest on the resultant borrowing is another huge cost. All these additional costs would disappear if the programs themselves were eliminated, so taxes could fall by even more than the reduction in benefits.

Of course, a lot of government workers would lose their jobs. But they would mostly end up with productive jobs in the private sector. It would be able to expand to utilize these added workers because a huge drag on the economy would have been removed. Taxes and other burdens on businesses would be reduced, while individuals, paying less in taxes, would have more money to spend, so demand for goods and services would grow and the whole economy would get a tremendous shot in the arm. This would further stimulate demand; a virtuous circle.

Understand, too, that bureaucrats pushing paper in government offices do not add to national wealth. Instead, those costs of running the government are a drain on the economy. What adds to wealth is the production of goods and services people want to buy. Shifting workers from government jobs to ones where they help produce saleable goods and services would increase national wealth. Those workers would now be contributing to a bigger economic pie for everyone.

So, not only would most people get a tax reduction to offset their loss of government goodies, but, in addition, they would benefit from a more robust and productive economy. The pie would grow faster. The aggregate benefits would surely exceed the losses.

Inevitably, such an earthquake in the economic landscape would make losers as well as winners. But there would be far more winners than losers; the average person would be better off and the nation, as a whole, would be better off. The utilitarian principle of "the greatest good for the greatest number" would be served.

This doesn't mean we could just say "tough luck" to those who do lose out, especially society's unfortunates. But note first that there would be fewer of them. With a bigger economic pie, the poor will get some of it. This is sometimes derided as "trickle-down economics," or making the rich richer so that some of that wealth will trickle down to the poor. But we're really talking about making nearly everybody richer. A stronger economy is good for everyone, providing more job opportunities and better pay for those at the bottom.

Second, if programs to help the needy were actually swept away with all the others, private charity would expand to fill at least a big part of the gap. This would happen because, between the tax reduction and the economic growth, the nation as a whole would be richer and more people would have more disposable wealth for such charitable activity. And there would surely be a bigger impetus for it if we all understood that there are no more government handouts for the needy. Most of my own donations are directed overseas because I know I already contribute through taxes to programs for less fortunate Americans. If that weren't so, I'd be a lot more inclined to make such contributions voluntarily, and so would many others.

Meantime, it is far from clear how much government programs really assist the less fortunate. (John Stossel, in *Give Me a Break*, bluntly asserts, in one of his chapter headings, that "Government Help Hurts the Poor.") As mentioned earlier, Lyndon Johnson declared war on poverty in the 1960s. Huge amounts were spent. Poverty did seem to decline, yet, crucially, the rate of improvement was no faster than before the "war," and, in some subsequent years, it was slower or even negative. Poverty statistics actually seem totally unrelated to what the government spends on antipoverty programs. (And if the poor had all the money spent, they'd be rich.)

It's the old adage: give a man a fish and feed him for a day; teach him to fish and feed him for life. Government programs are good (albeit inefficient) at handing out fishes, but quite lousy at teaching anyone anything except to clamor for more fish handouts.

Look at Native Americans living on reservations—they represent the ultimate in government paternalism—and the picture is totally disastrous. Life on reservations is awful. An Indian's only real hope for a decent life is to stop being a ward of the government. But the broader social pathologies and dysfunction created by government handouts have already been noted. They were what finally prompted the welfare reform of the 1990s, to get people off the dole and into work. Liberals howled that this would cause catastrophic hardship. They were proven wrong. When told to sink or swim, the great majority of affected people found they could manage to swim after all; seven million went from welfare into jobs. Instead of taking, they were now contributing to the economy. They were better off for it, and so was the rest of society.

Government intervention in the name of social welfare too often works out not to help society's weakest members, but, actually, to favor the strong over the weak. After all, it is, again, the politically strong who can exert their power to get what they want, often to the detriment of others. A good example is European job security legislation. The intent, as ever, sounds noble. And it does protect people fortunate enough to have jobs—at the expense of the less fortunate unemployed. They get locked out because job security laws penalize businesses for cutting staff, which makes them very cautious about hiring anyone in the first place. Likewise, high minimum wages are great for people already holding jobs but deadly for those trying to get a foot in the door.

Finally, this is not a purist answer to the question posed in this chapter—but, if all government handouts to the middle class, the well-off, and businesses were eliminated, I would be quite content to leave in place the lesser share of government spending that is at least intended to help the truly needy.[115] In fact, we could do far more. We could actually satisfy all reasonable social welfare concerns at a cost that would be quite affordable if only all the other government boondoggles were ditched. Voters imagine that a large share of government spending goes to the poor and, thus, they justify the big budgets in the name of compassion. Again, this is mistaken; only a small share of government outlays reaches the disadvantaged. The sad truth is that supposed compassion for the needy has been a Trojan horse for the expansion of government in so many other directions that the neediest are actually crowded out.

I am enough of a realist to understand that the last few chapters will not prompt readers to rush out and launch a revolt against big government. The aim, instead, has been to place the whole picture of govern-

---

115. Economist Milton Friedman suggested doing this via a "negative income tax" (or guaranteed annual income). If there is a consensus to provide a social safety net, why not rationalize into one straightforward program the crazy quilt of disparate welfare schemes that have built up over time? At least we might shed some of the usually inefficient bureaucracy needed to administer all these complex programs. We could, instead, simply give every citizen a single equal check. For most, it would be offset by correspondingly higher taxes. But someone with no other income would pay no taxes.

ment and political issues in a properly broad perspective. In the real world, political controversies are played out at the margins; our debates concern the details and minutiae of government programs. We rarely tackle seriously the larger issues. Still, when considering any political questions, it is important to see the overarching issues that lie behind them,[116] to point you in the right direction for answering them.

---

116. You may have to twist your neck to see something overarching that lies behind something else.

Wrongful Rights

The most important words ever written were the Declaration of Independence's assertion of fundamental human rights. But there can be too much of a good thing, and too many rights; that is, when rights for some undermine those of others.

The Americans with Disabilities Act (ADA) was passed in 1990 by politicians drenching themselves in self-congratulation for their humanitarian virtue. Promoting decent treatment for disabled people is, indeed, laudable, but here is yet another case where, in service of a laudable goal, government created a monster.

The ADA gives the disabled the right not merely to reasonable accommodation but to whatever is needed for them to function as though they were not disabled. This means that every bus has to be wheelchair accessible and that every bus, therefore, costs a lot more. This, in turn, means that every city can afford fewer buses, which results in less frequent bus service. Furthermore, the loading and unloading of wheelchairs makes buses slower.[117] The end result is that a pregnant woman may need to wait half an hour in the cold, in a dangerous neighborhood, for a bus. Doesn't she have rights too?

Instead of expensively modifying every bus, cities might have pro-

---

117. Intercity buses can even be required to make detours to pick up wheelchair passengers.

vided the disabled with their own special transportation at vastly lower cost. That might have been reasonable. But the ADA gives the disabled a right to ride on every bus. That conflicts with the rights of everybody else.

Similarly, it might be reasonable to require in every apartment building some wheelchair friendly units, but the ADA gives a disabled person a right to live in any apartment he chooses. That means *every* apartment in *every* building has to be wheelchair friendly. This makes no sense; the cost is huge, making apartments more expensive for everybody so that some people can't afford to live in decent apartments at all. What about *their* rights?

This book has stressed the basic human right to live the best life one can. But all of us have our limitations. I'd like to play the piano like Vladimir Horowitz, but no legislation could give me the right to live as though I had that ability. Giving the disabled the right to live as though they aren't disabled is really the same thing. What they should instead be entitled to is fairness and reasonable accommodation for their unavoidable needs. For that, society and its members should accept some burdens and compromises. But compromise is a two-way street, and this concept seems to get lost in legislation like the ADA. It doesn't allow for reasonable compromises on buses or apartments or wheelchair ramps. It's a one-way street with the rights of the disabled overriding those of everyone else.

One might arguably justify all this if it truly helped disabled people. Yet in some respects that's questionable. The ADA gives disabled employees all sorts of legally enforceable rights to be accommodated in the workplace. But guess what? Now many businesses try to avoid hiring anyone disabled because the ADA has made such employees lawsuit time bombs.[118]

---

118. John Stossel in *Give Me a Break* notes that, after it was sued and fined right and left because a drunken tanker captain caused an Alaskan oil spill, Exxon Mobil instituted a policy barring employees with drug or alcohol problems from safety-sensitive jobs. And guess what? Exxon employees with a history of alcoholism sued the company under the ADA, claiming discrimination.

Congress also legislated a right for handicapped children to be educated at public expense. Yes, very high-minded.[119] This right applies regardless of the disability's severity or the cost to accommodate it. In one case, parents insisted that the only program suitable for their disabled child was in Tokyo, so a court forced the local school district to cough up the money to send him there. This kind of thing busts school budgets all across the nation, as the high costs of dealing with severely disabled children swallow up resources and, thus, degrade educational quality for everyone else. Disabled children now have special rights; gifted children have none. A thousand times more money (literally) is spent in public schools on disabled children than on programs for gifted kids. While the disabled should be treated humanely, don't we need to nurture intelligent people too? Furthermore, disabled children are now entitled not only to special programs but to be in regular classes too if their parents so choose, no matter how unsuitable that might actually be. And in thousands of classrooms, the presence of severely disabled children is so disruptive and occupies so much teacher time and effort that the normal kids might as well stay home. Don't *they* have rights?

It's not only disabled kids who have been granted rights in schools. Of course children don't surrender their basic human rights when entering a schoolroom. But we have gone too far the other way, giving kids such wide rights to challenge and resist disciplinary procedures that it can be almost impossible to deal effectively with troublemakers. This is a big factor in the terrible state of inner-city public education. Children can't learn where teachers cannot control the classroom. The troublemakers should have some rights, but not at the expense of good kids who are trying to learn. They have rights too.

Congress has even conferred rights on animals, with the Endangered Species Act (ESA). Protecting endangered critters is a good thing where it can be done reasonably and feasibly, but such common-

---

119. Though it wasn't Congress that had to figure out how to pay for this; nor does the government pay for all the wheelchair ramps and suchlike it has required the private sector to install. Virtue comes cheap when someone else has to pick up the bill.

sense criteria are no part of the absolutist ESA. So, to preserve the habitat of the northern spotted owl, the government put loggers out of business. The owls had rights; the loggers did not. Nor did taxpayers—they got stuck with a $1.3 billion bill to retrain the loggers. And, incidentally, it turned out that this wasn't the owl's only habitat; the same species (with a minor color variation) was thriving elsewhere. Somehow that didn't matter under the ESA.

In a 1993 California wildfire, the only way to save twenty-nine homes would have been to dig a firebreak. But that would have disturbed the habitat of a rat species protected under the ESA, which contains no exceptions for fires. One homeowner broke the law and dug a firebreak. The other twenty-eight homes were incinerated. (So too, of course, were the rats.)

A common feature of all these congressionally mandated schemes of rights is that the chief vehicle to enforce them is litigation. This has spawned an explosion of lawsuits as zealots try to push their entitlements to the limits and communities try to resist the often crippling cost burdens involved. One might think Congress enacts all these rights not so much to help the disadvantaged as to help trial lawyers (who are among the biggest contributors to campaigns).

All this litigation is itself a huge societal cost, with wide-ranging impacts. We need the courts to provide recourse and compensation for genuine injuries wrongfully caused. But the system has been perverted into an extortion racket. If a medical situation does not turn out well (and in the natural course many don't), get an aggressive lawyer to cook up a case against the doctor or hospital, and even if that case is basically phony, the insurance company will probably agree to pay something to settle it because to fight it in court would cost a fortune, and besides, the hospital might well lose anyway, because juries are notoriously sympathetic to unlucky people and hostile toward hospitals and insurance companies.[120]

---

120. Class action suits can be another type of racket. Some have merit—but most are merely vehicles for lawyers to milk the system. They

Because insuring doctors and hospitals is so risky and expensive for insurance companies, they have to charge ever-higher rates for that insurance; this is a big element in the rising cost of healthcare. And, of course, money spent on litigation, settlements, and insurance is money that can't be spent to provide actual health services. It makes medical service less available. For example, a leading fount of litigation is obstetrics; not every birth goes smoothly, and if one doesn't, there will likely be a lawsuit, even if the doctor did nothing wrong. Accordingly, insurance for obstetricians is astronomically expensive. Fewer and fewer doctors are willing to shoulder these costs and risks; fewer are willing to deliver babies.

This is a growing general problem in our society. Countless organizations, projects, and proposals run up against it—insurance is required because the threat of litigation is so great; and because that risk is so great, the insurance is unaffordable. Hence, many worthy ideas, projects, and programs are strangled in their cradles.

The fundamental rights of the Declaration of Independence and the Constitution are rights *against government*. They tell us what government may *not* do. It may not restrict freedom of speech, or religion, or the press; may not deprive anyone of life, liberty, or property without due process of law. These are the basic rights upon which America was founded; their thrust is to protect citizens against government. (And of course government protects us from each other.) These rights are a shield. They protect everyone; no one's rights have to be compromised.

But the new rights being handed out by government are very different. They give to certain people and interests not a shield but a *sword*, a weapon to use against others to get their way. They are rights for some at the expense of others.

---

get the big bucks while the "injured" class members they supposedly represent get crumbs. I was a class member in one such case. At the end, I received a notice saying that, my share of the settlement being less than ten dollars, they wouldn't even bother sending me a check!

We should not object to decent treatment for the disabled and disadvantaged. And charity is virtuous because it represents the free choice of the giver. Some might even see it as virtuous for government, acting on behalf of society, to dispense charity, even though it employs the coercion of taxation. But creating an entitlement goes even further than that. Where there is entitlement, the concept of charity cannot apply. And the coercion factor is even larger. An entitlement is a stick, given to some, to beat others with and to enforce demands upon them. Thus, we have disabled zealots selfishly litigating to impose enormous costs on the rest of society, forcing other people to spend untold billions to make every nook and cranny wheelchair accessible, and preventing those billions from being used to provide more critical help to people more in need (including those in other lands). No virtue is to be found here.

What we have, instead, is absolutism as opposed to balance. A sensible and fair approach to any issue requires considering all competing interests and striking a balance among them, making necessary compromises. This is what, ideally, government should do. Ideally, it should balance the needs and wishes of the disabled against those of other people and society at large by coming up with solutions that accommodate the disabled to a reasonable degree without unreasonably hurting others or imposing undue drains upon limited resources that could be better spent elsewhere. Unfortunately, government seems unable to do this kind of thing. Instead, it makes heedlessly unbalanced laws like the ADA and the ESA.

We also too often forget that rights are entwined with responsibilities. We hear, for example, a great deal about women's reproductive rights, but little about reproductive responsibilities. Conceiving a child surely creates big responsibilities. Yet we are told that a woman has a right to do it, even if she is not situated to properly parent her child—thus, without regard to any rights of the child. And, of course, a child's rights are of no account as against his mother's right to abort. What is missing, in either scenario, is any notion that rights entail responsibilities.

Likewise, the disabled do have rights, but also responsibilities to the rest of society, as do we all. The "live and let live" principle applies yet again—it behooves even the disabled to "let live" with regard to others, to make reasonable compromises and accommodations with the rest of us, and not to seek their own rights and welfare at others' expense.

Much in this chapter (including some examples) owes another major debt to Philip Howard's *The Death of Common Sense*. He argues that one of our fundamental mistakes is to seek certainty through law. We don't trust people, or government for that matter, to do what is right, so we try to circumscribe their paths with clear, detailed, rigid laws, rules, and procedures. The result is that no one can use judgment. Chicago was flooded because an official could not use his judgment to quickly repair a dangerous leak instead of going through tortuous contracting procedures. Homes burned in California because people could not use common sense to dig a firebreak in a rat habitat doomed to burn anyway. We look to law and government to fix all our problems, but it fails to fix them, and indeed multiplies them.

No wonder many people feel cynical and powerless toward government. They see it not as their servant but as their master—and a capricious master at that.

America the Beautiful

The preceding pages have harshly critiqued American government, as a vastly overbloated viper's nest of political dysfunction that undermines our freedom and the true national interest. And yet, when I look upon that white Capitol dome, it still brings to my eyes tears, not of frustration, but of reverence.

Winston Churchill said that democracy is the worst form of government, except for all the others. And gazing on that Capitol dome, I see what Churchill saw—not the defects of democracy, but rather the alternative. I never forget that for thousands of years ordinary people had no say, no rights, and no freedom. In that light, the failings of American democracy are as nothing.

Plato called for rule by philosopher kings. Our founding fathers rejected that vision, rejected the whole ancient paternalistic idea that someone knows better, has greater wisdom, or is anointed to rule over everyone else. Those founders were not philosopher kings, but they were philosophers. They understood that if people give government a monopoly on force (to protect against private use of force), such government power could not be left open ended, but had to be circumscribed by law. They had to ensure that not just citizens, but government itself, would have to obey the law. They also understood that the great power vested in government would be a magnet for people ambitious to gain control of it for themselves; such usurpations had occurred over and over throughout history.

Furthermore, they had to be concerned about power grabs not just by individuals, but by groups—even political majorities. Of course, majority rule is fundamental to democracy, but that doesn't mean a majority should be able to work its will without constraint, taking advantage of an outvoted minority. There has to be protection for minority rights.

These were formidable challenges, never successfully met before. The conventional wisdom said that this experiment in self-government couldn't last. The ancient models, such as Athenian democracy or the Roman Republic, always reverted back to autocracy. To avoid that, our founding fathers had to create something new and different.

And they succeeded—spectacularly. The government they devised did keep to the idea of the social contract, optimizing liberty by protecting citizens' security and rights at a generally small cost in rights sacrificed, while also restraining the power of majorities and maintaining the rule of law, permitting no one to gain power outside the law.

And it has endured. Ours is the oldest national constitution in the world. It has lasted through two centuries that saw more change than all civilization's previous centuries combined. The world today would, in so many ways, have been unimaginable to the Constitution's framers; yet their scheme continues to work as intended. It does so despite a gigantic increase in the size, population, wealth, and power of this nation; despite massive social upheavals, including a bloody civil war; despite immense technological and cultural change.

America has actually grown even more democratic over time. Voting was originally restricted to white males with property; it has since been extended to all other adults.[121] And America has also grown more socially democratic, with ever more openness, opportunity, and

---

121. Some see low voter turnout as a problem in American democracy. But nonvoting bespeaks consent to the status quo and unconcern about what government might do. That may actually be seen as a good thing, an indication that (in spite of all I've written) government is still performing a properly *limited* role in society. If government loomed larger in people's lives they would have more impetus to vote.

economic mobility for women, blacks, and other previously disadvantaged minorities; and ever more tolerance of lifestyle diversity.

And so, we may make many bad decisions through our very imperfect democratic process, but more important by far is that *we* make them, we the people. We're all too cynical about democracy and voting, often glibly saying that it's meaningless, that we don't have real choices, and that it's all controlled by powerful interests. This book has certainly lamented special interest politics. Yet in the end, it's still voters who hold the power and responsibility, and nothing important can be done against their will. In a democracy like ours, ultimate authority resides in the ballot box; the people really do rule. And for all the badness of our political decisions, they are not nearly so bad as they would be under an unaccountable autocracy. That was how the Soviet Union was run, and it collapsed completely.

These are all the things that flood my mind when I see that white Capitol dome. This is what I see when a hundred million people go into voting booths all across America to choose their government. Against the backdrop of all of human history, and the long struggle to get where we are, that democratic spectacle is breathtaking. And when I myself enter that booth, it is for me a sacrament.

In late 1776, the American army lost battle after battle to the British, who chased it out of New York and all across New Jersey. Finally reaching the Delaware River, the Americans grabbed every boat they could find to escape across it. The British, snug in Trenton, were content to wait until the river froze to finish them off.

There wasn't much left of them, just a few thousand weary stragglers, many hurt, sick, ill clothed, hungry, shoeless. Many of their enlistments were due to end in days.[122]

---

122. Tom Paine, encamped with them, now wrote, in *The American Crisis*, that "these are the times that try men's souls." ("Try" meant "test.") He declared that, unlike "summer soldiers" and "sunshine patriots," those who stand with their country in this darkest hour would be remembered. He was right. I remember them. You should too.

What was General Washington to do in these desperate straits? What he did, on Christmas night, was to risk everything; taking those men back in those boats, back across that river, through a foul blizzard, to then march nine miles through snow to attack the British and Hessians at Trenton. The bad weather ruined his plan to surprise them before dawn and Washington was warned that the British had probably been alerted. But there was no turning back.

We won the battle.[123] It may have been the most important ever: had we failed, the Revolution probably would have been over, the Declaration of Independence not a beacon for humanity but a beaten idea. I hate to think how different today's world might be.

But the 1776 Delaware crossing means more to me even than that. To me, it stands for everything that is splendid about America and about the human soul.

One of the most untrue famous lines ever penned was F. Scott Fitzgerald's, "There are no second acts in American life." America is all *about* second acts! It's all about the opportunity for people to reinvent themselves. People have always come here precisely to start new lives. And that's what Washington did in crossing the Delaware. On the whole a failure until that moment, faced now with his toughest challenge, he rose to it, seized destiny in his hands, stepped into a boat, and into a transcending triumph. That was George Washington's second act.

And that's my America—a nation of boldness, of builders, of dreamers, achievers, and pioneers; a nation of undaunted spirit that declares, "the difficult we do at once; the impossible takes a little longer."[124] America is a vibrant perpetual motion machine made of

---

123. The British commander actually *had* received a spy's warning about the attack but had complacently put it unread in his pocket—where it was found on his body. So pivots history.

124. Many deemed impossible the building of a Panama Canal after the French tried and failed catastrophically (leaving twenty-two thousand workers dead). But America was not deterred. We had confidence in ourselves and in the power of human reason to solve the engineering and disease problems that had defeated the French; and that faith was vindicated. We got the job done.

people ready to pick up stakes, look for something better, and try something new.

And while we steadfastly believe anyone can succeed who is willing to work at it, while we may worship success, we don't despise failure, and we give people second chances. Our history is full of failure followed by success; full of people like Abraham Lincoln, who suffered defeat after defeat in politics but never gave up, and so won the biggest prize. People who pick themselves up off the floor and rise to their second acts—like those bedraggled men, blessed be their memory, who got back into those boats on a freezing night in 1776 to make the supreme effort for an idea larger than themselves.

We saw it again after September 11, 2001. How proud we can be of the nobility of spirit America showed in those days; so much generosity, so much strength and resilience, so much positive human feeling. Such a fountain of virtue gushed forth that one might even say the attacks did us more good than harm.[125]

Of course, all these admirable human traits are not unique to America; they are universal. This dreaming, daring and doing, this striving in the face of adversity, this refusal to be beaten, inspires my love for all humanity. What I love especially about America is that it's the one place where these human qualities have their finest flowering, where the best that is in us can be most fully realized.

My father started out poor; my mother started life rich, but arrived here as a refugee shorn of that wealth. They did what Americans do: worked hard, played by the rules; went into business, failed, went back to work, then tried again in business, succeeded for a time, then failed again; worked some more; and built good lives for themselves and their children. Most Americans take their lives for granted. But looking at

---

125. In 2005, victims of Hurricane Katrina were let down by a shamefully bumbling government response. Such bureaucratic failure to meet human needs shouldn't now surprise you. But America is more than its government, and legions of individuals and private companies rushed in to fill the breach. (One firm, Wal-Mart, often lambasted by social critics, here won credit for doling out relief supplies far quicker than government did.)

how much we have makes me misty-eyed. It didn't all fall down to us from heaven. It came to us because of the kind of country America is and the kind of people we are. I too have worked hard to achieve a good life for my own family—but it's America that made it possible.

Give thanks, and love, to this blessed land.

We are living now in the age of America—and of anti-Americanism. The voices, not only foreign but also American, denouncing this country and calling it ugly names are numerous and shrill. So many people bear hostility toward the United States, always thinking the worst about this nation, its government, its leaders, its policies, its motives, its society, and its character. Self-styled sophisticated advanced thinkers see America as a cesspool of racism, economic injustice, militaristic imperialism, environmental rapine, and social pathology, whose history is nothing but crimes, scandals, and atrocities. They sneer at patriotism as vulgar—except when they insist that it is somehow the height of patriotism for them constantly to rubbish the United States.[126]

Such vilification of America today far outstrips any cold war criticism of the Soviet Union, which Ronald Reagan called an "evil empire." For that he was ridiculed by many of those now spewing venom against the United States. Is America really worse than the Soviet Union was?

Reagan also famously called America a "shining city on a hill." This, too, was derided by the moral poseurs of the Left, most notably in a Mario Cuomo speech that recited a familiar litany of America's imperfections. Well, of course it's imperfect; Reagan never said otherwise. But his vision was the broader and truer. One can only pity those Americans whose crabbed thinking keeps them from appreciating that they indeed inhabit a shining city on a hill.

Unique in the world, this nation was founded upon an idea. The

---

126. Decades ago, the philosopher Eric Hoffer wrote, "Nowhere at present is there such a measureless loathing of their country by educated people as in America." It has since gotten much worse.

Declaration of Independence is the American mission statement. And, to a very remarkable degree, we have lived up to it.

Yes, we had slavery. It was a terrible crime; we spent most of a century wrestling with it and then sacrificed six hundred thousand lives in a war to end slavery and liberate its victims. End of story? Of course not. We spent another century wrestling with the continuing problem of racial injustice. We were slow about it, but ultimately we roused ourselves to mighty efforts. So are we finally perfect now? Of course not; nothing in human affairs ever is.

But whereas America-haters see a nation mired in racism, I see the exact opposite. I see a nation that has made titanic efforts to right these wrongs, to lift up their victims; and with great success, so that America today is a completely different country from the one of half a century ago. People ignorant of history have no idea how bad blacks had it in the past, and hence, do not perceive the improvement.[127] Today we see blacks everywhere integrated into society, into the professional world, as doctors, judges, corporate executives, and so on, and don't even give it a thought. Today, Americans of diverse races and ethnicities rub along together with a lot of amity and goodwill and really very little conflict. As against the bloody history of ethnic and religious strife throughout the rest of the world, one must give America extraordinarily high marks.

Native Americans? Certainly wrongs were done. This is, again, the kind of story that has recurred throughout human history, but what sets America apart is how we've tried to make amends for our wrongs. Admittedly there have been bumps along the way. The reservation system is a sorry mess and the government made a hash of its trusteeship of Native Americans' oil and gas royalties (the courts have given the government a black eye over this; our independent judiciary is a

---

127. After the Civil War, black voting in the South was suppressed with brutal violence. In the 1960s, blacks recovered their voting rights; today, half of Mississippi's elected officials are black; and, this time, there is general white acceptance. That's real progress (and shows again the power of political freedom).

powerful force for the righting of wrongs). But meantime, in a lot of ways, we have bent over backward in favor of Native Americans (some would even say too far in giving them legal privileges not enjoyed by other Americans).

Wrongs and injustices are endemic in human affairs. What makes America special is not a lack of wrongs, but a broad-spirited will to make them right. The important story is not racial injustice or mistreating Indians, but the sincere dedication this nation has brought to the task of remediation. The WWII internment of Japanese Americans was another terrible wrong, but here again we repented and made amends. We have plenty of problems, as does every society, but we try to resolve them with generosity and goodwill, in honest efforts to do what is right.

It's ironic that liberals have been in the forefront of such battles, and so greatly succeeded in making the United States a more open, democratic, and fair society, far less racist, sexist, and homophobic; yet those advocates of social change refuse to acknowledge and rejoice in their success. Instead, they perversely deny their own achievement and, against reality, continue to badmouth a caricatured America as though nothing has changed.

But most Americans know better; indeed, they tend to be far more patriotic than other nationalities. Europeans consider our flag-waving gauchely jejune. They see little reason to wave their own flags much; and where nationalism does flourish it's often mainly with a sense of grievance (as in the Balkans). But Americans, in contrast, love their country so proudly because they see it as standing for uplifting ideals. If that makes America different, *vive la différence*!

Social critics berate America's suburban lifestyle and "sprawl." They prefer people being packed together in cities. Paradoxically, at one time, the same species of elitist critics condemned city living, with the development of suburbs advocated as a humane relief from densely crowded high-rises plagued by noise and grime and lacking greenery and open spaces. Most people then could choose only between those gritty cities and the farm, since leafy suburbs were largely nonexistent. And today, all the mockery of suburbia for its alleged cultural sterility and so forth misses one crucial point: people like it. They flee the cities not because they're somehow misguided or deluded but for the very reasons social critics themselves once invoked against urban living. People feel the sprawling suburbs give them a better quality of life. They want some elbow room instead of living right on top of their neighbors, they want spacious homes instead of cramped apartments, and they want lawns and gardens and not just asphalt and concrete.

These are entirely reasonable human desires. Yes, to fulfill them requires giving up some benefits of city life; as always there are trade-offs; and, like anything, suburban sprawl creates its own problems that must be addressed. But millions of Americans gladly accept those trade-offs and embrace the opportunity to live in a way that few people in earlier times or elsewhere have been able to enjoy. This is not something to disparage; it's a singular blessing of modern America. The social critics, who deem themselves tribunes of human values, seem oblivious to what actual humans actually want.[128]

Life changes. True, we've lost some virtues of the "good old days." But those days weren't all good and, on the whole, today is better.

Critics also see a country riven by economic inequality, where the rich grow richer and not just the poor, but everyone else, grows poorer. Yet, the politics of class resentment has never really succeeded in America, because even most of the poor understand why it's misguided. If they thought they were condemned to hopeless poverty, they might revolt. But a high proportion of America's poor see their poverty as way stations on the road to the American dream, which they have every hope of achieving.

Poverty is indeed only temporary for a great many of America's

---

128. The "big box" store phenomenon is similarly a favorite whipping boy. Yes, these stores do create problems. But the reason they succeed and proliferate is because they ultimately serve human needs and wants. One local columnist, fulminating against such a store, admitted that he loves shopping there.

poor. Some, for example, are simply students, with little or no income; many are just starting out in the world of work and family life, they expect to rise, and they do. This is the key reason that poverty and economic inequality statistics, so beloved by America's detractors, can be highly misleading: much of the bemoaned "inequality" merely reflects the normal population distribution among different age groups at different stages of life. Obviously, someone just starting out is going to look very unequal, in terms of income and wealth, when compared to people decades older and with years of working life under their belts.[129] Likewise, the figures are obviously skewed by new immigrants, starting at the bottom. Thus, data for 1996–99 (reported by *The Economist*) showed that only 2 percent of Americans remained "poor" through the four years. And a University of Michigan study of seventeen thousand people from 1975 to 1991 found that *only 5 percent* of those who began in the lowest income fifth ended up there—while nearly 30 percent had vaulted into the top fifth.[130]

Meantime, if there are "two Americas," it's not rich and poor but, more accurately, rich and very rich. Poverty is a relative term, and there is no comparison between the lives of low-income Americans and the genuinely poor throughout most of history. And in many other countries, even today, a lot of people live on a dollar a day or less. Against that true poverty, most low-income Americans would indeed

---

129. Another misleading statistical gambit is to focus on stagnant or even falling "household income." But the average household itself has been shrinking, what with smaller family sizes, more single-parent households, and so forth. Wealth and income *per person* can rise even while for the average "household" it declines.

Watch out, too, for inflation-adjusted comparisons over time. Standard measures of inflation tend to exaggerate it (by looking only at prices and not changes in the quality or the mix of things people buy). The result is to underestimate gains in wealth and income. Compounded over time, the differences are sizable.

130. Even back in 1860, Karl Marx himself said, "The position of wage laborer is for a very large part of the American people but a probational state, which they are sure to leave within a longer or shorter term."

be rated as rich. According to Stossel, of US families classified by the government as "poor," 97 percent own color TVs (half own two), 75 percent own cars, and nearly half own homes. Meantime, even those "poor" are a small minority; most Americans are middle class, who today live every bit as well, in terms of material comforts and luxuries, as did society's highest echelons not so very long ago. The big economic story of modern America is not inequality; it is mass affluence. Look at the cruise industry. The passengers are mostly ordinary average people. A luxury cruise would have been unimaginable for commoners of past generations.

Yet America seems afflicted with what columnist George Will called "economic hypochondria," constantly obsessing about every tiny wobble in the economy (the fretful locution "these economic times" has been ubiquitous for decades), when the big picture really cries out stupendous economic robustness. George Will noted that over the fifty-five years to 2004, seventy-nine million jobs were created and GDP *nearly sextupled*.[131] Home ownership approaches 70 percent.

We do have fewer manufacturing and farming jobs, fewer telephone operators and milkmen, and the typewriter factories are all closed. The only constant in human life is change. But more new jobs have been created than lost. And fewer people employed in manufacturing and farming is not a symptom of something wrong—rather, this is productivity improvement—less labor producing more goods and services, which is precisely the source of our rising standard of living.

Some think we are gaining mostly low-wage "McJobs" and losing the good jobs. But the reality is the opposite. Over recent decades, as more Americans got more education, a higher proportion moved into well-paying professional jobs. Average annual family incomes for people aged twenty-six to fifty-nine now exceed $60,000.

---

131. Many of those jobs were added because of women joining the workforce in huge numbers—a major factor in rising family incomes and living standards. The more people do productive work, the richer we all are. And, of course, this huge social revolution has been an immense boon to women, giving them far broader life choices than ever before.

True enough, many middle-class Americans have trouble paying their bills. This is not because incomes are falling, but because consumption has grown even faster than incomes. Modern culture offers ever-expanding temptations of goodies to buy, and many people don't know how to balance their wants and means, especially with credit cards enabling them to buy now and worry later about paying. Admittedly, a serious medical situation (absent insurance) can be a budget buster, as can higher education (absent loans and financial aid). But it certainly isn't true that the average American can no longer afford a good lifestyle—though many of us have a greatly enlarged notion of what that requires. Many might include in that category broadband internet, cable TV, and cell phone charges, which take big bites out of our budgets. Of course, such modern "necessities" were not even available to prior generations.

Anyhow, even if there is still some real inequality—which of course there is—America is the most open economy in the world, truly a land of opportunity, where everyone can hope and dream, and make their hopes and dreams come true. Sure, it isn't a cakewalk, our streets are not paved with gold. Certainly, someone born to a poor, single, inner-city teenaged mother is at a tremendous disadvantage compared to anyone reared in affluence. That will always be true; luck plays a huge role in life. And there has admittedly been some evidence that social and economic mobility may be declining.

But still, America is very much a meritocracy, where a person with talent and drive, who plays by the rules and works hard to pursue a dream, has a decent chance at making it and enjoying a rewarding life.[132] In the nineteenth century, Horatio Alger wrote stories of plucky boys who made good. That scenario actually became far more common in more recent times; such rising from humble and deprived beginnings is no freakish rarity in America but instead it's a story

---

132. The poor shouldn't be blamed for their poverty. Yet, statistically speaking, a few simple rules enable most people to avoid poverty: don't have children before marrying, finish high school before doing either, and avoid credit card buying when you can't pay bills in full.

repeated over and over and over—it is *the* American story. One big factor is that, whereas in past times higher education was the almost exclusive province of upper-class scions, after midcentury almost anyone with brains and ambition could get a degree. This made for another huge social revolution.[133]

America's economic openness is why so many people throughout the world strive so mightily, even risking their lives, to get here. For all the harshness of worldwide anti-American rhetoric, people still vote with their feet for the United States. They may avow hatred for America, but still they want to be American. They understand what Reagan understood in calling this a shining city on a hill. Its beacon of economic opportunity still shines through the fog of anti-Americanism.

And this nation is a haven for them, a refuge for the world's downtrodden and oppressed. As the Emma Lazarus poem declares, the Statue of Liberty lifts her lamp beside a golden door. That door is not open as wide as I'd wish—but still enough to make us a thoroughly polyglot nation, derived from migrants seeking a better life—something, again, unique in the world. No other country has anything like America's human diversity, and nowhere else is there such tolerance and even cooperation among diverse people. We do a good job accepting newcomers and integrating them into our society. One thing I enjoy about my daughter's soccer games is seeing the names on the players' backs, always an ethnic kaleidoscope. One teammate was born in Rwanda in 1994; her mother barely escaped the genocide, then was welcomed into our community and enveloped with love and support.

People come to America not only for material betterment but also to breathe free. Is our freedom perfect? Again, of course not. It is

---

133. And if, as some claim, social mobility has stalled or even fallen, the real cause is likely to be found in the education picture. While the educated class is good at making sure its kids follow in its footsteps, poorer people are often ill served by public schools. More spending there wouldn't hurt, but that's no cure-all; what's really needed is more accountability for results, and competitive choice—ideas that liberals, who claim compassion for the poor, unfortunately resist.

always difficult and contentious to balance civil liberties against society's main function of protecting its members against harm. Throughout our history, that balance has been struck differently at different times. Yet, never has America given up its fundamental character as an open, free, and democratic nation under the rule of law. In fact, the broad consistent trend over two centuries has been the expansion of individual rights. Even post-9/11, with civil libertarians in full cry denouncing things, our fundamental freedoms of speech, of the press, and of religion remain close to absolute, and criminal defendants still have more rights than almost anywhere else.

Some fret that America is moving toward theocracy. Well, most Americans are religious, many are very religious, and, inevitably, such core beliefs color their politics. Their viewpoints do influence public debate—as they ought to, America being a democracy. But our democracy guarantees minority rights and protects minority religious beliefs. Indeed, for all their political assertiveness, religious fundamentalists are mostly fighting a losing rearguard action against advancing social liberalization (for example, gay rights). Theocracy? America doesn't even allow prayer in public schools. To see theocracy, try a country like Iran, where religious dissent will get you not a hearing but a death sentence.

Civil liberties were restricted in the name of security by various measures during the John Adams administration, the Civil War, and both world wars, and in all those episodes people were jailed on account of their political activism. One might think the cumulative result of all this would be the death of political liberty. Yet surely the opposite is true. In the back-and-forth history of civil liberties, the forces pushing their expansion (including a clear trend of Supreme Court decisions) have been stronger than those for curtailment. Indeed, since 9/11, anti-administration political agitation has been more widespread and shrill than ever, but this time not a single person has been prosecuted for that. The post-9/11 reality actually demonstrates that, far from being destroyed or endangered, civil liberties in America continue to flourish and even grow. No other nation in history—none, anywhere, ever—has so consistently honored the values of freedom, democracy, and human rights.

We have upheld those values not just within our borders, but throughout the globe. The anti-Americans brand this nation arrogantly imperialistic; Noam Chomsky calls it an empire seeking to rule the world by violence. This viewpoint is just grotesquely twisted.

Exercising our great global power is a commensurately great responsibility, a burden that is perforce extremely difficult to discharge to anyone's satisfaction, let alone everyone's. The United States is the most powerful nation since Imperial Rome. It seemingly bestrides the globe as a colossus—economically, culturally, and militarily. Many throughout the world resent that and would still resent it no matter how impeccably America behaved. We must be a responsible world citizen, yet are entitled, indeed obligated, to mind our own national interests as well. This means always walking a fine line. And the fact is that any exercise of US power, no matter how responsible, is bound to antagonize people who feel dwarfed and disempowered by it.

Particularly resented is what is seen as American "cultural imperialism," undermining and supplanting local culture. Of course we don't force our culture on anyone; it spreads because of its vitality and attractiveness. That's not an American crime. But many people blame the United States not only for that, but for just about everything in the world they don't like. America is a natural magnet for blame, a handy scapegoat for the inadequacies and failures of nations with chips on their shoulders. America's power and cultural dominance are manifestations of its immense success—and, thus, a source of envy and resentment for nations and cultures not quite as successful.

All this is understandable because America certainly looms large in reality—but even larger in the imagination, its power often wildly exaggerated in people's minds. They fantasize that the United States controls and manipulates world events far beyond its true capability.[134] But if the United States is really so all-powerful, why can't it do anything about rampant anti-Americanism? In fact, anti-Americanism is itself just one factor among many preventing the United States from working its will throughout the globe. For all our influence, it's far from limitless, especially when so many people worldwide would rather be caught dead than be seen to cooperate with America.[135]

As to America's alleged imperialism of the more conventional sort, our record is not blemish free, but no balanced assessment can sustain a broad indictment.[136] To the contrary, we can be proud of how America has behaved. We went to war in Afghanistan to oust a horribly repressive regime; in Kosovo, with no motive other than to stop murderous "ethnic cleansing"; before that, to thwart the Iraqi aggression against Kuwait, to free Panama from rule by a drug gang, and to stop North Korea's aggression against South Korea, aggression by the

---

134. Facts and reality don't often get in the way of anti-Americanism. Iran demonizes the United States based on a litany of alleged past misdeeds that are largely mythologized; the obsessive Khomeini once declared (actual quote), "The Great U.S. Satan has dominated our country for the past 2,500 years!"

135. Meantime, would all the critics of American power really prefer a world in which America followed their advice to mind its own business? Who would fill that power vacuum? Historical experience does not inspire optimism for such a scenario. And the fact is that US military presence gives huge numbers of people unprecedented security against warfare. It's often said that America should not be the world's policeman. But would we want to live in a society without the law and order that the cop on the beat provides?

136. We eventually gave the Panama Canal to the Panamanians. We did take the Philippines from Spain in 1898, and did battle an insurgency afterward. But we later gave the Philippines independence, amicably, without their having to fight us for it. We also liberated Puerto Rico from Spain. We have let Puerto Ricans vote on their status and they've rejected change. That's not surprising—they have all the privileges of their US citizenship, except paying income tax! (But, okay, the Mexican War was imperialistic. I'll give the America haters that one.)

Axis nations in WWII, and aggression and violations of international law by Germany in World War I.

After WWII, we occupied Germany and Japan. Did we seek to exploit them as colonies, to subjugate them, or to annex their territory? Throughout history, that has been the fate of nations conquered in war. That's what imperialism actually means. But instead, we rebuilt Germany and Japan, put them back on their feet, and reformed them from militaristic tyrannies into free, democratic, and responsible members of the world community. Having accomplished that, within a short time, we left. And when General MacArthur said good-bye to Japan, the Japanese wept. In all of history, one will not find more noble conduct by a victorious nation.

The 2003 Iraq war was not launched for bad reasons either. We did it to liberate the country from a viciously murderous regime that had defied seventeen United Nations resolutions requiring it to account for its weapons of mass destruction—weapons it was known to have been developing and stockpiling and which it had used already in two heinous wars of aggression. With Iraq concealing whether it still had such weapons, we couldn't take the risk that it did. Furthermore, the Iraqi regime's evident long-term objective of gaining a stranglehold over Middle Eastern oil—vital to the whole world's economy—was a dire threat that had to be removed.[137] And this was no imperialist conquest. As in the case of Germany, Japan, Afghanistan, and the Philippines, our aim has been a free, democratic, and peaceful Iraq, whose people can thrive, providing a positive model for a region sorely in need of one.[138]

Then there was Vietnam. Conventional wisdom deems it a moral stain on American history. And we did do a lot wrong there. But consideration of this war has tended to focus exclusively on faulting the

---

137. Saddam Hussein was also one of the world's worst environmental destroyers. Yet, strangely, few greens endorsed his ouster.

138. The Iraq war represented a clash between my idealism that says we should strive to achieve great things and my distrust of government to achieve them. That distrust was certainly borne out by the invasion's thoroughly botched aftermath.

US role, with rarely a critical word about the other side. The United States was demonized, the other side romanticized as a "national liberation struggle" by indigenous Viet Cong rebels. In reality, it was a war of aggression by North Vietnam seeking to extend its communist dictatorship to the South, which we tried to help defend. That may have been a mistake, but it wasn't ignoble. And once we failed, the Viet Cong were brutally brushed aside by the invading Northern army. The imposed tyranny was so harsh that a million people tried to escape by sea; many perished. This humanitarian catastrophe was what we had been fighting to prevent.[139]

Thomas Jefferson held the ideas in the Declaration of Independence to be universal human values. The last thing he ever wrote was a letter saying he was too ill to attend a fiftieth anniversary celebration for the Declaration; but he there expressed his conviction that its idea of self-government and human rights would in time spread across the globe: *"to some parts sooner, to others later, but finally to all."*

It was a breathtaking dream in 1826, when America still stood virtually alone in upholding those values; even the French Revolution had fizzled out. Yet Jefferson's vision has since come a long way toward fulfillment. In my own lifetime, I have seen more progress toward it than I ever dared imagine. Just as he said in that final letter, we Americans, in 1776, ignited a beacon light to lead humankind from

---

139. We also fought to prevent a "domino effect" of other nearby nations falling to communism. That idea is today derided as though it epitomized American foolishness. Yet, in fact, following South Vietnam's fall, Cambodia, too, was seized by a communist force, the Khmer Rouge, which proceeded to murder 1.7 million people, a quarter of the population. This is a fact America haters can't shrug aside—so, instead, they insist that (like every other bad thing) the Cambodian genocide was actually somehow caused by the United States. (More logically, it was caused by the success of America's peace movement, which cleared the way for the Khmer Rouge takeover—another example of the law of unintended consequences and how "peace" can carry a heavy price.)

darkness. I share his dream that one day every person on Earth will enjoy the right to life, liberty, and the pursuit of happiness.

And that is, in fact, the core of American foreign policy. It's not to subjugate the rest of the world under our heel. That is not even our self-interest as we see it. Our aim, instead, is a world of free democratic nations, respecting human rights, promoting economic integration and growth, and cooperating peacefully with each other. As John F. Kennedy said, "We seek not the worldwide victory of one nation or system, but a worldwide victory of men." That is the American vision, and we see it as consistent with our own true self-interest. We want a world that is not just good for America, but good for everybody, and we know such a world would be even better for America.

Are we imperfect in our pursuit of that vision? Sure. Do we make mistakes? Certainly. But America is a big-hearted nation that at least tries to do good. When Nazi Germany or Soviet Russia did bad things, that was a reflection of something systemically wrong; when America does bad things, it's in spite of a fundamental goodness. An example is the abuse of Iraqi prisoners and Guantanamo detainees. Amnesty International called Guantanamo "the gulag of our time." But the Soviet gulag camps were not only vastly larger in scope, they were intrinsic to the political system of crushing dissent; and, in the Soviet Union, no media could investigate and expose the gulag, nor could any court have intervened, both of which were major elements of the Guantanamo tale. To see equivalence between America and Soviet Russia is moral blindness.

Meantime, no other nation has ever done more to promote democracy, freedom, national self-determination, human rights, peace, and economic betterment for all people. It is a raw fact that if the United States does not take the lead when fundamental human values are at stake, no one else will. And we do take the lead, again and again and again. Whether it is the Marshall Plan to rebuild post–WWII Europe, the Berlin Airlift, saving the Muslims of Kosovo, brokering peace in Bosnia, preventing anarchy in Haiti, relieving starvation in Somalia, standing up for human rights in China, stopping the execution of a leading dissident in South Korea, ending civil war in Sudan, gaining freedom for political prisoners in Egypt, spearheading negotiations to open up world trade, trying to make peace in the Middle East, rescuing Liberia from chaos, giving food aid to North Korea (despite that nation's bitter enmity), liberating Kuwait from Iraqi conquest, or supporting democracy in Afghanistan, it is America that takes the lead.

That is American foreign policy.

My love for America is not blind chauvinism. It is rooted in my deep study of history and understanding of realities throughout the world. Put against that background, America shines as the most noble, most idealistic, most generous, most moral nation there has ever been. America stands for free will, free people, and free enterprise; a triumph of the human dream of opportunity and hope.

Verily, it is a shining city on a hill.

The Morality of Free-Market Capitalism

Many critics deem free-market capitalism morally base. They see it as an engine of inequality and social injustice, making some people rich and others poor. That a capitalist should profit from the labor of others they hold likewise immoral; so too that the whole system is fueled by greed.

The Left's traditional remedy of choice was to remove business and commerce from private hands altogether and put them, instead, in public hands, with the state owning and operating businesses on behalf of society.[140] Another tack the Left takes is to redistribute wealth and income from rich to poor and put up obstacles to people getting rich in the first place.

All of this does have a certain superficial moralistic appeal. It does seem wrong that some are very rich while others are poor. It might seem unjust for a businessman to reap the profits from what his employees produce. And supplanting private greed by establishing common public ownership for the good of everyone does sound like a fine idea.

---

140. This, again, is socialism or communism; but even in the "free world" the state has gone heavily into business. A spate of privatizations (government selling off its businesses) begun in the Thatcher era rolled back some of this, but not all.

And it might indeed be so—if government were run by disinterested angels with omniscient wisdom. Of course, as we have seen, the reality falls rather short of this ideal. Politics pervades government, distorting all it does and hampering its ability to serve the true public interest. And government officials can never possess the depth of understanding, the immensity of information, or the proper tools to effectively supervise a complex national economy.

This is by now widely acknowledged, after the clear failure of nations trying central economic planning and state control. Even at the microlevel of a single business, the state always fails. Government-run enterprises always lose money (that is why so many have been privatized).[141] Soviet factories were renowned for churning out shoddy goods that no one would buy, while things people did want were never available. Instead of "adding value" to raw materials by turning them into finished products, Soviet economic bosses actually managed to *subtract* value by turning raw materials into worthless goods. Thus, where Marx wanted workers to reap the wealth benefit of added value, communism, in practice, actually gave them the impoverishment of subtracted value. And of course, it operated by coercion—government telling everyone what to do.

Contrast this with the free market. Its definition is that participants are left free to act in their own self-interest, in their buying and selling, in their production and pricing decisions, and so on, with government steering clear. Adam Smith put his finger on what makes this work out so well. He saw the economy as being guided by an "invisible hand," comprised of all those myriad little individual decisions made by all its participants. The price system, together with the law of supply and demand, acts as the regulator, the gyroscope, of the marketplace. If buyers want a certain thing keenly, they will bid the price up, and its makers will be able to sell lots of it, so they will make more of it, and

---

141. Many complained when Amtrak, the government-run railroad, discontinued food service on which it was losing millions. Who else but government could manage to lose money selling overpriced food to captive customers with no competition?

soon others will be attracted into the business of making it. Supply will increase, forcing prices back down as suppliers compete with each other for customers. Contrariwise, if demand for an item weakens, prices will fall, signaling suppliers to make less of it, or even exit the business.

Thusly do prices of all goods tend to move toward an equilibrium level where supply is matched with demand. This is what makes the marketplace function smoothly and efficiently, with societal resources being utilized to maximum benefit. Desired goods will be produced; goods not desired won't. Raw materials will tend to go where the most value can be added (because those businesses will offer to pay the most to get those raw materials); and likewise, labor will tend to be put to the most efficient and productive uses.

To bring it down to the smallest example, in my own little rare coin business I have to make innumerable decisions about what coins to buy and how many of each type; negotiating deals, bidding in auctions, and trying to price coins to maximize my profits. I do all this based on long years of experience dealing in coins and my knowledge about them, about the market, and about what my customers like. I am a participant in a wholly free market. The coin trade is not very important in the national economy, but the same picture holds for all markets and for all goods produced, bought, and sold. What I do in my little business is multiplied millions and millions of times over throughout the economy. You can readily grasp how impossible it is for government bureaucrats, sitting in offices and removed from the hurly-burly of the marketplace, to substitute their own price and supply decisions and achieve anything approaching the economic efficiency produced by the free market's invisible hand.[142]

---

142. It's true that capitalism is subject to periodic ups and downs. But note that the worst such, the Great Depression, actually reflected not some inherent flaw of the free market, but poor decisions by the very government body (the Federal Reserve) set up to prevent such things. The Depression would not have become "Great" without government meddling. (And, as Milton Friedman has argued, any system giving fallible government officials such vast power is a bad one.)

* * *

In the early days of car making, Henry Ford attracted the best workers by offering the highest wages, which he was able to do because he could use that labor more efficiently than his competitors due to his innovative assembly process and because the resulting product was one that millions wished to buy. Ford also realized that he benefited if laborers earned enough to buy his cars.

That sort of positive dynamic belied Marx's narrow conception of economic life. And it also points up another key concept that is too little understood. Henry Ford was helping to create a virtuous circle: the more his workers earned, the more cars they could buy; the more cars were sold, the more workers he could hire and the more he could pay them. And, when this is happening throughout the economy, it's not the rich getting richer while the poor get poorer, it's everyone getting richer.

The economy is all about Joe selling things (including his labor) to John while John in turn sells things to Joe. And realize that Joe won't buy John's widget unless he values it more than the money he pays; and John won't sell it unless he values the money more than the widget. Thus, it is not a zero-sum game with a winner and a loser, with one getting rich at another's expense. Joe and John are both winners; each winds up with something he values more than what he had before. Both increase their effective wealth. That is how the market economy enriches everyone.

This may seem counterintuitive if viewed from the standpoint of a two-person economy, Joe and John, as though they are lifting themselves by their bootstraps, making something out of nothing. But, of course, the real economy has millions of participants with complex webs of interrelationships among them. And it does not make something from nothing. What really underlies society's enrichment is productive effort and labor creating goods and services people want to buy. Those goods and services are what constitute the material wealth of society. The more of them an economy produces, the richer its participants become.[143]

---

143. However, when effort is expended and resources are used up without satisfying human needs and wants, that is the opposite of wealth pro-

Incidentally, there is a common mistake that only manufacturing—making "things you can drop on your foot"—is genuine productiveness, whereas a service economy doesn't produce anything real. But the true criterion of value creation is people's willingness to pay. If customers willingly pay as much for a service that merely makes them feel good, as they do for a droppable manufactured item, the two are worth the same, and society benefits equally from production of either.[144]

And as Adam Smith saw, the beauty of the whole system is that, even while individuals act out of naked self-interest, seeking the best deals to make the most profit for themselves, the net result of all such activity benefits everyone. Desired goods and services are made available at prices people are willing to pay, the purchasers enhance their lives, and everyone participating in this commerce is better off. In effect, the "invisible hand" harnesses all the individual acts of self-interest to advance the public good.

Most of us today do understand that free-market capitalism delivers the bacon. Yet many still regard this as a Faustian bargain—accepting the system because it gives us material abundance, even while condemning its moral dimension.

One point, already mentioned, is the Marxian objection to worker "exploitation." Of course workers deserve to share in the profits from their labor—and they do share—that's where their pay comes from. Without profits, business owners wouldn't be able to hire and pay workers at all; an entrepreneur does his workers a boon by providing

---

duction; it is wastage—as in the case of military spending. The costs of war may be justifiable on other grounds, but never because they are in any sense "good for the economy."

144. Note that in my mentioned coin business I am a merchant, not a maker. But such trading also adds to societal welfare. I buy coins from those who value them less and sell to others who value them more. The difference is my profit. But I am not the sole beneficiary; both my supplier and my customer also benefit. All three of us are better off.

them with an opportunity for employment. And the owner who does that—puts up the capital, coordinates the investment and all aspects of the enterprise, manages it, and assumes the risk of failure—is certainly entitled to share in the profits as well. The share going to each is something decided by negotiations between them. Their relationship is mutually beneficial, not "exploitation."

The chief indictment of the free market's morality centers upon inequality. Yet, if the choice is either a society with large inequality (some people rich and others poor), or else one with no inequality and everybody poor, then surely the former is morally preferable to the latter as it is better in human terms. Equality is not a moral thing if it means equality of poverty. Of course, redistributionists would say they don't just want to eliminate the rich, they want instead to spread the wealth so that no one is poor and everyone's needs are met. However, the rich don't have nearly enough money to achieve that (not worldwide, certainly). Redistributing all the wealth from the rich would not raise the rest all that much; and more important, you could only do that once, because afterward no one will exert himself to get rich, knowing that his wealth is subject to confiscation. The more the rich are taxed, the more wealth is taken from them, the less reason there is to work hard to get rich. Remove the incentive for people to get rich, to exert themselves, to take entrepreneurial risks to produce things, and pretty soon everybody will be poorer than when you started.

The fact is that we need the rich. More precisely, we need the *opportunity* for people to become rich, which is such a tremendous motivator for them to do the kinds of things that ultimately make us all better off. That conflation of private ambition and public good is, again, the beauty of the free market. Letting some people get rich is the price we pay for its benefits—if you call that a price. There's nothing morally tainted about someone getting rich through providing things that enhance people's lives. Such wealth isn't gained at the expense of the poor or by "exploiting" anyone. It is not immoral to profit from your industry and enterprise, to reap the fruits of your labor. And the resulting inequality is not social or economic injustice.

Note, too, that people's drive for self-betterment is not just a matter of making more money for themselves. For many, improving themselves is quite literal; in order to rise they must become better people, more educated, more skilled, and more creative, because it is actually by making a bigger contribution to the betterment of others that they gain more for themselves. And, in general, if people do earn more, it is because they contribute more to society and create more value for which others willingly pay them. Of course, this isn't universally true; but it is generally true. The inequality produced by the free market is, in great part, a consequence of inequality of human enterprise, effort, and productiveness. Though it is an imperfect process, in the main, the rewards in a country with economic freedom go to those who do the most to earn them.

Furthermore, we must realize that people's striving for money, and for the good things in life, has another crucial dimension beyond the material one. They also do it as a way to assert their pride and human dignity in relation to their peers; to gain status, respect, and self-respect. This is fundamental to human nature. Likewise, it's noteworthy that democratic rights, too, don't serve just people's material interests, but also this natural craving to honor their dignity and human worth. Even if an individual cannot be equal in material terms, democratic freedom gives him an important element of psychological equality. Here, again, we see how economic and political liberties are deeply intertwined.

The Left worries too much about redistributing wealth and not enough about how to produce wealth in the first place, nor about how the former affects the latter. They want to have their cake and eat it: to redistribute wealth from rich to poor and to have the flow of wealth magically keep coming for redistribution. Well, it doesn't work that way. Remember the fable of the goose that laid golden eggs? Her owners thought they needn't wait for one egg a day, there must be many more inside her. So they killed her and cut her open. End of golden eggs. Those who seek to redistribute the wealth of the rich are really proposing the same policy of cutting open the goose.

So the choice is really as stated—either a society with rich and poor,

The Morality of Free-Market Capitalism 209

or else everyone poor. And in the latter case, the poor would be even poorer than in the unequal society produced by free-market capitalism. That system at least generates far more resources with which to help the poor.[145] But the ultimate answer for poverty and other social ills is not found in transferring wealth from one part of society to another; it is, instead, to build a thriving free economy where people have opportunities to earn decent incomes through contributing to societal wealth.

And, of course, that's pretty much what we've done. Once more, it's misleading to talk of "rich and poor" in a modern capitalist society. The free-market system has enabled the great majority of us to enjoy an altogether decent standard of living, which would indeed be considered "rich" on any relative global assessment. What inequality exists is by and large an inequality of riches.

And to try to undo such inequality requires great heaping gobs of coercion. It is another fundamental reason for the failure of socialist/collectivist economics that it can only work by fighting human nature. It asks people to relinquish their self-interest and their thirst for betterment and status. It requires compelling them to do what they don't like and to give up what they cherish, enforced by the clang of prison gates.

Where is the morality in this? Where is the virtue in one group of people arrogating to itself the right to confiscate the rightly earned possessions of others? The plain word for this, again, is *theft*. It is precisely what the social contract is intended to protect us against. When society itself is the perpetrator, it tears up the social contract.

Contrast, once more, the virtue of free-market capitalism. It functions not by fighting human nature, but by working along the grain of human nature, harnessing it to serve the greater public good. In the free market, the natural human motivation to improve one's status and condition of life is the driver, rather than coercion exerted by the state.[146] It works through consensual transactions, voluntary cooperation—not theft.

---

145. As Margaret Thatcher said, "No one would remember the Good Samaritan if he'd only had good intentions. He had money as well."

146. But it bears repeating that selfishness is not the only human motivation, and people are naturally cooperative social animals. Thus, by no means is *laissez-faire* a recipe for zero social cooperation.

Hence, there is far more social and economic justice in a free market, where people benefit from their efforts, merits, and contributions, than in a socialist system that seeks to achieve equality by coercion and confiscation, by stealing from the productive members of society the fruits of their sweat. That is no way to achieve any justice worthy of the name.

Ultimately, to seek equality of economic outcomes is the wrong goal. The correct aim, instead, is to provide equality of rights, equality before the law, and equality of opportunity. And this equality can be extended universally without curtailing anyone else's rights, without taking anything from anyone.

Leftists throw around the phrase "the contradictions of capitalism." The only "contradiction" is that individual ambition is made to work for the benefit of all. It is actually anticapitalism that is shot through with contradiction—the idea that social justice can be attained by seizing from people what they've earned and the contradiction that, despite the lofty aim, this actually impoverishes everyone.

A cartoon shows a child at a lemonade stand with a sign, "Charlie's Lemonade, 25¢." Beside Charlie is a rival: "Arnie's Lemonade *with a cherry* 25¢."

That's competition. Arnie realizes that to attract business he must offer his customers something extra. By doing so, he makes more profit. Customers benefit too; they get more for their money. And maybe Charlie will respond with a different tack—cutting his price. So now buyers will have a real choice. Cherry lovers may go with Arnie while those who don't care for cherries will find Charlie's offering more attractive.

This is the beauty of competition in a free market. In the long run, businesses never gain any permanent advantages—what extra profits they may garner by one-upping their rivals will, in due course, be competed away as others figure out new ways to lure customers. For similar reasons, monopolies never last either. There will always be alternative ways to satisfy demand. Meantime, Adolf Berle, the pioneer analyst of the modern corporation, concluded (in *The Twentieth Century Capitalist*

Revolution) that what it really seeks is just "a steady job—the job of producing goods at roughly predictable cost, under roughly predictable conditions, so that goods can be sold . . . at a roughly predictable price." But, again, such comfortable stasis is unattainable.

The marketplace is, in fact, a never-ending Darwinian struggle for survival. Economist Joseph Schumpeter called it "creative destruction." Like a new predator in an ecosystem, a new competitor, with a new and better way of satisfying customers, will wreak destruction upon other firms unable to withstand the challenge. The new top dog will reign until it, too, is ultimately destroyed by something newer and better still. And the real beneficiaries are consumers, because as the process plays out over time, with competitors continually striving to beat out their rivals, products are constantly improved and consumers get ever better value and ever more choices.

That is why in any supermarket you'll find so many different breakfast cereals, with myriad permutations catering to every taste or predilection. Cereal companies must never stop trying to learn what buyers want and how to make products to satisfy them.

And this, too, is why the free market works so much better than government in meeting human wants and needs. Indulge my reiterating the obvious point that government is not engaged in any Darwinian competition against rivals. It has none; hence, it has no similar impetus to satisfy its "customers." This is why in a Soviet store you'd never find many breakfast cereal choices—or much of anything else you wanted. Their bureaucrats had no incentive to understand customer desires. They didn't even have to worry about selling the goods produced; that didn't matter (to the bureaucrats).

But this really applies to anything government does, and more important things than breakfast cereal are at stake. Education is a prime example. Most public schools don't face competition; there is scant penalty for failure. Layers of bureaucracy stifle, if not penalize, innovation. Entrenched interests fiercely defend their turf against reform and resist allowing education consumers (students and parents) the kinds of choices that a free market might provide.

Those with limited imagination tend to see direct government action or provision of services as the only option. Indeed, they often demonize "privatization," as though private action must be less virtuous than anything done by government (and as if government is not itself captive to private interests, as we've seen). Yet we've also seen how much better the free market can do, by enlisting private interests to serve the public good, compared to ham-fisted government trying to regiment people. Often, we can utilize the market rather than government to accomplish our goals.

It's true that the market is not a universal panacea. Economists refer to "market failure," where individuals seeking personal advantage cannot be expected to act for the broader public interest. Pollution is an oft-cited example, with businesses having no impetus to curb it, so we need government action. Yet even here, government can act by utilizing the market. America's sulfur dioxide trading scheme to control air pollution gives a firm an incentive to find economical ways to cut its emissions and, thereby, earn "pollution rights" it can sell to some other firm for whom reducing emissions would be unfeasibly costly. Thusly, businesses are motivated to use their own know-how to target pollution-control spending where the cost-benefit picture is optimal—instead of government trying to figure out exactly what every factory should do. The result is that the country's acid rain problem has been essentially solved at a fraction of the cost originally estimated for a governmental command-and-control approach. Similar measures, using tradable fishing quotas, have helped to reduce overfishing, and bottle deposit schemes utilize pricing to give people incentives to act in desired ways.

Price is, again, a key element of market economics; it's the regulator matching supply with demand, and it also promotes economic efficiency by rationing resources according to how people truly value them. As seen above, government can beneficially utilize this tool; but when it, instead, intervenes in ways that distort the economy's price signals, the results tend to be bad. Many of the world's water supply problems are caused by users being shielded from facing the true costs. Why bother fixing a leak if you're not paying for the water? So an awful lot literally goes down the drain. The same factor looms large in America's healthcare problems. Most users of medical care simply aren't concerned with what it costs because they aren't paying. The bills go elsewhere; the patients often don't even see them. So they don't shop around, don't negotiate with providers, and consume a lot of costly medical care that they could do without. Is it surprising that health costs are out of control?

Another example is highway congestion. Road use is mostly a nonrationed free-for-all, with gridlock the only control valve. But through pricing we can ration road use according to the differing values drivers place on it. We are actually starting to see this, with tolls that vary by time of day and traffic conditions, and choices between toll and nontoll options. Relaxed drivers may be content with the more congested free road while those in a hurry can opt to pay the toll. If too many do so, its benefit will disappear, shifting traffic back to the free road—a far more efficient and rational control valve. And London now charges drivers for entering the city. Some motorists resent this—but most like it because it means they suffer less in traffic.

The fact is that, while government dictation is so bad at achieving desired results, the free market, with its price system, is an extremely powerful mechanism for doing so. And it's better to get results, not by forcing people to act contrary to their interests, but instead, by finding ways to align those private interests with the public interest by providing proper market-based price signals, and by giving people choices, rather than government making choices for them.

For all that, government, nevertheless, remains a popular recourse to fulfill societal needs. Many people really don't *want* choices. They are bewildered by row upon row of breakfast cereals. They want life to be simple. Making choices, making their own decisions, can be onerous; personal responsibility is a burden. This is why the idea of private accounts within Social Security gets so little support. People seem more comfortable with the seductive notion of a benignly paternalistic government, with all-seeing wisdom, making the choices for them, with their best interests at heart.

And some people believe in Santa Claus too.

* * *

Money has been called "the root of all evil." Many evil things are, indeed, done for the sake of money. But it isn't money that's evil, it's the doers. Money was actually one of the greatest inventions of all time, one of the keystones of civilization. Direct barter of goods is very cumbersome and inefficient because, when you want to trade your pottery for old MacDonald's pig, he may not need any pottery. But sell your pottery for money and you can easily buy a pig. Thus, the invention of money made possible the division of labor, with people able to pursue different specialized occupations, always able to sell their products, labor, or services and then buy whatever different products and services they need. Money is the universal language of commerce; everything traded can be translated into terms of money, and that's what makes commerce flow. And it is that flow of commerce that gives us such a rich society.

A recent newspaper column decried that our healthcare system "now" has "making money" as its primary mission. Well, it is certainly true that people working in healthcare do it to make money; they have to feed their families and pay their bills, after all. They provide healthcare to make money, just as the columnist, herself, provides columns to make money. There was never a halcyon time when selfless healthcare workers ministered to the sick without wanting to get paid or people ran healthcare businesses without wanting to make money.

Concededly, some healthcare in our society is provided on a charity basis (though employees of such charities still want salaries). But, in general, there is no reason why people should not expect to pay for the goods and services they desire, with the providers thereby making profits. After all, that's why businesses strive to satisfy people's needs and wants. And, again, there's nothing morally wrong there.

Marx proposed a different model: "From each according to his ability; to each according to his needs." Sounds fair? But it disconnects what people receive from what they contribute—so why bother to contribute? And indeed, under communism, where the profit motive and rewards commensurate with work were abolished, people had no incentive to exert themselves, so they didn't. You know the rest.

The philosopher John Rawls urged achieving social justice by focusing on all those born in unfavorable circumstances or with lesser native assets and trying to fix all those deficits. And he posed the question of what kind of society you'd choose if you didn't know beforehand how well off (or not) you'd be. According to polls, most liberals believe a person's life is shaped mainly by that kind of luck, whereas conservatives think it's merit and action. Rawls and liberals feel that success is really an arbitrary roll of the dice, so fairness requires equalizing outcomes, while conservatives see that as unfairly negating what people deservedly achieve by their own talents and efforts.

In truth, success in life is molded by both factors, luck and pluck, intertwined, and it's impossible to untangle them for any individual, let alone for a society. It's been said that the key to success is to choose your parents carefully, and that's the element of luck liberals mainly have in mind. Yet, many born with such advantages squander them while many born without them nevertheless do succeed in life through ability, hard work, enterprise, and drive.

But having such personal qualities is also lucky in a sense, which renders problematical the idea of rectifying outcomes produced by luck. Not only being born with a silver spoon in the mouth but also such attributes as artistic talent, athletic prowess, physical beauty, or entrepreneurial ingenuity are, likewise, matters of luck, the results of a great cosmic lottery. Does trying to level that playing field really make sense?

It is reasonable for society to ensure that the unlucky disadavantaged at least live minimally decent lives. But beyond that, the goal, once more, should not be equality of outcomes but equality of opportunity. A level playing field should mean that the same rules apply for everyone—not that everyone is somehow made equal in capability so that all will achieve the same score. Of course, that cannot be done by strengthening the weaker players so much as by hobbling the stronger ones. Society does not gain by trying to squelch people with talent and drive, cut them down to size, or redistribute away what their efforts garner for them. Instead, society, and all its members, are best served if such individuals are given the maximum scope and incentive to make the most of their gifts. Success should not be condemned and punished but, rather, celebrated and encouraged. That is the best way to tap into and spread widely the prizes that the cosmic lottery bestows on people.

And there's my answer to Rawls's question. I would pick the society in which the greatest number of people have the greatest opportunity to live good lives. That means one with the greatest possible freedom—not one misguidedly seeking an egalitarian utopia by undoing all forms of human inequality. In the latter kind of society we'd all be poor—because it would require virtually totalitarian coercion and confiscation, producing their predictable grim results. And, without freedom, can there be any social or economic justice worth having?

The final conclusion, from everything we've discussed, is that the free market is a better vehicle than government for improving our lives. The free market does better because it utilizes human nature, allowing people to pursue and realize their ambitions and to benefit from their efforts. Government works against human nature by forcing people to do what they don't want to do, and by taking away the fruits of their efforts. That this doesn't work as well and doesn't deliver the goods is no surprise. And trying to achieve results by compulsion and confiscation is not moral or just either. Government should aim not to *substitute* for the workings of the free market or change its results but, rather, to *facilitate* its working and to work along with it. That is the best way to improve life for everyone.

Wherever we can choose between a government answer and a free-market answer, between letting people gain from their actions and preventing it, between compulsion and choice, and between more freedom and less, my answer is clear:

I choose freedom.

Globalization and World Poverty

Inequality is a worldwide concern. Too many people do live in squalid poverty. Some folks believe there is only so much global wealth and income to go around and, hence, the rich enjoy their affluence at the expense of the poor. This is, once more, considered "injustice," tantamount to the rich robbing the poor.

But, like the free market, the world economy is not a zero-sum game wherein one person's (or nation's) gain is another's loss and everyone is scrambling for the largest piece of a pie of limited size. To the contrary, the pie's size depends entirely on what people *produce*. Americans consume ten trillion dollars' worth of goods and services annually not by grabbing them from the hands of the world's poor, but rather, because America *produces* goods and services that people are willing to pay ten trillion dollars for.[147] Africans are much poorer because they produce much less. If they produced as much as Americans, they would be as rich as Americans. And America does not need to become any less rich in order for Africa to become less poor.[148]

So the wealth of the rich is not part of the problem. In fact, it is

---

147. Well, almost. In fact, we're spending more than we produce and borrowing the difference.

148. This was well stated in a leader (editorial) in *The Economist*, March 13, 2004.

part of the solution, because the rich nations have the means to buy and consume what the poor nations produce, enabling the latter to rise out of poverty. Impoverishing the rich nations would not help the poor ones—it would make them even poorer.

Population control is not the answer either. Yes, a family with two children might be less poor than if it had ten. But in the big picture, the problem is not insufficient resources, not that there isn't enough food to go around. It's that some people can't earn the money they need to buy it. Look again at Hong Kong, with scant resources and lots of people—whose productive energies nevertheless made them rich. Africa, even if it had half its current population, would still be poor if that half was not more productive. Giving people opportunities to be productive is the key to fighting poverty.

Some critics try to make "globalization" and even "free trade" dirty words, as though they are tools for the rich to exploit the poor and keep them down. The opposite is true. "Globalization" means the integration of the world economy, dissolving the importance of national boundaries and distances, and unfettered movement of investment, production, and goods. It means people and businesses communicating, exchanging information, and collaborating to mutual benefit. Most important, it means free markets, opening up economies, and removing barriers to trade. And while some see globalization as empowering corporate interests, in truth, it empowers individuals far more, greatly widening human opportunities.

Of course, as with any change, there are winners and losers. But those nations embracing globalization and openness have been the ones climbing out of poverty. South Korea was one. Half a century ago, its per capita income was on a par with Zambia's—today it is *thirty-two times* that of Zambia. China did likewise starting in 1978, and India in the early nineties, and both have seen phenomenal economic growth, poverty reduction, and huge numbers of people now able to enjoy better, healthier lives.[149] In contrast, those poor nations

---

149. Yet some critics actually dispute the desirability of such growth, fretting about "externalities" like environmental impacts. Well, it's true that

that have failed to move toward globalization, free trade, and free-market economics have remained stuck in poverty.

This is because, far from thriving on economic "injustice," as seen by the critics, and perpetuating global inequality and poverty, market economics and trade are powerful engines *combating* poverty, *by making the pie bigger.* In fact, even if you believe globalization increases inequality (which is debatable), on balance it is still good for the poor, because that rising inequality reflects the poor not gaining as fast as the nonpoor—but nevertheless gaining—and most of them gaining more than they would without globalization. Furthermore, globalization is also a force for peace, which is another factor in fighting poverty, because war sucks up resources and disrupts economic activity. Nations making money trading with each other are less likely to go to war and throw that benefit away.

Archaeological evidence confirms that trade in goods, among tribes, goes back to the very beginnings of humanity, for these very reasons. It was profitable, it made tribes better off, and it promoted peace among them. And even globalization is not as recent as many think; worldwide economic integration had actually progressed quite far before the process was temporarily interrupted by the two world wars.

In the global market economy, trade benefits *all* participants. This is another crucial point that is widely misunderstood. The economist David Ricardo called it the law of "comparative advantage." It decrees that a nation always benefits by exporting what it is best (most efficient) at producing in trade for things it isn't as good at making. If what Slobovia makes best is widgets, it doesn't even have to be the world's best widget maker. It need only make widgets better than it makes other things. That comparative advantage in widgets means it will benefit by

---

growth is not cost free. But Benjamin Friedman, in *The Moral Consequences of Economic Growth*, shows how rising living standards contribute to healthy social dynamics whereas a stagnant or shrinking economy generates a culture of resentments and societal conflict. Thus, economic growth also entails important (though unappreciated) positive externalities—beyond the bare fact of people living better.

trading them for goods in which other countries have their own comparative advantages. Everyone benefits. Everyone gets richer.

The explanation made before bears reemphasis. When anyone buys anything, it is because he values the item more than the money. But the seller values the money more than the item. The transaction improves welfare for both. That is why trade happens. And it's just as true for nations as for individuals. It is how nations improve the conditions of life for their inhabitants.

The notion of self-sufficiency ("autarky") can seem attractive—a nation striving to meet all its own needs without dependence on outsiders. Notably, Mahatma Gandhi preached this for India. The problem is that this cuts you off from the wealth effect of trade and comparative advantage. There is nothing gained (and much lost) in trying to make for yourself things you can't make well when you can get them from others who can, through trade. You could build your own computer but you're better off trading your money to Dell for one. The same applies in world trade. India did not begin to rise from poverty until it gave up the mistaken dream of self-sufficiency and instead embraced trade. The world's premier devotee of autarky is North Korea—with literal starvation the result.

The major obstacles to free trade are tariffs and subsidies. A tariff is a tax on goods imported from foreign countries. Adding that tax to the cost of production (and transport) makes importation less competitive pricewise against locally produced goods. And that's the whole idea; not to get revenue from payment of the tariffs, but to hobble foreigners in competing against domestic businesses. A subsidy is a government handout to a producer, by grace of which he can sell his goods at a lower price and still profit (because the subsidy makes up the difference). That, too, helps firms compete.

Suppose an American factory makes widgets costing $9 to produce and priced at $10 apiece, while Slobovia, with its comparative advantage, can sell them for $8. If Slobovian widgets are imported, the US firm cannot successfully compete, and may go bust, with its workers losing their jobs. But if the US government slaps a 50 percent tariff on Slobovian widgets, that will force them to be priced at an uncompetitive $12, which means Slobovian widgets will actually not be imported at all, and the American firm can go on its merry way selling its $10 widgets.

This is called protectionism, and it does protect the US firm and its jobs, so it has much political appeal. Yet what is the consequence for the US economy as a whole? Widgets will cost us more than if we got them from Slobovia. Consumers overpaying for widgets are subsidizing the profits of the US widget maker and the paychecks of its workers. But if Slobovia can sell us widgets cheaper than we can make them ourselves, isn't it in our national interest to stop making them and buy theirs instead? By failing to take advantage of the Slobovian widget bargain, we make ourselves poorer (and make Slobovia poorer too, of course). Our economy would be better off if the investment tied up in the widget firm were shifted to some other business (where the United States does enjoy a comparative advantage) and its employees, likewise, worked in some other industry.

Critics also make a big issue over "unfair trade." Yet, in our example, we still benefit from importing Slobovian widgets even if Slobovia's competition is somehow "unfair." Maybe its widgets are cheaper because its workers are paid less than their US counterparts. Or maybe Slobovia is engaging in protectionism itself and subsidizing its widget industry, enabling it to undercut American prices by dint of government handouts to make up the difference. This is indeed "unfair trade." And we even have laws against other countries trying to sell us goods below production cost; it's called "dumping."

But all forms of protectionism are ultimately self-inflicted wounds. If Slobovia is willing to hurt its own true economic interests by "unfairly dumping" widgets below cost, we are better off if we let them than if we subvert our own true economic interests by trying to stop them. Adam Smith, too, said what common sense tells us: if another nation will sell us something cheaper than we can make it ourselves, we should buy it from them and put our own industries to work making things where we enjoy a similar comparative advantage. Indeed, it was to highlight this key point that he titled his 1776 book *The Wealth of Nations*; this is how a nation gains in wealth.

Two centuries later, we still haven't learned the lesson. While many blame persistent poverty on capitalism, the true cause is actually insufficient capitalism. Latin America is a prime example. Its economies have perennially been mired in heavy-handed protectionism and state intervention, still refusing to heed Adam Smith's prescription. Latin American poverty is not the product of free-market economics because Latin America has never really tried free-market economics.

Protectionism is yet another example where narrow special interests can get their way against the interests of the nation as a whole. We have already seen how big agribusiness parlays a few million dollars of political contributions into billions of dollars of subsidies. Similarly, a business threatened by competition from foreign imports will lobby Congress and hand its members money to get a tariff enacted and will even win broad public support to "protect American jobs." The harm to consumers, to the broader US economy, and to the world economy, is overlooked.

So President George W. Bush imposed tariffs on steel imports to protect the US steel industry and its workers from competition from cheaper foreign steel. But what about all the US industries that *use* steel? Because of the tariffs, they now had to pay more for steel, which made *their* products (such as cars) more expensive to produce, higher in price, and, hence, less competitive against foreign rivals. In fact, the steel tariffs may have destroyed more jobs in the auto industry than were "saved" in the steel industry, and certainly consumers' wallets took a hit. We might actually have been better off simply paying the steel workers to stay home, rather than imposing tariffs to keep out cheaper foreign steel. (Bush eventually saw the light and canceled the tariffs.)

So more is always better when it comes to world trade. It is always beneficial to reduce obstacles to trade. Remember the controversy over NAFTA (the 1993 North American Free Trade Agreement), cutting tariffs, and fears of a "giant sucking sound" of US jobs moving south? Didn't happen. A Carnegie Endowment study found that NAFTA caused no net US job loss, and may even have done the opposite. But what NAFTA unquestionably did do was to boost economic investment and growth in the region, and to make a greater variety of goods available at lower prices for consumers, all of which meant improving incomes and living standards.

Did some individuals lose their jobs because of NAFTA? Yes. Change is always happening (again, "creative destruction"), and change always means some winners and some losers. Social and economic policy should aim for more winners than losers, and that's what free trade does. And, of course, we don't just write off the losers as human sacrifices for the greater good. We must for policies that will give them new opportunities. The goal should be to carry as many of us as we possibly can across the Jordan into the promised land.

Much rhetoric is also spouted about low wage rates in developing nations, which are viewed as both economic injustice and unfair trade competition, with overseas workers stealing American jobs. International wage disparities are frequently exaggerated for political effect through dubious statistical methods.[150] But anyhow, worldwide wage differences tend largely to reflect productivity disparities. If an American factory worker earns five times the pay of his Slobovian counterpart, that is mostly because his labor is more productive, resulting in far more output than does the Slobovian's work. The Slobovian earns less because he produces less and, hence, his labor is worth less. But, over time, such wage differentials are bound to narrow in a globalized economy because a lot of the productivity difference is related to technology (i.e., the American works with better equipment, computers, and so forth), and entrepreneurs will see an

---

150. Comparisons are often based on official currency exchange rates. Wages in China, expressed in US dollars, may seem a pittance—but a dollar actually buys much more in China than in America. Thus, Chinese workers are not really paid as little as bare numbers can make it seem, nor is China so poor; such statistics exaggerate global economic inequality too.

economic opportunity to profit by making investments aimed at boosting the productivity of Slobovian workers.[151]

Meantime, most of the angst over the supposed injustice of "sweatshop" foreign wages is misplaced. Even if the pay and work conditions of Slobovians hired by some multinational corporation are well below Western standards, they usually surpass the norm among local Slobovian firms because the multinational wants to attract the best workers and can afford them. What an American would view as "sweatshop" labor, a Slobovian might well regard as a ticket to a better life—thanks to global trade, which, as we see again, benefits more people than it hurts. To censure and discourage corporations that employ such labor condemns the affected workers to even worse jobs and can only serve to keep poor countries poor.

Likewise, while some Americans feel guilt when they buy things made in lower-wage countries, as though they are contributing to exploitation, the opposite is true. Buying such goods, helping to create a market for them, gives people in the manufacturing countries more and better economic opportunities. Your buying a shirt made in China doesn't hurt Chinese workers, it helps them.

It is also mistaken to see foreign workers as somehow stealing American jobs. Critics of free trade and overseas outsourcing make the same mistake as Luddites who fret that technological advances destroy jobs. They see only the downside but not the job-creating benefits. Again, we gain by buying Slobovian widgets if Slobovia can make them cheaper than we can—or by importing clothing, toys, or electronics manufactured more cheaply in China. If, in consequence, a US factory closes, those job losses are very visible. But meantime, US consumers get the benefit of lower prices not just on Chinese imports but also on all the goods from other countries and companies

---

151. Actually, the world of manufacturing is becoming one without borders. Many Japanese cars are now built mostly in America, and even the Airbus, the flagship European rival to America's Boeing, is half built in the United States.

whose prices are forced down by Chinese competition. The total effect is huge. This raises Americans' standard of living, giving them more money to spend on different goods and services, which, in turn, spurs creation of new jobs to supply that increased demand. Those added jobs are less obviously visible, but they, too, are a consequence of globalization, trade, and outsourcing. And, likewise, America gains from getting software or call center services from India if Indians can do that work cheaper (and/or better). Such outsourcing by US firms enhances their productivity, profitability, and competitiveness, better enabling them to prosper, expand, innovate, develop new and better products and services, and tap into new markets. And furthermore, free trade, by forcing firms to compete against foreign rivals, also inhibits monopolistic practices. All of this is good for the US economy, for US consumers, and for US paychecks.

Just as America is not rich at the expense of the poor nations, they are not getting richer at America's expense either. To think otherwise is, again, the error of viewing the world economy as a zero-sum game of competition for slices of a static pie. When American firms turn to poor nations for labor, this enlarges the pie. And as foreigners thusly rise out of poverty, they are able to buy more goods from the United States. Thus, freer trade means more exports as well as imports; we obsess about import-related job losses while overlooking the export-related job gains. America would not benefit by keeping other countries poor; it is good for America if the rest of the world becomes as rich as we are.[152]

For decades now, we've been hearing how foreign competition— at one time from Germany, then Japan, more lately China—will ravage America's economy. Similarly, we've been hearing for *cen-*

---

152. Those who bemoan outsourcing and back protectionism see no contradiction when they also urge buying pharmaceuticals from Canada if they are cheaper—no worries about US pharmaceutical jobs. And, while decrying low third world wages, they also complain about good American jobs going overseas. But doesn't a Bangladeshi have as much right to a good job as an American?

turies how automation will destroy jobs. Yet the economy never seems to heed all this; it just continues to grow and create jobs. More Americans are employed today, and in good jobs, than ever before.

So let's stop talk about "Benedict Arnold" companies outsourcing jobs. Benedict Arnold sold out to an enemy. Overseas workers are not our enemies. Instead, they are America's partners in making a better world for everyone.

Anyhow, low foreign wages are very much the wrong thing to worry about. In fact, as author Thomas Friedman argues, the real threat to America's economy is not a "race to the bottom," where other countries beat us out with low labor costs, but rather a race to the top, as others swiftly get up to speed in education and technological advancement. No longer are we importing just low-end labor-intensive products from China; the Chinese are moving briskly into high-tech markets. In too many ways, America is failing to maintain its competitive edge in technology and innovation (its true comparative advantage). The world is changing ever more rapidly. We are not endangered by peons working in overseas sweatshops, but by the inability of our own schools to equip graduates to compete with today's worldwide best and brightest. They will make a richer world—but America may not share fully in that growth if we don't smarten up and keep up.

We started this chapter talking about inequality and poverty and have seen how globalization, trade, and free-market economics are the right medicine. But they are not panaceas and cannot by themselves cure poverty. Unfortunately, it's not that simple, and economic health requires some additional factors.

One is the rule of law. This we take for granted in America. It means that people can know what the laws and penalties are, that laws are enforced on a reasonably consistent and fair basis, and that the court system is available as a forum for settling private disputes, such as contract disagreements, again, on a reasonably fair basis.

Many countries have none of this. Laws are opaque, haphazard, and applied arbitrarily, often unfairly, and often corruptly, with bribery a big factor; and their courts cannot be relied upon to provide any reasonable hope of recourse in a dispute (again, often due to corruption). Such conditions are, obviously, major impediments to trade, business, and investment. For example, in today's Russia, entire businesses have been stolen by fraudulent and strong-arm tactics, with the original owners unable to get any help from the courts or legal system. This sort of thing is devastating to the functioning of the country's economy.

Some might imagine that the legal system is a tool for the rich to oppress the poor. But, actually, it is the poor and powerless who suffer most when the rule of law is weak, when they are milked for bribes, when they have no recourse for abuses, and when they can be exploited with impunity. And, of course, rule of law helps the poor by providing the foundation for a growing economy that attracts investment; poverty is perpetuated by its lack.

Private property rights are also taken for granted in America—though some leftists still regurgitate Pierre-Joseph Proudhon's old absurdity that "property is theft" (from the propertyless). Yet ironically, it is their own preferred remedies that entail true theft, theoretically for the benefit of the greater population. In reality, such confiscations never benefit anyone but the ruling elites who perpetrate them. (Look at Robert Mugabe's Zimbabwe.) They are, indeed, excellent means for impoverishing entire populations (like Zimbabwe's) because, if no one's property is reasonably secure, you won't be inclined to make investments in private property such as a business, which provides employment and economic opportunity. Thus, like the rule of law, secure property rights are essential for a properly functioning economy.[153]

And poverty in the developing world is not somehow caused by the institution of private property. The truth is exactly the opposite. Poverty in many backward nations is perpetuated not by institutions of private property, but by their lack. In such countries, where legal sys-

---

153. A government official in Hugo Chavez's Venezuela, engaged in confiscation of farms, was quoted as saying that legal niceties should not stand in the way of social justice. He forgot that without the rule of law and property rights, no justice worthy of the name is possible.

tems are a shambles, few people have secure, documentable, and legally enforceable titles to their homes or the lands they farm. This makes it impossible to use such property as collateral for loans and deters investment in them—once more keeping people poor.

Red tape is also a big factor. This, of course, refers to bureaucratic procedures, rules and regulations, fees, forms to fill out, and so on. Most people think of it, with a weary smile, as a mere annoyance. But many of the world's poorest economies are the most entangled in red tape, and that partly explains their poverty. Business activity in such countries is suffocated by red tape. In 2004, it took 203 days to register a new company in Haiti—versus two days in Australia. To record a property sale in Nigeria, it took twenty-one procedures and 274 days, with official fees eating up 27 percent of the property's value; in Norway, one day, costing 2.5 percent.[154] It's no surprise that few legitimate businesses are started in Haiti, few people are keen to buy property in Nigeria, and few decent jobs are to be had in either place.

In such countries, admittedly, much gets done outside the law. But that is no way to run an economy. Illegal businesses don't pay taxes, must keep a low profile, and can't raise credit, so they can't grow. Meantime, some red tape can't be avoided except through bribery, so countries with lots of nuisance regulations tend to develop a culture of corruption.

Ideally, government regulations are promulgated for good reasons. But we have seen how, even in advanced countries, this often backfires, and it's even worse in poorer ones, where any nexus between governmental regulations and the public good can be hard to find. Often regulations are really aimed at coddling some entrenched interest. An existing business benefits if red tape makes it hard for a competitor to get started. And some countries seem to create red tape not in spite of, but to promote, corruption—they pay their police and bureaucrats too little for them to get by without bribes. Government's legions love to have a lot of regulations they can be bribed to ignore.

Physical infrastructure is another factor. Trade in goods is ham-

---

154. *The Economist*, September 11, 2004.

pered if there are no roads, railroads, or ports, and a communications network is also vital for disseminating the information that markets need to function effectively. One of the best investments a poor society can make today is in cell phones.

Education is also important. Often, poor countries can't afford to spend much on it and poor families can't afford to let children go to school instead of working. Then there's healthcare, clean water, and sanitation—chronic sickness and early death diminish what a person can contribute to economic betterment.

All the foregoing factors reflect quality of governance. While government *can* be a force for good, many countries are poor because the opposite holds true. Look again at Zimbabwe. The Mugabe regime, operating as a criminal enterprise and doing ill in almost every possible way, managed to bring living standards down by half or more in the quarter century following independence.

The problems of poverty are formidable and complex; again, there is no panacea, no simple solution, no shortcut. Many African nations, in particular, seem caught in a poverty trap, beset with so many disadvantages, and too poor even to get a foot on the ladder's first rung. Fixing this requires outside help to create the conditions for these poorest nations to attract investment and get their economies off the ground.

The rich countries have, of course, given a lot of aid. But it has tended to be insufficient and often misdirected and wasted. Much has gone into misconceived grandiose schemes instead of down-to-earth initiatives that tackle the mundane problems stymieing ordinary people, like water, sanitation, healthcare, and education. Much aid has been swallowed up by corruption—not just the Mobutus funneling money into Swiss accounts, but poor individuals, themselves, will often seek ways to pervert donor intentions for personal benefit. Aid can engender the pathologies of dependency, giving recipient countries disincentives for their own economic development. And the law of unintended consequences always lurks. Local farmers can't survive in competition with free food handouts; similarly, much used clothing has been donated to Africa, which is well intentioned, but this has undermined Africa's own textile industries.

Rich nations do finally seem to be growing smarter about how they deploy aid, as well as more open handed, so there are grounds for hope. But the bigger fact is that the true path for nations to improve their condition is through earning money, not receiving it. The rich nations would help the poor ones more by opening up their markets and embracing free trade than by handing out charity; it wouldn't even cost the rich nations anything. It would actually make them richer.

And, while freedom is, again, not a cure-all, it is the best antipoverty program. History teaches that all measures for combating poverty that curtail freedom (e.g., socialism) do not work and only make things worse. Trying to cure poverty through different schemes to carve up the economic pie can only serve to make it smaller; the only sure way to fight poverty is to make it bigger. And freedom—giving people the maximum impetus to improve their lot and the greatest scope for doing so—is humanity's great pie enlarger.

A study by the Fraser Institute, a Canadian think tank, measured countries' economic freedom, as defined by low tax rates (i.e., allowing people to keep most of what they earn), protection of private property rights, freedom of contract, free trade, and monetary stability (due to restrained government spending). The study found that the freest nations attracted forty times the economic investment of the least free, investment was used 70 percent more productively, and between 1980 and 2000, nations at the higher end of the freedom scale had a 3.4 percent annual GDP growth as against only 0.4 percent for those at the lower end.[155]

It is no coincidence that the freest nations are the richest. To relieve poverty, give people not money, but freedom.

---

155. GDP, of course, directly correlates with standard of living. Annual growth of 3.4 percent may not sound like much; but, at that rate, national wealth would *double* within just twenty-one years.

Why Corporations Are Not Totally Evil Scum

We demonize corporations—big bad corporations—caring only for profits, doing evil deeds, manipulating consumers, controlling the world economy, and so on. This is the dark picture painted by popular culture—the "Erin Brockovich" scenario in which the sinister mercenary corporation is the villain that has to be stopped from laying waste to everything good and wholesome.[156] Nazis used to be the movie and TV bad guys everyone loved to hate. Today it's businessmen.

Now, I have never worked for a corporation myself, and I frankly have a sour view toward big impersonal organizations of any type. Corporations, being collections of people, are subject to all the failings and foibles that individual people have. In such large organizations (certainly in government, too) there is a tendency to function by bureaucratic habit, to take the path of least resistance, to get ensnarled in procedures, and, generally, to lose sight of what the real mission

---

156. In the movie, Erin was fighting a power company whose use of chemicals was allegedly making people sick. The company settled the lawsuits to cut its losses, but there was never any valid evidence that its chemicals were harming anyone.

is.[157] And corporations, like all things human, are indeed capable of evil. But there's another side to the picture.

What, actually, is a "corporation," and why do we have them? The corporation evolved to enable a group of people to organize a business too big for anyone to handle alone. The owners ("shareholders") get shares in the business proportional to how much they invest. Shares can be bought and sold (on the stock market). Shareholders generally hire other people to actually run the business for them, including the boss, the "chief executive officer" (CEO). But the key feature is *limited liability*. This means that shareholders cannot be held personally responsible for anything the corporation does. If you are the direct owner of a business that harms someone or owes money, you can be sued. Of course, a corporation that does injury or owes a debt can be sued too—but not its shareholders.

If it meant being exposed to losing not just the money invested, but far more, who would take the risk of investing in the shares of a large business? No one. Exxon Mobil's Alaskan oil spill meant billions of dollars in fines and lawsuits. If its shareholders could be made to pay personally for things like that, no one would be crazy enough to buy shares in Exxon Mobil, or any other company. The stock market could not exist; nor could any large firms, because no investors would be willing to put up the money to build their factories, hire their workers, and so forth.

So the invention of the corporation was a great blessing. It made possible the large business enterprises that are essential to modern life. You can romanticize about the precorporate world of the Middle Ages when all business was conducted by individuals personally. That worked fine for producing things that a single craftsman could make.

---

157. The German sociologist Max Weber pioneered the examination of bureaucracy as the modern form of institutional organization. He saw it as turning people into parts of a machine, divorcing them from traditional moral precepts. However, Weber was not particularly fearful about corporate bureaucracies; he considered government bureaucracy far more powerful and, hence, far more dangerous.

It would not have worked for producing things like cars or refrigerators. We don't have to love corporations, but we should give a thought to where we'd be without them.

All the products that make modern life what it is, all the comforts and conveniences, all the well-made things that are so useful or pleasurable, yet so taken for granted, come to us by grace of the free-market capitalist system and corporations. Sometimes I look at the most commonplace manufactured product and reflect that not so long ago it would have been looked upon as a marvel, with wide eyes and gasps of wonderment, and would have fetched a fabulous price. Even so lowly a thing as a glass jar—perfectly made and perfectly transparent—would have been highly prized. But we today have so much, we throw glass jars away.[158]

Products do not fall into stores like manna from heaven. We get them because corporations make them, and because people invest capital in corporations, giving them the means to make such things. And, moreover, they are made because people can afford to buy them—which, in turn, is also a result of the capitalist free-market system. We have already seen how that system is all about John selling to Joe and Joe selling to John, making both richer. Multiplied billions of times over, this has produced the expansion of affluence that enables people to buy all the goods and services that make their lives better. It is a virtuous circle in which the corporation plays a key role.

It is true that corporations have to earn profits to stay in business, make all these products, and provide livelihoods for all whom they employ (which, of course, is most of our population). Still, even if we recognize this, many of us view the idea of private profit with distaste and consider it a necessary evil. This is wrong. "Profit" is not a dirty word. In fact, it is a positive social good.

The word "profit" often gets sullied by association with the negative word "greed," but the two are not the same. Greed is indeed ugly, a heedless self-indulgence, and really far removed from a rational

---

158. In ancient times, there was really no such thing as garbage. Everything was reused somehow. People couldn't afford to do otherwise.

desire to improve one's lot through enterprise that produces deserved profit. Greed is fed at the expense of others; profit is earned through others' betterment.

And the desire, the necessity, of people to earn money is, again, what drives our economy. Without that, who would build a factory or run a business to produce the things you want and need? If we were all selfless altruists instead of seekers of personal advantage, the whole economy would come to a dead screeching halt, plunging us into poverty. As Adam Smith wrote, "It is not from the benevolence of the butcher, the brewer, or the baker, that we expect our dinner, but from their regard to their own interest." And once more, his great insight was that the beauty of the free market is how it harnesses all that self-serving activity for the good of everyone.

Let's look more closely at what private profit actually represents. The price you willingly pay for a product or service reflects what it's worth to you. You wouldn't buy it otherwise. Producing it costs society something. If what you pay exceeds that cost, society gains and the company earns a profit. When a business uses $6 worth of fabric and $10 worth of labor to make a shirt it sells for $20, society comes out $4 richer.

Profit is thus a measure of value created for society. The bigger the profit, the bigger the societal gain.[159] Hence, we should all wish to see a world with more profits being earned, not less.

True, there may be production costs, such as pollution, which a company may escape paying for. That's, again, something appropriate for government to address. But, in the big picture, we mustn't see corporations as somehow profiting at society's expense. The opposite is true. Today's quality of life came about in large part through corporations making things like that shirt, turning $16 worth of inputs into $20 worth of goods, again and again and again. Corporations have profited—and so have we all.

Meantime, while profit is a key driver of corporate behavior, sev-

---

159. Clive Crook lucidly discussed the above ideas in the January 22, 2005, issue of *The Economist*.

eral further points must be noted. In the first place, it is not true that corporations serve only shareholder interests. The real scandal is that shareholders get short shrift because, although, in theory, they own it, they do not actually control a corporation. Instead, it is controlled by its managers, headed by the CEO. And while, theoretically, managers are the hirelings of the owners, in reality, shareholders have no say, with managers actually being a self-perpetuating elite, running the corporation mainly to serve their own purposes.[160]

The bigger point, though, is that profit isn't everything. A corporation, again, consists of people, and people are not purely economic beings. Does a person go to work in the morning thinking, "how much profit can I generate today for the company?" Or does he more likely see himself as helping to provide a good product or service? Obviously the latter is a big motivating factor. We don't regard ourselves as simply moneymaking machines. Ask someone what he does and he will say, "I repair cars" or "I sell shoes" or "I'm in medical research." Most of us feel good about ourselves and our jobs not just because we bring home a paycheck or enhance corporate profits but because we do something worthwhile that makes the world better. That human reality refutes the view of corporations as soulless machines caring only about profits.[161]

This applies even to those at the top who run corporations. They

---

160. This is a common feature behind corporate scandals of the Enron and Tyco sort. But a more widespread problem is CEO pay. Again, the CEO is supposed to work for shareholders and his pay should be negotiated with the board of directors whom they theoretically elect. But, in practice, the CEO can pack the board with his cronies, often fellow CEOs, who support each other in grabbing as much pay as they can. The pay of Richard Grasso, CEO of the New York Stock Exchange, gobbled up virtually the firm's entire profit.

161. For years my job was fighting utility rate hikes. Yes, the utility people wanted higher profits. But why and to what end? I grew to understand that it wasn't because of greed. They sincerely saw healthy profits as enabling them to better serve the public. (And I grew doubtful that the public was truly served by government regulation of utilities.)

don't want to be seen—or see themselves—as bad guys. They, too, want to feel they are serving some larger mission, contributing to society through good products (and providing incomes to employees and returns to shareholders). And many big companies genuinely strive to be good citizens as well. Indeed, "corporate social responsibility" has become not just a catchphrase but a virtual industry in itself, with major firms actually buying into the agendas of their fiercest critics when it comes to environmental sensitivity, sustainable development, protecting third world employee rights, workforce diversity, and all that seemingly wholesome stuff, not to mention cash charitable giving.[162]

Further, it isn't just the incentive to profit via good products that aligns corporate interests with those of the public. Jared Diamond, in *Collapse*, details the extraordinary environmental carefulness of a Chevron oil facility in Papua New Guinea (contrasted against the irresponsible practices of one nearby, run by government). What accounts for Chevron's virtue? It reckons that this is actually better for profits in the long run than to cut corners and risk the huge costs of an environmental disaster like an oil spill or the Bhopal tragedy. Responsible corporate behavior also benefits the bottom line through enhanced employee morale and public acceptance, helping Chevron win new contracts. Good citizenship turns out to be good business.

Undeniably though, corporations do sometimes behave egregiously. While the people who comprise them often have the good motivations mentioned, they can also be corrupt, self-serving, and heedless of harm to others in their pursuit of self-interest. This is, of

---

162. *The Economist* (January 22, 2005) argues *against* all this corporate do-gooding. It rejects the premise that unvarnished capitalism is a bad thing. *The Economist* holds that social and economic policy are best left to governments accountable to voters, while business most truly serves the public by building shareholder value through providing products and services people want to buy; and further, since corporate managers are custodians for shareholders, any activities inconsistent with shareholder interests can be seen as unethical violations of their foremost duty.

course, true of all human activity. And just as we need laws to deter individuals from crime, some government regulation of corporate behavior is appropriate too. But the free market also has a self-regulating aspect and punishes those who do not offer genuine value for money; businessmen who succeed in the long run are those who satisfy customers. Bill Gates did not become the world's richest man by scamming. He did it by supplying products that benefit millions.

A recent ad placed by a public organization said that certain careers—it mentioned nurses, teachers, doctors, curators, and so on—"inherently add value to our culture" and "contribute to society." Business was not included. And few of us think of business careers in that way, as contributing to society like nurses or teachers do. This is wrong. We benefit from what teachers do, but we also benefit from what people in the business world do. In fact, we all benefit beyond calculating. Every hour of the day we use products and services made available by business. And without the enormous societal wealth generated by business and commerce, we could not afford the teachers and curators and others lauded in that ad. Business does not merely contribute to society—it makes everything else possible.

We often tend to think of "consumer products" derisively, as fripperies, gizmos, and tchotchkes that we could just as well do without, or might even be better off without. And people do buy a lot of stuff they could live without. But we make our own choices; I might not emulate or approve of someone else's choices, yet everyone is entitled to seek happiness in his own way. The cornucopia of products showered upon us by the corporate world makes that possible.[163] And many of those products are no mere fripperies. Before the advent of modern conveniences and laborsaving devices, daily life was exhausting. That's part of why life spans were shorter. And while everyone hates

---

163. I laugh at people spending two dollars for a plastic bottle of plain water. But obviously, they feel they are getting two dollars of value; and the worth of anything is, again, measured by what people are willing to pay for it. Thus, the company using a few cents' worth of plastic and water to make something for which people willingly pay two dollars is creating value for society.

the pharmaceutical industry, look at what it gives us—products that make us healthier, better able to enjoy our lives, and that literally save our lives. That's just one example.

Many of the great visionaries who built our civilization were capitalist businessmen. Had you proposed to me in 1810 a transport system requiring hundreds of miles of steel rails, I would have replied, "That's nuts." Or how about a communication system needing thousands of poles spanning the entire countryside? This I'd have deemed even crazier. Yet some bold men had the supreme breadth of vision to actually undertake such schemes; surmounting tremendous obstacles, they laid their rails from sea to sea and laid their cables even across the seas (and after the first one failed, tried again). They did it to make money—some succeeded, others lost their shirts—but more important, they made life better for all humanity.

So let's give at least two cheers for people who work in commerce and industry. And maybe even three for entrepreneurs—visionary people who put their money and careers at risk to start businesses, to give us things we want or need, providing employment and making all our lives richer and better. They are really heroes of society, yet they get little respect—more typically being labeled "greedy capitalist bloodsuckers."

Many of us think corporations control and manipulate consumers, ensorceling us with advertising to desire things we wouldn't otherwise covet, to make us buy things we don't need. It has even been argued, for example, that America's obesity epidemic results from a corporate conspiracy to ensnare people to eat unhealthy foods in order to bloat profits. But couldn't corporations earn just as much profit promoting healthy foods? In fact, since many consumers seem willing to pay extra for food they think is healthful, such products could actually offer the greater profit potential. Why, then, is so much fattening food produced, marketed, and sold? *Because that's what most people want.* They buy such foods not because of some manipulative corporate plot but because that's what they enjoy eating. Consumers vote, with their spending dollars, for the products they want. Health-conscious eaters are outvoted. It is the consumer, not the corporation, that rules the marketplace.

If you doubt this, just look at the commercial landscape littered with the corpses of products that corporations tried but failed to market. Ford's Edsel car was the 1950s paradigm for this; in a later generation, it was New Coke. These products, and countless others, were quickly abandoned when it became evident that the public wasn't buying. In truth, corporations spend millions on marketing research not to figure out how to manipulate consumers into buying unwanted products, but instead, how to make their products more appealing to consumers—finding out what consumers really need and want, and trying to satisfy those needs and wants.

The consumer, not the corporation, is king.

In fact, this trend has accelerated dramatically. Consumers are savvy enough to disregard and discount advertising, and the Internet now arms them with an enhanced advantage of access to information. Researching price comparisons and product quality before buying has become commonplace. Car dealers find that most buyers come to the showroom already knowing exactly what they want—and exactly what they ought to pay. Thus does modern technology serve to further empower consumers, intensifying the pressure on corporations to offer good products at good prices, or else fail.

Nevertheless, some on the Left still imagine that corporations today are more powerful than governments, and that it is really corporations, not governments, that rule the world. If businessmen really controlled everything, one might expect they could get Hollywood to stop portraying them like Nazis. In truth, corporations are not only at the mercy of consumer preferences and whims, but we've already seen how competition puts them in a virtual straitjacket. Because of it, a corporation doesn't even have power to set its own prices. Instead, prices are effectively dictated by the market. It is up to the corporation to try to supply goods or services at the market's prices. If it cannot do this, and still make a profit, it will not survive.

In contrast, governments are not subject to the checking force of competition. And while corporations live or die by persuading people to buy their products, unable to force anyone to do anything, the state *does* have force at its disposal, and people have no choice about obeying. Indeed, governments can make laws that *corporations* must obey.

It is true, as we've seen, that corporations have a lot of influence upon what government does; of course they're heavyweight players in the political money game. But in this arena, too, there are important constraints upon the power of corporations. They're not the only players and often go up against other powerful interests, such as the AARP or the trial lawyers. And the corporate world's political clout is undercut by its totally negative public image. Politicians would far rather posture as crusaders against corporations than be seen as their tools. This can make corporations fat targets for political grandstanding.

In the last analysis, the greater power remains that of the state. Indeed, government has grown bigger and more powerful than ever. Any notion that it's somehow trumped by corporate power in today's world is simply absurd. Look at the collapse of AT&T, surely one of the most powerful corporations of all time. Its fate was sealed by government action, together with its failure to adapt swiftly enough to a changing world.[164]

And, if corporate malfeasance is a problem, government malfeasance is a hugely greater one. Government rips us off, by wasting our money, far more than does the business world. Corporate executives who don't deliver are fired every day; government bureaucrats, never. A bad corporate product will soon fail in the marketplace, but a bad law or regulation, or bad government program, that does more harm than good, may endure forever, if (as always) some interest group benefits from it.

No corporation could ever damage public welfare as much as does the federal agriculture program. Not corporate power, but government, is the Godzilla we must battle.

---

164. AT&T's remains were bought by SBC, which resurrected the brand name.

Territoriality and Tribalism

When a cat rubs up against things, he is actually marking them with his scent, his way of declaring, "This is my territory." People, too, care greatly about territory, defending against incursions, and wanting more of it. There is also a powerful "us against them" tribal psychology. All this has been a fount of untold grief in the world, contrary to the "live and let live" philosophy emphasized in this book.

The basic human tendencies to tribalism and territorial consciousness have resulted in our being organized into nation-states. That is actually a big step up from being organized into bands and tribes. Some would have us take the next step and establish a world government.

Europe actually has tried to move in that direction, its political elites pushing "ever closer union," to eventually govern the whole continent from Brussels. But we should distrust governmental bigness. Bigger government means government more distant from the governed and, hence, less accountable, and also means aggravation of all the previously discussed pathologies of statism. The European Union regime is mired in contentious economic subsidies, overbearing bureaucracy, and institutions of incomprehensible Byzantine complexity; it tries to force uniformity upon a continent of divergent societies, is disconnected from popular control, and has a genuine legitimacy deficit. A world government would be even more problematic.

The nation-state's government, at least, is less remote from its citizens than a world regime would be. And, because people and cultures are so diverse, we should want some variety in governance. Even while freedom and democracy are universal principles, that certainly doesn't mean Algerians should be governed in exactly the same way as Americans. Many even complain that, in the United States, our main political choice is between two presidential candidates who are usually more alike than different. Such political homogenization could hardly suit a worldwide electorate.

Of course, world government is not currently looming. What we do contend with, though, is what David Brooks has called "a squishier but equally pervasive concept: the 'dream of global governance.'" The idea is to subordinate nation-states to international and multilateral institutions that are deemed to embody greater legitimacy and right. And some people do seem to feel that taking action without the sanction of a United Nations vote is fundamentally illegitimate.

Solving global problems by cooperation among nations is desirable where they can be mobilized to act positively. But the problem, as Brooks observed, is that "there is no global democracy, no sense of common peoplehood and trust." The UN (and its bureaucracy) are totally insulated from any democratic accountability. The UN is the creature of an irresponsible majority of voting nations with their own agendas that are self-serving and often far from noble. It can posture grandly but tends to be feckless about any tough decisions. Thus, in 2004, it gave Sudan a thirty-day deadline to stop the killing in Darfur. After thirty days and no result, what was the upshot? Another equally toothless deadline. But even that was more than was done about Rwanda's 1994 genocide. In Bosnia, the UN did establish "safe havens" —but then allowed their inhabitants to be massacred. It passed seventeen resolutions warning Iraq of "serious consequences" for failure to comply with weapons control, but no consequences were ever voted. And the Iraqi "oil-for-food" program was a vast corrupt enterprise.

The UN can sometimes serve a useful purpose. It does some worthy humanitarian work. And again, international cooperation can be a good thing. But let us have no illusions that the world can function effectively as a single society with a global social contract. If we can do nothing without international consensus, then we can indeed do nothing. To quote Brooks again, "the forces of decency can be paralyzed as they wait for 'the international community'" and lofty pieties about global cooperation should not seduce us to trust in an undemocratic and unworkable ideal.

Still, some denounce the idea of the nation-state, decrying nationalism as evil and a cause of war.[165] But nationalism per se is not wrong; we must distinguish between rational love for one's homeland and the chauvinism of a Nazi Germany that seeks to subjugate others. The problem is not the institution of the nation-state, but with some people trying to impose their will on their neighbors. While, as we have seen, we have no duty to help strangers or share wealth, there is a duty to avoid harming others, interfering with them, taking from them, exerting compulsion on them. Territoriality is obviously part of the picture. People are always trying to take territory away from each other.

Many Palestinians want to drive the Jews out of Israel. Here is the perfect case for a "live and let live" resolution. Israelis and Palestinians are fighting over a piece of land plenty big enough for both. Neither side needs it all, neither deserves it all, and neither can get it all. They could have two perfectly nice countries, side by side, engaging in commerce, trading goods and workers, investing in each other's industries, helping each other, with everybody living decent and satisfying lives. Instead, they kill each other for no conceivable gain to either.[166]

---

165. Yet strangely, these same idealists who condemn the nation-state often also (when it suits their biases) reject interventionism, deeming national borders inviolate and insisting on the right of a regime to remain unmolested in perpetrating its crimes.

166. I am reminded of an old Laurel and Hardy film. They drive up to a man's house and get into a spat with him. In anger, he breaks a lamp off their

Is this hopelessly naive? No. "Live and let live" is actually in the true self-interest of both sides. If each were selfishly serving its own genuine best interests, they would agree to "live and let live."

A similar case is Kashmir. When my daughter was eight, she heard something about it on TV and asked me to explain the problem: India and Pakistan each believe Kashmir should belong to them. For over fifty years they have quarreled about it and have even gone to war over it several times. Her eight-year-old response: "Why don't they just split it?" That was, in fact, the correct answer. Two nations, at each other's throats for half a century, could not agree on an answer obvious even to an eight-year-old.

We just seem to have a blind spot over issues of territory. Boris Yeltsin let the Soviet Union dissolve, with all fifteen of its republics set free—a truly visionary act. Yet he then balked at the independence sought by Chechnya, a tiny peripheral piece of Russia, and launched a horrific bloody war, literally destroying the place rather than let it go. What did this achieve? Huge war costs, atrocious casualties, a Russia with a piece of it wrecked and inhabited by embittered people driven to terrorism, and a blot upon its moral ledger, instead of a Russia just a wee bit smaller but at peace with a neighboring Chechnya.

Then there was the Ethiopia-Eritrea war. Ethiopia had amicably agreed to let Eritrea secede—another remarkable deviation from the territorial imperative—only to fall into a costly war, with seventy thousand killed, over their conflicting claims to a tiny, barren, worthless patch of desert.

Indonesia seized East Timor, merely because it could, and held on for a quarter century, at great cost in blood and treasure, like holding a roaring tiger by the tail. And when it could hold on no longer, like a spoiled brat, it thoroughly trashed the place before giving it up.

And China insists that Taiwan is part of it. Taiwan has been a

---

car. Hardy responds by doing likewise to the house front. Tit for tat, and soon the duo is single-mindedly wrecking the house while its owner ignores them and works over their car. Each becomes solely focused on hurting the other, with no heed to his own damage. Both house and car are demolished.

separate country for over half a century,[167] yet China pretends this isn't so and bullies the world into endorsing the fiction. China deludes itself that it can eventually bully Taiwan into capitulating and threatens military invasion if Taiwan ever dares speak the truth that reunification is out of the question. A rational, reasonable, "live and let live" China might say, "We're both Chinese, we can just as well have two countries, be friends, trade with each other, and support and defend each other."

But letting go is so hard.

The lust for power (which Tacitus called "the most flagrant of all passions") afflicts nations as well as individuals. People imagine that, for nation-states, bigger is always better, and that a nation's greatness is defined by its power, its ability to impose its will on others. This "great power" fallacy has messed up people's thinking all across the globe and throughout history.[168] Russia went into a deep national funk when, after the Soviet Union fell, its great power pretensions were found hollow; and much of Russia's subsequent foreign policy centered on vain efforts to somehow recapture its lost "glory." France, too, is having a hard time adjusting to diminished influence. Of course, the poster boys for this power obsession were Germany and Japan in World War II, each striving to subjugate surrounding lands and to swagger as a great conqueror. The price each paid for this craven hubris was utter national catastrophe.[169]

So here is the crucial lesson: a nation's greatness does not hinge

---

167. When communists won control of China in 1949, the defeated side fled to Taiwan, an island off the coast, and it has been effectively independent ever since. Taiwan has been a tremendous economic success, in large measure due to its freedom, which, of course, particularly infuriates the undemocratic Chinese regime.

168. Matthew Arnold told his fellow Britons, "We have a great empire. So had Nebuchadnezzar."

169. Some accuse the United States of this very sort of national hubris. As I've stressed, what we actually seek is not American self-aggrandizement at others' expense but, rather, better lives for people everywhere.

upon how much land it rules, nor its ability to impose its will on anyone.

These are the fool's gold of nations. As is said of male sexual equipment, size doesn't matter, it's what you do with it. So too with nations; size doesn't matter, it's what you do with what you've got. What matters is the kind of life your people have. The lives of a nation's people are not enhanced or ennobled by its being a great power, by its conquest of others, by adding territory, or even by holding onto all its territory. In fact, such efforts usually degrade the lives of a nation's people, imposing costs on them that reduce their standard of living, not to mention the moral stain of wars like Chechnya and East Timor. There is no proper national pride, but only shame, in the "glory" of crushing victims.

What makes for a good and great nation is providing a safe, happy, prosperous home for a free people. Living at peace with its neighbors, avoiding the costs of war, engaging in trade and commerce and industry, with political and economic liberty, providing an environment in which the citizenry can thrive and lead rewarding lives at the highest possible standard of material comfort. That is what makes a great nation.

We often see debate over whether this or that small territory can be "viable" as an independent nation. As though bigness and a lot of resources are necessary to make it in the nation game. By now the reader should see the falsity of this. What makes a viable nation is the ability of its people to be productive. Look again at the success of little Hong Kong, with no resources but the energies of its people.

In fact, some of the truly greatest nations on Earth are among the smallest and least powerful.

Recall again how evolution programmed us for social cooperation and altruism—to help our band survive in competition against other bands. Accordingly, that cooperativeness centers upon an "in-group," to the exclusion of others. Indeed, the very process that made us social within our tribe at the same time instilled hostility and aggression toward those seen as outsiders, against whom our tribe competes. That is why xenophobia (literally, fear of strangers) and tribalism are actually intrinsic to human nature and so hard to overcome.[170] It's also why war has been so much a part of the human story. War is of course a manifestation of the group-against-group competitive impulse nature bequeathed us. This leads some cultural pessimists to a bleak assessment of our species and its future.

But history is not destiny. Just like individuals, nations can—and do—use the power of reason to rise above the brutishness our natures entail. And, meantime, as civilization has developed, we have expanded the in-group's scope, from small bands and tribes, to encompass nation-states, often ethnically diverse, and even groups of nations—and some people today include all humankind, while a few of us actually extend perceived kinship to some nonhuman creatures too. And so, the realm of cooperation and altruism steadily grows while that of competition and war shrinks. (War among members of the European Union has become virtually inconceivable; so too in the Western Hemisphere.) The prognosis is positive.

Still, xenophobia does persist, and people often have a hostile view toward others not like themselves, especially if those others want to move in next door, or even just into their country. There is much hand-wringing about immigrants adulterating and degrading a nation's culture.

The old metaphor was the "melting pot," blending disparate immigrants into an ultimately homogeneous citizenry. The modern politically correct metaphor is a quilt, wherein the pieces all retain their character and, together, form a pattern of diversity. The truth, and what is desirable, lies somewhere in between. We should expect and want immigrants to melt partway into the pot, to become integral members of a cohesive society, rather than see ghettoization and apartness. We have to learn from the murderous ethnic strife that has plagued so many

---

170. Shermer sees here an explanation of Old Testament morality, emphasizing humanitarian principles on one page while glorifying blood-drenched ethnic cleansing on the next. "Love thy neighbor" was meant literally—it didn't apply to non-neighbors.

societies where people have emphasized their differences rather than their commonality. Still, it is also desirable for immigrant groups to preserve their distinctive heritages, adding to the richness of our culture. We wouldn't want a quilt whose pieces are all shredded together to produce a monochrome; diversity is, indeed, one of the glories of American life. In a local annual Greek festival, Greek Americans celebrate their ancestral culture without separating themselves from the larger American culture and, in fact, invite non-Greeks to join in their celebration. This is not unique, and this is how it should be.

There is a widespread fear that immigrants take jobs from natives or soak up welfare payments or otherwise are a drain on the economy. Many studies have shown that, in reality, immigrants don't cost the economy anything and are almost certainly net long-run contributors. When New York City had an economic near-death experience in the 1970s, it was actually saved by immigrants and the revitalization they brought.

As to the job concern, this is another manifestation of the old "lump of labor" fallacy—another zero-sum game—the idea that there is only so much work to go around and that if someone takes a job, that's one job fewer for others. That may be true on a very temporary basis, but if there is more labor available, a free market can be expected to find uses for it. In the long run, national wealth is a function of people being productively employed, so the more people we have, the greater is our economic potential.

And realize, too, that so many people try to enter the United States seeking work because it pays more; and it pays more because it is more productive. So moving labor from places where it is less productive to where it is more productive means a net benefit to global productivity and, hence, wealth. This, again, makes the economic pie bigger for everyone.

There is another key consideration: in the advanced nations, affluent people are having smaller families, plunging birthrates below replacement level. Native populations are falling even though the death rate is declining and people are living longer. The result is a substantial aging of these populations, with dire implications for their economies and social welfare systems, since ever fewer working people support more and more pensioners. What this has to do with immigration should be obvious—taking in more work-hungry young migrants can help offset shrinkage of the employment base. America does exactly that; our population is growing because of immigration. So, rather than stealing away jobs, immigrants are instead bringing labor that we need.

The concern that immigrants will change a country's culture is not baseless. Of course they will. But the river of life is always changing. Sure, we want to keep what's good about our culture and society; not to remain static and prevent all change, but rather to keep the change going in healthy directions. We must continually adapt ourselves to our evolving demographic mix. But meantime, it's reasonable and appropriate to ask newcomers to make some adaptations too. In particular, if they are to live in an open society with an ethos of tolerance and diversity under the rule of law, they should be expected to absorb these principles and, thus, respect the rights of others unlike themselves. Accommodation is a two-way street and we should not be tolerant of intolerance.

Anyhow, America is quintessentially a nation of immigrants; everyone here (even, ultimately, Native Americans) is descended from migrants that strove for better lives. This made for a nation emphasizing liberty, acceptance of diversity, suspicion of bossy government, a powerful work ethic—and a welcoming attitude to new arrivals. These basic national virtues are not likely to be altered by new waves of immigrants.

For a person to uproot himself and move to a different country is itself a powerful expression of individualism, ambition, and self-reliance; such people already have more of the American pioneer spirit than do a lot of folks born here. Many literally stake their lives to get here, setting out on ramshackle rafts or across killing deserts. Some don't make it. Those that do, I want here. Anyone with the pluck to try to raft his way from Haiti to America, or cross a desert, has got to have tremendous personal qualities that surely will make him an asset to this country. It breaks my heart when such people are sent back.

Because America is such a great country, I want as many people as possible to enjoy its blessings—and we can accommodate plenty more with no detriment to those already here. The more people we have, the stronger and better we will be as a nation.

Why the Gloom and Doom Crowd Is Wrong

Doomsayers have been predicting catastrophe for humankind for centuries. They have always been wrong. They will probably always be wrong.

There is a bias in the pronouncements of professional Cassandras. They want attention paid to them, and, of course, that wouldn't happen if their messages were that everything's fine. Saying that things are terrible compels attention. Environmentalist advocates and their kin often have a vested personal stake in making the problems they work on seem as important and threatening as possible.

Most famously, Thomas Malthus, two centuries ago, projected that population growth would outrun the food supply. Of course he was wrong. World population has actually grown even faster than he foresaw, partly due to improvements in health science, infant survival, and longevity—but also, in part, because agricultural productivity and food availability have increased even faster than population, the exact opposite of what Malthus predicted. Yet, undaunted, environmental alarmists, even today, continue to spout neo-Malthusian warnings about running out of food.

We are also supposed to be running out of oil, coal, water, natural gas, metals, and virtually every other natural resource you might name. Now, granted, the Earth's resources are finite. But these doomsaying predictions have been commonplace for a very long time; yet, as time goes by, even as we consume natural resources, the remaining available supply, due to technological advances in search and extraction, actually grows. Thus, estimated oil reserves in 1970 were 580 billion barrels; between 1970 and 2000, 690 billion barrels were burned; but in 2000, estimated reserves had nevertheless grown to 1,050 billion barrels. Similar numbers are seen for copper, bauxite, and other mineral resources.

If the Cassandras were right, and supplies were approaching exhaustion, the market would logically have driven up the prices of natural resource commodities. But in fact, over a long time span, most such prices have actually fallen substantially in real-dollar terms.

I am neither an anti-environmentalist nor against everything environmentalists advocate. They are actually sometimes right. We do have serious environmental problems and do need to try to minimize pollution and resource consumption. But, as I've said, to be "for the environment" is too facile and simplistic. You have to confront the hard choices and real difficulties of these issues to figure out what really serves human interests. And you have to see the world as it really is—not as the negativists portray it.[171]

The twentieth century has been lamented as the worst in human history. Indeed, the bloody experience of that century has led some pessimists to reject the idea of progress itself; they say we are retrogressing. This shows ignorance of both history and the world's reality. The past century certainly witnessed unspeakable horrors, which are vivid to us because of our closeness to them. Everyone knows about World War II and the Holocaust. But how many have even heard of the Thirty Years' War or the T'ai-p'ing Rebellion? One can't say those

---

171. Bjorn Lomborg, in *The Skeptical Environmentalist*, discusses in compelling detail the ways in which some environmentalists have misused statistics to support their fearmongering. The book is highly recommended as a more objective, balanced, and realistic view of the state of the planet and of humanity.

earlier horrors make the Holocaust look like a picnic, but they do make it seem unexceptional.

In fact, contrary to what many of us suppose, the worldwide per capita death rate from war has actually steadily *declined* over recent centuries, reaching a historic low point in the twentieth. And furthermore, the twentieth century's war deaths were heavily concentrated in its first half. Peace is on the march.

And, despite all its horrors, the twentieth century was no setback in human progress. On the contrary, it produced spectacular advancement. The impact of the horrors was simply overwhelmed by the vastly greater importance of the gains—with the average person incomparably better off at the century's end than at its start.

If you look at worldwide historical graphs for the two key measures of human welfare—average life spans and incomes—what you see for all the centuries up to the nineteenth is almost invisibly slow improvement. Then, as technological and scientific advancement begins to bear real fruit, the trend lines bend upward. And in the twentieth century they *explode* upward. Where before the trend lines were almost horizontal, now they are nearly vertical!

The average prehistoric life span was twentyish; few cavemen reached forty. During all the subsequent thousands of years of civilization, until 1900, a very slow improvement roughly doubled the average life span. But in the single century since 1900, it has nearly doubled again. And the increasing trend shows no sign of slackening off. Centenarians are now becoming common. A hundredth birthday used to mean a letter from the president, but that had to stop—he was getting writer's cramp. Moreover, not only are people living longer, they are living better, freer of chronic sickness and pain. The stereotype of old age used to be physical decrepitude, but today the typical octogenarian is as healthy and active as were people of sixty in earlier times.

To listen to environmentalist scaremongers, you might think we are all being poisoned by all the terrible chemicals and toxins and pollution to which we are heedlessly exposing ourselves. The simple response is that if we are all being poisoned, how come the average human life span keeps going up and up and up, and people are not only living longer but are healthier in old age to boot?[172] This obvious reality is the answer to all the fearmongering about pollution. If the alarmists were right about pollution, we would be less healthy and dying younger.

Part of why we aren't, of course, is scientific and medical advancement. But also relevant is the other key human welfare index, the average income (in which, of course, technological progress again plays a key role because it makes people's work more productive). Higher incomes allow us to eat better, to get better medical care, to work less hard, and so, to live longer and healthier. During the twentieth century, worldwide average incomes, in real-dollar terms, rose approximately *fivefold*.

That's right, fivefold, 500 percent. The average person at the century's end earned five times more than at its start. Don't dismiss this as concerning "merely" money. Money is the difference between wretched poverty and a decent life. The stupendous income gain of the twentieth century improved conditions of life for the average person far more than occurred in all the thousands of centuries before. (These gains have not been confined to the better-off; World Bank figures show the global poverty rate virtually halved in just the quarter century after 1980.) All this means not only longer and healthier lives, but more education, more travel, more enjoyment, more flowering of the arts, more self-fulfillment, and more freedom and choices.[173] *That* is the biggest story of the much-maligned twentieth century.

---

172. And this is happening despite ballooning obesity, lack of exercise, and other lifestyle factors that are far more deleterious to health than the bugaboo of toxins and pollution.

This isn't to deny that pollution does harm and that we'd be even healthier without it. Of course we would. But it's absurd to imagine we could somehow eliminate all man-made pollution without eliminating modernity itself, along with the benefits that more than compensate for its drawbacks.

173. Some advocate focus not on incomes or Gross Domestic Product but, instead, on measures like the "Human Development Indicator" or the

Of course, this fantastic betterment is totally contrary to what environmentalist doomsayers (and Marxist economists) would insist should have happened. They would have you imagine population growth triggering a grim struggle over limited food supplies and other resources, with impoverishment and starvation for the losers. Yet life spans and incomes have vaulted upward at the same time that population, too, has exploded. World population likewise grew more in the twentieth century (despite all the killing) than in our entire previous history. But instead of being condemned to poverty, most of those extra people have managed not only to get fed, but to live, on average, far better than people ever did before.

How can the doomsayers have been so spectacularly wrong? Those who still rattle on with dire warnings about population growth see additional people as just more mouths to feed. But they also bring more hands to work.

That's the point all the "population bomb" poppycock misses. People have not just mouths to feed, they have hands (and minds) to work; and the past century's vast gains came about because so many of those extra millions of people were able to find ever-more productive employment, thereby increasing, rather than reducing, the wealth of humankind. Instead of the grim picture of a rising population scrambling for ever smaller slices of a static pie, the reality is a pie expanding even faster than population—quite simply because, thanks to technology, most people produce more than they consume.[174] So growing population won't increase poverty. In fact, poverty is decreasing, and

---

"Index of Social Health" to capture human welfare. This can provide some useful information; but it's an unassailable reality that income is the overriding determinant of quality of life in all the ways noted above. To ignore this, and to rely instead on other measures, leads to dubious results. (A "social welfare" study once tagged communist Bulgaria as the world's most paradisiac nation.)

174. "Overpopulated" and impoverished India always used to be Exhibit One for population scaremongers. They couldn't see how India's multiplying people could be fed. Yet, by 2000, India had actually become a net *exporter* of grain.

this itself will actually curb population growth because more affluent people tend to have fewer children. (That's why world population is ultimately projected to fall, after peaking around midcentury.)

Another great thing that happened in the twentieth century was the advance of freedom and democracy. The century did see a big outbreak of totalitarianism—but, in the end, it was largely crushed, and Jefferson's dream of extending liberty "finally to all" took a giant step forward.

There used to be an event called "Captive Nations Day." At the complex where I worked, tables bedecked with national flags featured people in native costumes beseeching freedom for Soviet-dominated lands: Latvia, Lithuania, Poland, and so on—even Ukraine. I would walk past with sympathy and sorrow—the cause seemed so hopeless.

But I was wrong. "Captive Nations Day" is no more because none of those nations is still "captive"—not even Ukraine. Not all are democracies, but at least now they're independent (and between 2003 and 2005, three of them overthrew undemocratic regimes). I'll never forget November 9, 1989, when I switched on the evening news and saw people dancing atop the Berlin Wall. It was a great day for humankind; the world had changed, and a chunk of that bygone monument to tyranny sits on my desk as a tangible reminder of the freedom that's been won. Further, throughout Latin America, where military dictatorship had always been the standard model, democracy now reigns in practically every land, and it has been breaking out all over in long-suffering Africa, and in Asia too, and there are even glimmers in the Middle East. And some nations, most notably China, that have yet to embrace democracy have nevertheless become more free in other ways.

The concept of human rights, and concern for them, is a modern development. We still have a lot of human rights problems; but in ages past they weren't even recognized as such. In today's small wired world, abuses are hard to conceal or ignore and consciences are mobilized. "People power" has become a force to be reckoned with, helping to sweep away the Berlin Wall, the Soviet Union, South African apartheid, and rotten regimes all across the globe. Bad guys from Goering and Tojo to Milosevic, Saddam Hussein and Charles Taylor are made to face justice. The world is getting better.

Freedom is not just an abstract virtue. It enhances not only people's inner lives but their material well-being too. It's a cliché that democracies don't make war on each other, but conflict certainly does seem highly correlated with absence of political liberty and governmental accountability. Freedom is a potent medicine for promoting world peace —which is good for business. And, as I've also stressed, freedom is the best tonic for improving economic performance and living standards.

This bodes well for the future. The last century's fivefold income gain was achieved in spite of devastating wars and a massive freedom deficit, with great parts of the world in the grip of totalitarian, central-planning, socialist, or statist regimes. Much of that brake upon humanity's fortunes is now gone. China, once more, is a key example, with stonking economic growth now that it has jettisoned socialist dogma. This story has been repeated in nation after nation. Though excessive statism in the advanced world is a real concern, the planet, as a whole, has become far more free. So, if incomes could rise fivefold worldwide in the last century, what might we achieve in the next one?

Environmentalist doomsayers seem afflicted with a chronic inability to grasp the power of human ingenuity to overcome problems and obstacles and improve our lives. The one constant throughout our history is resilience in the face of challenges, our ability to surmount them and rise to yet greater heights. It is knowledge and technology that has enabled people to produce more than they consume. Malthus was wrong because he couldn't have foreseen our explosive improvement in agricultural productivity; and the trend shows no sign of abatement as advanced farming techniques spread to the globe's more backward regions.[175] Likewise, burgeoning technology continues to

---

175. Much of this "green revolution" is actually *opposed* by many self-styled "greens." In particular, as already noted, they crusade against genetic modification, which holds huge promise for boosting agricultural yields, with risks that any objective scientific analysis must deem insignificant.

make all varieties of human labor more efficient, with most working hands producing more and more and adding to the size of the pie for everyone.

Of course, such dramatic developments in the human story could not occur without complications, problems, and downsides. That is axiomatic. Yes, all this economic growth and material progress has been accompanied by environmental challenges; it could not be otherwise. Some people-haters bizarrely talk as though we have despoiled the Earth wantonly, for no reason, like vandals; "pissing in our nest" one has said. But in fact, our environmental problems are the unavoidable costs associated with boosting human well-being. There is no totally green way to achieve that; we could never have risen out of the caves while leaving the Earth unspoiled or without consuming natural resources. And if multiplying fivefold in one century the living standard of the average human, lifting billions out of poverty, has created some environmental problems, surely the price is well worth paying for the benefit gained. We have helped humanity far more than we've hurt the planet.

If today we stopped exploiting natural resources, stopped producing and using energy, stopped manufacturing goods and driving our cars, ended our consumer society—if we went back to living in caves—Earth would revert to being a pristine Eden. But as long as we don't do that, as long as we choose to live as people rather than as animals, we must face and accept that there are unavoidable environmental costs—yet they are costs worth paying for what we gain.

And, just as they have proven so poor in grasping the power of technology to improve people's lives, so too have the Cassandras underestimated our ability to cope with our environmental challenges. Listening to them, you might think that Earth is "going to hell in a handbasket." But, just as they've been wrong about depleting natural resources, wrong about the impact of population growth, and wrong about a supposed world food crisis, they are also wrong that the environment is sure to be wrecked by human activity.

Not only does such thinking underrate humanity's capacity to meet challenges, it also fails to appreciate how affluence has positive as well as negative environmental impacts. We are told that the advanced nations have ravaged the environment and that China, India, and others are following in those footsteps. Accordingly, some of these negativists (while otherwise wringing their hands over global poverty) actually seem to want India and the others kept poor. It is true, again, that raising incomes does create environmental challenges—but it also creates resources to meet them. People value clean air, clean water, and a healthy environment; when they are poor, they cannot afford to worry about such things—yet they can when they get rich. And so, the rich nations, far from compounding the environmental downsides to their progress, are able to devote resources to fixing things. Doing so is politically popular. As a result, it is simply factually wrong to think environmental conditions in the rich countries are getting worse. On the contrary, because they can afford to tackle these issues, in the advanced nations, air, water quality, and so on are dramatically improved over conditions of the past. It is rich societies that can worry about protecting endangered species or ecosystems that poor people may be driven to exploit. So the answer to the potential environmental challenges posed by increasing prosperity in India and elsewhere is not to keep those countries poor, but to help them grow rich enough to be able to tackle their environmental problems as we in the West have done.

Certainly, humankind has grown hugely more sensitive to environmental concerns than in the past—when such sensitivity was, indeed, nonexistent. Just as we have made great strides in our material conditions of life, respect for human rights, and extending liberty and opportunity, so too have we gotten a lot smarter about the environment. The very fact that so many people have become environmentalist zealots is a big change, when in the past nobody cared at all. Indeed, so much newfound environmental activism actually creates a danger that we'll go overboard and unduly sacrifice human values to environmental concerns. At any rate, surely one has to see that our stewardship of the planet is getting better, not worse.

Someday, eventually, we will run out of oil and coal and natural

260　*Life, Liberty, and Happiness*

gas and a lot of other resources we use. Conservation can help postpone that day, yet, obviously, that's not a permanent solution. But before we run out of fossil fuels, for example, it seems reasonable to believe that our technological ingenuity will enable us to exploit new and better sources of energy. The blueprints for doing so are already well along. As Sheikh Yamani said, the Stone Age didn't end for lack of stone—and the Oil Age will end long before the oil runs out.

The same applies to all the other warnings that what we're doing to the planet is unsustainable. Buying that argument in full would, again, virtually mean going back to life in caves. But in 1800 no one could have conceived the planet capable of supporting today's six billion people. And it couldn't—not with 1800 technology. Perhaps with today's technology we can't sustain our way of life indefinitely either. But we won't have to. In another two hundred years we will have twenty-third-century technology, which we can scarcely imagine— just as people in 1800 could not have imagined twentieth-century technology, or an Earth supporting six billion souls.

Jared Diamond's book *Collapse* chronicles many human societies that failed, often from environmental factors and/or shortsightedness, suggesting it could happen to us. Yes, our history is full of cautionary disaster stories. But the bigger story is that for humanity *as a whole*, the trajectory has been upward, with ever more people living ever better lives. Our failures have been eclipsed by our successes in mastering our challenges. Our environmental problems are serious but not insoluble. In fact, Diamond holds that we can solve them even without new technology, that the real key is the will to do what's needed. We've done it before, and we're doing it now.[176] That's why he characterized his book as ultimately optimistic.

Problems, and dealing with them, are what life is about. There will never be a world without problems. Even if we somehow managed to solve all our problems, that would surely create unforeseen new ones.

---

176. Diamond cites a sustained US effort that reduced six major air pollutants by 25 percent over three decades, even while population and energy consumption rose 40 percent and vehicle miles driven by 150 percent.

My wife once said to me, "How can you be such an optimist when there are so many problems that so many good smart people are concerned about?" I replied, "That's precisely why I'm optimistic!"

One big environmental headache that human advancement seems to be affecting is global warming. We should certainly try to do what is reasonable to avoid aggravating it.[177] But let us put this in perspective:

Rhetoric about human activities "destabilizing" Earth's climate is surely misplaced because the climate has never been stable, but constantly changing. We evolved during an on-again, off-again ice age; there is some evidence that the last few thousand years have just been a warm spell within a longer icy period, so that the greater threat may be cooling, not warming.[178] But in truth, we really can't be sure—factors influencing climate are exceedingly complex. Science doesn't fully understand them all and even the most powerful computer modeling cannot reliably capture effects that, in the big picture, are really tiny (so that a very small modeling imperfection can produce a dramatically different projection of climate change).

So, while human activity has an impact, we don't fully understand how the story is playing out. That doesn't stop the environmental fearmongering machine from trying to make guesses and even fantasies sound like facts. And on such a big planet, with so many different things happening, it is all too easy to pick out isolated details and trends and claim they are proof of something. The truth is that one fact or even a hundred facts can be meaningless unless you look at the planet as a whole and can be sure there aren't an equal number of facts going the other way.

Second, while no doubt global climate change would have disruptive effects, the gloom-and-doom crowd naturally sees only the downside. But some areas would actually benefit from warmer temperatures; for

---

177. Greater use of nuclear power would help a lot, though, strangely, most greens oppose this.

178. In fact, as recently as the 1970s it was the prospect of global cooling, not warming, that environmentalists were agitating over.

example, though we'd lose some cropland, we'd also gain some, growing seasons would be longer, and more rain could help alleviate water shortages. The net overall result of warming would still admittedly be negative, but not as uniformly grim as some would have us believe.

Third, if we have proven anything during our time on Earth, it is our adaptability. We evolved out of the steamy African savannah, yet managed to cope with the European ice age, and then a return to warmth—and, of course, that was without the benefit of all the scientific knowledge and technological prowess we have gained since. Here, yet again, the gloomsters utterly fail to credit the human capability to deal with whatever nature throws at us and whatever messes we get ourselves into. For example, the 1930s dust bowl was a terrible man-made environmental calamity, but we recovered from it, learned its lessons, and have avoided a repeat. And when people awoke to the genuine danger of atmospheric ozone depletion, all the leading nations joined to ban the chlorofluorocarbons that were causing it; and ozone loss has been reversed.

Ironically, while environmentalists tend to discount our coping ability, at the same time, they vastly overstate our ability to combat climate change. Even the most ambitious and aggressive antiwarming proposals on the table would make only a minuscule difference in projected average temperatures, far in the future, while entailing gigantic costs in productivity and living standards today. Global warming might not be catastrophic, but following the antiwarming prescriptions of environmental extremists surely would be. Resources are not unlimited. Should we expend them trying to shave a degree or two off temperatures rather than on sanitation, AIDS, malaria, and so forth, which would greatly improve conditions for millions of the world's least fortunate?[179]

Humanity is certainly profligate in many ways. But, just as Winston Churchill once said of America, "It will always do the right thing, after exhausting all the alternatives."

---

179. Over ten million third world children under five die annually from illnesses that would be cured in the West.

Why the Gloom and Doom Crowd Is Wrong

* * *

This book's very first words portrayed a familiar litany of negativity and pessimism. Depressing facts to feed it are never in short supply in a huge complicated world. Studying history and current events certainly rubs my own nose in them and often makes me heartsick. But the antidote is to stay mindful of all the countervailing, and big, good news. Yes, people have done and still do horrible things, and many still do suffer blighted lives. But understanding this should only intensify our passionate appreciation of what so many of us have gained: comfortable, affluent, peaceful, well-fed, healthy lives full of recreation, pleasure, entertainment, satisfaction, happiness, joy, love, and the blessings of freedom.

This is the big picture, the gigantic accomplishment of humankind. This reality is the nub of the case for optimism and positive thinking. It is my dream that someday every person on Earth will cross that river and reach this promised land. But not just my dream—it's my conviction.

Man, Technology, and Nature

There is a popular little epigram, *"O God, your sea is so vast and my boat is so small"*—bespeaking human insignificance in the face of nature's power. Some people actually relish that idea, even believing that the world would be better without us, or at least with less of our rumbustious presence. They may think of themselves as humanist but they actually detest humankind, ashamed of their species like teenagers embarrassed by their uncool parents.

The preceding chapter showed the error of pessimism about progress and about the environment. Why then are so many of us so receptive to it? One reason is that the Cassandras are vocal, insistent, and adept at trotting out statistics, which may be misleading or manipulated, to seize our attention and advance their agendas. And their message resonates with many who feel a deep-seated guilt about their pampered lives (especially when, despite all the advances, some people are still poor). Others, falling away from conventional faiths, have substituted what is really an environmentalist religion, worshipping Earth and displaying messianic fervor. Like old-time religionists, they regard the rest of humanity as a pack of sinners deserving damnation.

Some are hostile toward modernity itself, seeing undue reliance on reason and technology as incompatible with our true nature, causing spiritual alienation and dissatisfaction, despite our outward comforts, and corrupting us with greed and violence. Again, they deny the idea of progress,[180] believing instead that we are actually in a downward spiral. They cleave to nonrationalist "new age" thought and idealize more primitive societies as supposedly embodying blissful pacifism and harmony with nature. This myth of the "noble savage" has been proven factually false,[181] yet still it informs the cultural pessimism that pervades so much modern intellectualizing and badmouthing of civilization and its achievements ("our sick modern society," and so on).

Technology also elicits fear. We are fundamentally conservative creatures who cling to our familiar ways and fear change, especially change we don't understand. And, certainly, as technology progresses, it becomes ever harder for ordinary folk to comprehend. However, human advancement is a product of our ability to maintain and build upon our body of knowledge and understanding. This is a collective venture—and the fact that our collective knowledge overwhelms what any one of us can grasp is not a problem but rather our strength. This is what has made us the most successful species ever; it is the great fact of our evolution. And so technology (itself an evolutionary process),[182] rather than being somehow alien

---

180. Yet curiously, such people often label themselves politically as "progressive"!

181. Harvard's Steven LeBlanc said, "Anthropologists have searched for peaceful societies much like Diogenes looked for an honest man," that is, without success. And a study of 186 hunter-gatherer societies by University of Michigan ecologist Bobbi Low found their environmental conduct shaped not by responsible stewardship but, rather, by practical limits to their destructiveness; and nevertheless, environmental degradation was often severe. Michael Shermer, noting all this, succinctly concluded, "Savage yes. Noble no."

182. Ray Kurzweil, inventor and author, suggests that the cutting edge of evolution on Earth has, in fact, now moved from the realm of biology to technology, as carried forward by humans, with each new stage of development creating more powerful tools for spearheading the next one. This hugely accelerates the pace of advancement.

to our humanness, is, on the contrary, absolutely integral to it. We are, first and foremost, toolmakers and tool users; that's what technology means. A more accurate label for us would be not *Homo sapiens* but *Homo techniens*. Technology, then, is not antihuman but the highest expression of what it is to be human.

Still, there is widespread fear that technology, instead of being controlled by us, will control us. We are haunted by the Frankenstein story of a hubristic scientist, "playing God," who subverts nature, creating a monster. Thus, technological advances get tagged by critics with the prefix "franken" to frighten us. And there are fantasies of a future world ruled by computers and robots that make humans their slaves or brush us aside.

These are surely fantasies indeed. Though computers sometimes seem to have minds of their own, we know that they actually don't have minds at all; they are incapable of doing anything but what humans tell them to do. If we someday succeed in creating artificial intelligence, it too will be to serve human purposes.[183] Real scientists are not in the business of making monsters.

But, even if human slavery to technology never becomes literal, many of us seem to feel that we are already slaves, chained to our computers, cell phones, and myriad other devices. Yet that very sense of inescapability actually reveals how essential technology has become for us. We could easily forsake all our gizmos if they were not so gosh darn useful and if we did not love them so (even if it is something of a love-hate relationship).

And, while many Americans feel they're working harder than ever, the facts show differently. There was, of course, far more backbreaking toil in earlier times, eliminated by technology. But further, while job hours actually haven't changed much in recent decades, household work—cooking, cleaning, washing, shopping, and so on—has been hugely reduced by technological changes. Moreover, the wealth effect of technological productivity enables us to support a far

---

183. Isaac Asimov, robotics' foremost prophet, decreed its Three Laws to ensure that humans are always in charge and never harmed.

higher share of the population in retirement. The bottom line is a vast increase in our collective leisure time.[184]

Thus, far from controlling people, technology has actually done the opposite, empowering and freeing us. There is no better example than the automobile, a revolutionary technology giving masses of people more mobility and independence than was ever possible before. We've been liberated from numerous debilitating health problems. The pill gave us newfound control over procreation, another social revolution. We may mock those whose cell phones seem glued to their ears, but their ubiquity testifies that this new technology fulfills a huge human social yearning. And, of course, computers and the Internet have likewise been transformative. The latter, in particular, a supremely democratic technology, has opened up for us a whole new window on the world, whole new landscapes of options for exploring life.

But meantime, technology's biggest impact has simply been to make people richer—and there is nothing like money for widening your choices in life. The standard of living now enjoyed is directly traceable to technological advancement, which makes us ever more productive. And the resulting increase in affluence gives ever more people ever more independence, more autonomy, more options. Thanks to technology, we are gaining more control over our lives, not less.

Are science and technology unmitigated blessings then? Of course not. We should not make a religion of them either. Yes, inevitably there are problems and downsides, and sometimes science and technology backfire on us. Those who rail against such evils make technology itself seem a Bad Thing. For example, Stuart Chase, in *The Proper Study of Mankind*, wrote that Henry Ford "gave us the Model T, and presently the robot on the assembly line, and traffic jams." But surely the benefits of industrial automation surpass its drawbacks, and to give up cars to avoid traffic jams would be throwing the baby out with the bathwater.

---

184. If many of us still feel overstretched, perhaps it's because modernity facilitates multitasking. Thus, we try to squeeze ever more activities into our available hours, while our high incomes make us feel each hour is worth more.

Of course, any technology can be misused, whether it's a hunting spear turned against men, or atomic power. We have to be careful and we have to use our advancements in humane ways that truly serve us. Food is a perfect example: modernity has produced a cornucopia that has contributed to improved health and longevity; but it's not good if we overindulge and "supersize" ourselves. The point is that science and technology have given us the expanded choices; how we use them is up to us. But let's keep our eye on the big picture. The benefits have vastly outweighed the negatives. I'll say it yet again: but for science and technology, but for our "tampering with nature," we'd still be cave dwellers.

And meantime, environmental extremism and antitechnology crusading are not without harm too. They keep people in poverty by denying them the benefits of advancing knowledge.[185] And if science can be misused against human interests, more so can antiscience—recall again the misguided crusade against GM foods and how banning DDT promoted insect-borne diseases.

It's ironic that some intellectuals who loathe technology often make icons of the likes of Che Guevara and romanticize the idea of leftist revolution to refashion society. That sort of revolution, wherever it's been tried, has never liberated anybody, never given people better lives or more control; indeed, it's always done exactly the opposite. Whereas technology—demonized by those romantics—has, in fact, been the truly liberating revolutionary force in the world. It's technology, not leftist political revolution, that has remade society, and for the better, smashing the shackles of humanity and lifting people up from squalor. It's science and technology that take us to the promised land.

* * *

---

185. It's said that a good lawyer doesn't tell you why you can't do what you want; he finds a way that you can. Too many environmentalists are scolds who are just negative toward human needs and wants, focused on fulminating about all our "crimes." A good environmentalist should, instead, be like a good lawyer, seeking out positive ways to make human development more compatible with environmental constraints.

So let us turn away from those who curse technology, denigrate reason, and despise humanity as out of tune with nature.

It's a truism that we are part of nature; it made us what we are. We cannot separate ourselves from that reality. And nature is a fount of beauty, wonder, and awe. Any living thing is a marvel, an almost miraculous defiance of entropy. The existence of even the lowliest insect, if you ponder it well, seems improbable; that nature could evolve beings like us is an even grander leap. So, a humble reverence toward nature is in order; and it isn't wrong to lament a loss of connectedness with the natural world, a realm that has become an alien one for many of us. This is, indeed, a sad consequence of our modern technological way of life. Cavemen did live in greater intimacy with nature. But would we trade places with them? I think we've gained far more than we've lost.

The planet we inhabit is uniquely hospitable to life, veritably a lush oasis in a vast desert. We are cosmically lucky to have this beautiful Earth, and it, too, commands reverence. And yet we're in no Garden of Eden where the living is easy. Earth gives us an environment to thrive in, but still, we have to work terribly hard to do it. Notwithstanding all its rare blessings, the planet is not some nurturing mother but is, in many ways, a hostile and unforgiving place. Humanity's whole story is an eternal struggle to overcome the challenges and obstacles of the natural environment. In that struggle, reason and technology are our most potent tools. We should glory in our victories. I love my species, and I celebrate what we have done.

Yes, cruelty, crime, and war are part of our legacy—but also music, poetry, and art. We produced Hitler, Stalin, Mao—but also Shakespeare, Einstein, and Mandela—for every crime, a hundred acts of courage, charity, and love, a hundred unbelievable achievements—for all the evil, so much beauty, so much good, so much sublime. On the backs of men who slaved and suffered to serve a ruler's megalomania, the Great Pyramid of Giza rose over Egypt, never equaled since, a monument to man's inhumanity but also to his bold reach for the magnificent.

In 1970, two hundred thousand miles from Earth, a catastrophic explosion rocked the *Apollo 13* moon ship. Intensive breakneck efforts were launched to somehow save the crew. The difficulties were gigantic and the odds were grim. But the episode showcased everything splendid about humankind: our daring courage in exploration, how we hold precious every single human life, and how we don't give up, no matter the challenge. And that we actually did get those astronauts home alive displayed a technological virtuosity dazzling beyond belief.

We emerged in this world as naked animals, equipped with nothing but our bare hands—and masses of gray stuff in our skulls—to carve out an existence, somehow, from that often unforgiving and hostile land. We started making tools from the only things we had, from rocks and sticks and bones. We made language; mastered fire; learned to grow food; and then to melt rocks and extract their metal; and, with that metal, we made better tools and then machines and cities and much more. And thus have we made lives for ourselves worth living.

Wherever I travel, looking out the window at the passing scene, or even just walking, my heart is filled with awe and love for what I see. It is love for human civilization, for all that we have accomplished in building a home for ourselves on this planet, to provide the good life that I see being lived all around me. That a naked animal, hardly removed from the apes, has somehow managed to make steel, glass, bricks, and plastic; to make factories, airplanes, and telephones seems utterly astonishing to me. And knowing the awfulness of most of history, awfulness that still afflicts so many even today, my heart swells when I look out upon a quiet tree-lined street of neat houses with cars parked at the curb, flower gardens, mailboxes, children's toys on the lawns, and suntanned people wearing shorts and comfortable shoes, walking their dogs. What mountains we had to move to achieve this!

We did it by questing after knowledge, teasing out the world's secrets. We have wrestled with her mysteries, deciphering the music of creation, to penetrate the innermost truth. We're naked animals who came to learn how the world began, how it works, and even how we came to be here.

The magnitude of our achievement is impossible to overstate. As Charles Murray suggests in his book *Human Accomplishment*, look at any natural phenomenon, forget what you know, and try to imagine figuring it out. How would you even begin to tackle the challenge of truly understanding fire, or changing seasons, or tides, or wind, or rain, let alone how Earth and life were made? The difficulty would loom so large as to crush any thought of even trying. Yet humankind, with our insatiable thirst for truth, would not be deterred. And by incredible, indefatigable effort, we did prise out the truth.

No loving Goddess Nature did we discover—but instead, a mindless force, driven just to duplicate a molecule, with living things as copiers, heedless of the pain and suffering it takes. She only wants for us to reproduce and then is happy to discard us; but we refuse to be discarded. We battle against our frailties, as crusaders waging war on Death itself, gaining every day another precious inch of ground. And nature batters us, too, with earthquakes, hurricanes, and tidal waves—with wind and water, fire and ice—knocking down much that we build. But out of the ashes, from the rubble, we clamber up and build anew.

The planet has no consciousness, no mind; but *we do*. Rocks, soil, trees, and water do not feel, or love, or suffer pain; but we men and women do. And if soil and water we bend to our will, if we melt rocks and cut trees, taking from the Earth the things we need so that we who breathe and feel may suffer the less and live the more, this is no crime; it is a triumph.

After four billion years, at last, there are beings on this globe who are not helpless playthings but, instead, the masters of it, and of our own destinies. By toil and strife, up from squalid caves we've climbed, to the mountaintop—by our bootstraps—by ourselves.

Yes, the sea is vast, and our boats are very small. But with that gray stuff in our skulls, our eyes to the horizon, and our faces to the wind, we set out upon our journey.

And reach for the stars.

History and Its Lessons

"History is bunk," Henry Ford famously declared.

He was all wet. Arthur Schlesinger has said that history is to a nation as memory is to a person. Think what you'd be without all your memories. Those memories—the sum and substance of everything you've done and been and seen—are what make you the person you are. Without them, you would be cast adrift, your life would lose its meaning. That's why amnesia is so awful; it's the loss of one's identity, virtually of life itself.

In the same way, our collective memory—our history—makes us who we are as a people. Once more, the richness of human culture is a product of all our past experience. History, memory, is our identity, the foundation of our lives, as individuals, as a nation, and as a species.

This applies with special force to America. Far more than do most countries, this one derives its identity and meaning from its history. We are a nation forged from an idea that springs directly from our history, going back all the way to the first colonists who came here seeking the freedom to choose their own paths. We are defined by our history: the Revolution, the Civil War, the opening of the West, the immigrant waves, the Great Depression, WWII, and the Cold War.

This isn't an exhaustive list, but subtract any of its elements from our history and America would be a very different place. If we lose touch with that history, we lose touch with what this nation is all about. National amnesia is the death of the civic soul.

Take the Civil War. A century and a half later, some might imagine that's just ancient history, hardly more relevant to us now than the Punic Wars. This couldn't be more wrong. Every day we are living the legacy of the Civil War. Look around. Do you see any African Americans? That's our history staring us in the face. This is why William Faulkner said the past isn't dead; it's not even past.

So to understand history is central to understanding the world we live in. One cannot do so without knowing how it came to be the way it is—cannot know where we're going without knowing where we've been. Moreover, history gives us not just the facts that made the world what it is, but important lessons concerning life and human nature. Columnist George Will has quoted Lord Bolingbroke: "History is philosophy teaching by examples." And Yale Professor Donald Kagan observes that with religion waning as a source for moral judgments, "It is natural and reasonable to turn to history, the record of human experience, as a necessary supplement if not a substitute." My whole outlook upon the world is shaped by what I have learned from history.

And don't think history is dry. Maybe some lousy teachers can desiccate history, but that takes special talent. "Story" is part of the word because that's exactly what it is, the story of people; many stories, really. Many are absolutely amazing, eye-popping stories that, if found in fiction, would be dismissed as an insult to credulity.[186] And,

---

186. How about Byzantine emperor Justinian II—after a decade of misrule, in 695, they threw him out and cut off his nose so as to bar his return. But, undeterred, Justinian went into the wilds, found a barbarian princess to marry, and raised an army of her tribesmen to retake Constantinople and his throne in 705. This "Comeback Kid" preened in the hippodrome with his foot on the necks of both his successors. But, in 711, failing to heed the lesson of his first ouster, he was deposed again. The populace, however, had learned its own lesson—this time they killed him.

whatever may be the pleasures of fiction, the stories in history are far more powerful because they are true.

Of course, some postmodernist intellectuals would dispute that statement; we have already addressed their notion that all supposed knowledge is tainted by biases and, hence, nothing can really be deemed "true." That idea is a bad one concerning science, but when it comes to history there are indeed problems. Facts are facts, but history is mainly all about how we interpret and contextualize facts, an endeavor in which prejudice and preconception do loom large. To take a simple example, the sixtieth anniversary of WWII's end spotlighted the chasm between Russian and Baltic views of the events of the 1940s. Russia thinks the Balts voluntarily joined the Soviet Union; they, in contrast, believe they were brutally subjugated. Moreover, history can even get the facts wrong—witness our previous discussion of the Sudan "pharmaceutical plant" bombing. The process by which some assumed facts get incorporated into the received version of history, while others fall by the wayside, is a very imperfect one.[187]

Where does that leave us? The answer surely is not to turn our backs on history as too fraught with uncertainty to merit study. Less information and knowledge is never preferable to having more. If history can be problematical, that means we must give it all the more attention; its importance to us is undiminished and obliges us to make the effort of grappling with its challenges. That is why historians do us a service—if history were nothing but straightforward facts, we wouldn't need historians. We read them not for facts but for understanding.

Further, here again, the mere existence of multiple viewpoints doesn't make them equally valid. There is still such a thing as objective truth. Russia's take on Baltic history is a self-serving denial of reality, and crackpot Holocaust deniers do not cloud the Holocaust's significance in the human saga. While history may get some things wrong, the bigger a story is, the more likely it is to be fundamentally true. You can

---

187. History also seems now to take as fact that Jefferson fathered children by his slave Sally Hemings. In truth, the evidence is suggestive but by no means conclusive.

quibble over details, but the larger truths about the Holocaust are undeniable; the big picture of history cannot be dismissed as bunk. And besides, history's inaccuracies or distortions are not the real problem for most people; it's that they know too little of history altogether.

The point about taking responsibility for our actions applies to nations as well as individuals. It's not just our history itself that makes us who we are; it's also how we go forward from that history. America's past is not unblemished, nor is our record of dealing with it, but, on the whole, this is an open nation willing to look critically at itself and to try to right its wrongs. Germany, too, has done a pretty admirable job of facing up to its past, and that says a lot about what kind of nation Germany is today. Japan has done somewhat less well and Russia considerably less. Meanwhile, Turkey's refusal to atone for the 1915 Armenian genocide only serves to keep the modern nation needlessly complicit in past crimes. Lady Macbeth found that no effort of scrubbing could get the blood off her hands. Just as for individuals, a nation trying to sanitize its past really only deepens the stain.

I once read a commentary saying that the Wright brothers don't mean anything to anyone anymore; they're just facts in a history book. What a pitiful idea. Every time I board an airplane, I can't help but think about that history—how for thousands of years people gazed up at birds in the sky and dreamed of flight. Even as the technological age unfolded, that dream remained elusive. The birds seemed to mock us. To make an aircraft go where you wanted was a fiendishly complex, difficult scientific and engineering challenge. It repeatedly defeated numerous efforts by the best minds, including the US government's own major project led by the head of the Smithsonian. Yet, through hard work and painstaking scientific analysis, a pair of bicycle makers from Ohio succeeded—gloriously. When their machine lifted into the air at Kitty Hawk on December 17, 1903, it was a sublime moment in human progress.

The Wright brothers are history. But history is not just dry facts and dates. It is alive in everything we experience. It is what we are made of and it is who we are.

So I don't take flying for granted; it has great meaning for me. When I sit in an airplane soaring through the sky, this is to me the epitome of our history—our rise from being the plaything of nature to controlling it. To me, December 17, 1903, is not just a date in a history book—it shines with the brilliance of a supernova. And when I look upon that first airplane, hanging from the ceiling of the Smithsonian, I venerate it as a holy object.[188]

But most people seem casually to take for granted not only flying but everything about modern life, as though everyone has always lived as we do today. They even, if anything, frequently romanticize the past as "the good old days," a nobler and more blessed time, lamenting the comparison with modernity.

No one with a firm grip on history could make that mistake.

Were some things in the past better than now? Of course. But would we really trade all we've gained to get back what we've lost? Of course not. If you think your life is hard, a visit to the past would quickly change your mind. War and violence loomed vastly larger. Life meant ceaseless grinding toil, and then you died. You had a lot of children because you knew a lot of them wouldn't survive. Women often died in childbirth, if they didn't die of exhaustion from all the washing and cleaning and cooking they did by hand. Healthcare was essentially a fiction; doctors hardly knew how to cure anything. If you had a pain, you had to live with it until it killed you. I could go on, but you get the picture. History teaches us the truth about "the good old days" and, thus, helps us see the world and our own lives in proper perspective.

History isn't even just about the past. It continues to happen every day, right before our eyes. Many people seem interested only in events in their nearby surroundings, in only what they think affects them. They're not interested in news from China, for example. But we don't live just in our neighborhoods; we live in the whole world. There is a saying (not literally true) that a butterfly flapping its wings in China

---

188. Of course, since September 11, 2001, air travel confronts us with history in a further and less uplifting way.

can cause a thunderstorm in Chicago. But events and trends in China can have a big impact on the whole world, because everything is so interconnected and interrelated.

Most folks similarly tend to regard people in faraway places as somehow less real and of lesser concern than those close to home. They don't identify with distant people and events. If, in my town of Albany, ten men were chained together and burned to death, it would be big news, to say the least; but let atrocities like this, and others, befall tens of *thousands* in Sudan (it happened in 2004), and it hardly even registers with people in Albany. They will identify with fellow local residents, as people just like them: "Gosh, that could have been me!" But they don't see Sudanese that way.[189]

Yet people are very much alike everywhere. Recall Shylock's famous speech in *The Merchant of Venice*—"If I am cut, do I not bleed?" He was talking to his own neighbors who thought Jews were somehow less human, a mistake repeated over and over throughout history and practically everywhere on Earth. Perhaps Shakespeare was way ahead of his time to glimpse the commonality of humankind four centuries ago, but there is no excuse for not understanding it today.

The more one learns about people, the more obvious it is that their similarities, all across the globe, overwhelm any differences.[190] Cultural quirks, ethnic variations, racial characteristics—these are all the merest details, while the big picture screams out alikeness. People everywhere have the same sort of consciousness. They suffer pain just as you do; they experience joy, hope, sorrow, fear, just as you do; they love their children just as you do. Their lives mean as much to them as yours means to you.

Maybe it's too much, asking people to actually empathize with

---

189. The news media is partly to blame. An event like this, in Albany, would be given a special local newspaper headline and hyperventilating TV coverage—but the Sudan situation is barely mentioned.

190. In fact, 99.9 percent of genes are identical in all humans. The attentive reader may notice that I've also emphasized how all people are different. That remains true too. People everywhere are much the same but, happily, not *exactly* the same!

everyone else. But at least let's accept that we're all equally human. Refusing to do even that, calling some group, nationality, or race "subhuman," is factually nonsense, and has led to untold horrors too well known to recount. Those who deem some other people less than human only demonstrate their own lack of humanity.

What happens to inhabitants of Sudan is just as significant as what happens to those in Albany. And, indeed, it is apt to be more dramatic. We lead very insulated, protected, and cosseted lives in America. People here might think that losing a dollar to a malfunctioning soda machine is a big injustice. Most Americans have no idea what it is like to deal with the really awful things that so many people in so many places suffer.[191] To know about such things, to understand them well and truly, once again puts your own life and problems in clearer perspective.

This all may sound like a parental "Eat your spinach because it's good for you," even though it doesn't taste good. But I don't keep informed about the world just because it's good for me. I do it because it is actually full of flavor.

Most guys follow pro sports. They devour every tidbit about the players, watch the games on the edge of their seats, and go wild if their favorite team wins a big one. Playing on your own sports team is a worthwhile activity, a meaningful part of your life—but, if you think analytically about it, whether the Dolphins win the Super Bowl can mean absolutely nothing to your life.[192] Yet so many people are mes-

---

191. This affects how people look at world issues. During the Cold War, Americans mostly tended to imagine Soviet life as somewhat different from ours to be sure, but they had scant idea how huge the difference was. Similarly, regarding Iraq, most people recognized that its dictator, Saddam Hussein, was nasty, but seemed to have no true grasp of the human suffering he caused.

192. Some sports fans may be psychologically projecting themselves into the players or teams they follow, so the teams' triumphs effectively become their own and a source of meaning in their lives—though ultimately ersatz, imaginary meaning. It is interesting that men can identify (and concern) themselves so powerfully with sports figures who are actually quite remote and different from them, but not with ordinary foreigners who, in reality, may be much more like them.

merized by such things while remaining oblivious to the genuine dramas played out on the world stage.[193]

I actually follow world events and politics like other guys follow pro sports. To me, history, as it continues to unfold every day, is the most fascinating of dramas, competitions, and soap operas. I know the players, the "teams," and their records. And, unlike the triumphs in pro sports, which are devoid of true meaning, victories and defeats on the world stage have tremendous impacts on real people—life or death impacts.

I'll never forget the August 1991 Soviet crisis. It was the cusp of history; the outcome could have gone either way. I held my breath and lapped up every news broadcast with goose bumps. And when the evil empire fell, it was like my team winning the Super Bowl, the World Series, and sweeping the Olympics, all rolled into one. That was a *real* triumph to celebrate. To this day it still makes my heart soar.

---

193. The same applies to the antics of pop culture celebrities, with zero real meaning for the lives of the people watching them. Lots of folks can name all the members of the latest hot rock band but none of the members of the US Supreme Court, whose doings are a bit more important.

Freedom of Expression

Freedom of speech was enshrined in the Constitution not only because it was considered a fundamental human right but also because it was deemed essential to the idea of self-government. If citizens are to participate in decision making, there must be free debate of all public questions. That's why the First Amendment stipulates in absolute language that "Congress shall make no law . . . abridging the freedom of speech."

It is, once more, the natural right of all people to do as they please, limited only by the need to avoid harming others; and if we restrict that freedom, there better be a strong reason that promotes the welfare of all. As we have seen in discussing individualism, a person is not the creature of society, obliged to submerge his individuality into a societal homogeneity, as bees in a beehive do. To the contrary, society and government exist to promote our self-realization. And there is nothing more salient here than freedom of expression.

A powerful thirst for self-expression seems universal in human nature. Whether it is through "open mike" poetry, karaoke, letters to the editor, creating art or music, clothing, body piercings, or even just ordinary conversation, people everywhere just love to express themselves. (That's what I'm doing in this book!)

Because it is thus so fundamental to the primacy of the individual, freedom of expression should command great deference, with any restrictions upon it facing a particularly high hurdle. The First Amendment does make freedom of speech absolute. And surely your right to do as you please means *saying* what you please, so long as you harm no one.

Now, you could harm another with libel or slander. Of course, this is an obvious exception to absoluteness of freedom of speech, which the law recognizes and fully and properly addresses. The courts have also sensibly made an exception for some types of "action speech," like Justice Oliver Wendell Holmes's oft-cited example of shouting "Fire!" in a crowded theater. So far, so good. The only other possible way speech could harm people is by *offending* them. And here's where many of us have a problem with free speech.

First of all, it is impossible to draw bright lines between offensive and nonoffensive speech, because everybody has different ideas, and a consensus today may change tomorrow. This is a classic "slippery slope." Good people may agree that the word "nigger" is offensive, but if today it is prohibited, then tomorrow someone will demand banning some other word, and pretty soon freedom of speech is out the window. If inoffensiveness is deemed a requisite for free expression, then free expression is meaningless, because almost any expression is bound to offend *someone*.

And second, if offending someone is the price for free expression, then it is a price well worth paying. It is vastly more important to have a society with freedom of speech than one where no one is offended. American values are threatened far more by undermining the First Amendment than by the most offensive statements. The proper response is not to ban them but to answer them. As Jefferson said, "Error of opinion may be tolerated where reason is left free to combat it." That kind of open debate is, again, the objective underlying the First Amendment. We want people to be able to express themselves freely. A requirement that no one ever be offended must make for a bland, sterile, and pallid landscape of expression.

This doesn't mean it's perfectly okay to say "nigger." Of course it's not; that isn't the point. We should always try to avoid offensiveness. Civility is important. But what we shouldn't do is tell anyone, "You're not allowed to say that." The proper response instead is, "You're wrong, and here's why."

This is also another aspect of the democratic tolerance discussed before—of "live and let live" social contract reciprocity. If you want to live in an open society where you can express yourself freely, then you must reciprocally accept the other fellow's right to do likewise, even if what he says offends you. You can criticize him, but you can't demand his persecution or suppression.

Further, concerning this bugaboo of offensive speech, there is wisdom in the ancient children's ditty, "Sticks and stones will break my bones but words can never hurt me." Remember our discussion about the fallacy of caring how strangers see us. If someone labels me a "kike" that is his problem, not mine; it needn't affect me. I can, and should, shrug my shoulders and ignore it. The same goes for all racial or ethnic slurs and other forms of disrespect. As Eleanor Roosevelt said, "No one can make you feel inferior without your consent." Our hand-wringing over this whole realm of offensiveness is way overblown.[194]

In fact, sometimes being offended can be good for you. Recently, a local history teacher asked her class to devise arguments supporting Hitler and Stalin; a big hoo-ha erupted over the "offensiveness" of this and how (the horror!) it made students "uncomfortable." Well, encountering an idea that makes you uncomfortable, that challenges your thinking, can open up your mind and be a positive step toward greater wisdom. If that teacher got her students pondering in new ways about Hitler and the lessons of Nazi history, they were better for it— even if they were offended.

In 2006, Muslim countries had violent riots over a Danish newspaper cartoon deemed offensive to their faith—obeisance to which they insisted should trump press freedom. David Brooks commented that "we don't just have different ideas; we have a different relation-

---

194. Some people elevate the taking of offense into a performance art. Nothing delights them more than to encounter something offensive, to serve as a launching pad for their high dudgeon act.

ship to ideas"; as heirs of Socrates and the agora, Westerners inhabit a bustling marketplace of ideas and are generally accepting of its untidiness. From that cacophony, we recognize that greater understanding can emerge. We *allow* ourselves to be offended. That intellectual openness is integral to the vibrancy and dynamism of Western culture—and its lack is a key failing in the Muslim world.

We often hear that freedom of speech is under assault in post-9/11 America. The very frequency with which this complaint is aired belies it. Some on the Left seem to have a persecution and martyrdom complex. This, and their disaffection toward America, always seeking cudgels to beat it with, leads them to actually cherish the idea that their freedom of expression is somehow being stifled—an idea that America permits them to shout from the rooftops. It is a little weird to hear people endlessly speaking out about how they can't speak out.[195] Of course, the truth is that America unstintingly provides megaphones for even the most nonmainstream viewpoints.

But the one place where free expression really is being stifled is the one place where you might least expect it—in colleges and universities. At one time, their insularity against outside pressures—the "ivory tower"—served to protect free inquiry, thought, and expression; but more recently it's been the opposite. To be sure, there is much prating on campus about free speech and academic freedom, but many of the prattlers seem to believe in freedom only for themselves and their ideas. They harp upon "diversity," but definitely don't mean the kind of diversity that matters most: diversity of opinion.

"Political correctness" is the term for this mind-set, dominant in university faculties and before which our whole society cowers. The term may have originated as semisardonic "communist chic," evoking Soviet politics under Lenin and Stalin, where the penalty for a political "mistake" could be death. Political correctness exalts race, gender, and class

---

195. They are also especially fond of complaining against being labeled "unpatriotic" for their views. One hears this complaint about a thousand times more often than one ever hears anyone actually being called unpatriotic.

as the touchstones of politics and uses them to indict American society. I find this mostly wrong and pernicious, but truly believing in freedom of expression, I wouldn't stop these people spouting their views. But the politically correct, in contrast, tend to be highly intolerant of diverging viewpoints. They hold sacrosanct their right of "dissent" but not dissent from their dissent. While academic freedom is invoked to protect the Left's attack dogs, any critique of them, in an Orwellian twist, is deemed to be an assault on academic freedom, even McCarthyism,[196] which can get you drummed out of the university. Many on the Left simply refuse to allow their dogmas to be debated, responding with hysterical indignation to any such challenge. In this they are, indeed, the intellectual heirs of Lenin and Stalin, and of the Inquisition, whose answer to religious dissenters was to burn them alive.[197]

Many campuses have actually adopted "speech codes," banning utterances deemed offensive,[198] with students subject to discipline, even expulsion, for things they say.[199] Transgressors against this

---

196. Senator Joseph McCarthy, in the early 1950s, crusaded against supposed communist influence in government and elsewhere. "McCarthyism" has come to mean persecuting people for their political beliefs. Those on the Left, when criticized, are quick to squeal "McCarthyism." They are also highly adept at practicing it themselves.

197. We've already noted the firestorm when Harvard's president queried whether engineering and science aptitudes might differ between genders. For raising this obviously valid but politically incorrect question, he was not executed, but he ultimately resigned after the Harvard faculty voted for his ouster. And its members still talk with a straight face about "academic freedom" and denounce "censorship."

198. After numerous court decisions holding such rules to violate the First Amendment, academia now often labels them "harassment codes." But they're still really censoring free speech. (These trends are documented in *The Shadow University*, by Alan Charles Kors and Harvey A. Silverglate.)

199. In one prominent case, a student kept awake by (black) late-night carousers outside his window called them "water buffalo." He, not the noisemakers, was brought up on charges. A big debate ensued over whether "water buffalo" was offensive from a racial standpoint in violation of the university's speech code. Lewis Carroll did not make this story up.

thought control are typically forced to undergo "sensitivity training"—eerily reminiscent of communist "reeducation" (brainwashing) camps. The University of Maryland prohibited "distribution of written or graphic materials that are derogatory." Derogatory? Of *anything*? John Stossel points out that his own book would run afoul of that rule—as would much of the world's great literature. And the university also banned "sexual looks, such as leering and ogling, licking lips or teeth," and "holding or eating food provocatively."

What kind of bland dehumanized robots is this university trying to create? The rationale is that nobody should have to confront anything they're not comfortable with. Of course, that's a recipe for intellectual sterility—entirely the opposite of what a university is supposed to be all about.

But freedom of speech does not mean freedom from the consequences of your speech. You can say anything you like, but the next fellow has the right to say you are a darn fool. Such back-and-forth, such criticism, is integral to the public debate the First Amendment was intended to foster. If you take part in public debate, you must accept that others may criticize what you say.

In the McCarthy era, some people were not only criticized for pro-communist politics, they even lost their jobs; many in Hollywood were blacklisted by the studios. They are widely lionized today as heroic victims. But even if they had a right to be communists—their freedom of speech and thought—does anyone have a right to be both communist and employed in Hollywood? And does academic freedom mean a professor cannot be fired no matter what vile rubbish he spews to his students?

These are not simple issues. But I would suggest that university speech codes and Hollywood blacklisting are not analogous. The difference is between the public and private spheres. The First Amendment bars *government* from punishing you for what you say. A university acts analogously if it punishes a student for something he says—he is subject to its authority just as a citizen is subject to government's authority—and in neither case is it okay to punish speech. But outside the exercise of such governmental or government-like authority, people should be free to act toward you as they see fit. So a university should not be allowed to expel a student for saying "nigger," but a club to which he belongs may do so. And the Hollywood studios had every right to refuse to employ communists.

Another point is that freedom of expression does not mean the right to an audience. The word "censorship" is much misused. "Censorship" means preventing or punishing something being said or printed. Of course, we don't have that in America.[200] Yet the word is thrown around all the time. If a library decides not to put a certain book on its shelves, or to remove one, people will cry "censorship!" as though the author's freedom of expression includes the right to have the library buy his book and put it on the shelf. Well, of course it doesn't. You can print anything you want, but you can't make people read it; you can say what you want, but you can't make anyone listen.

---

200. With some very limited exceptions, of course (child pornography, for example).

Race

The first thing to be said is that "race" is, objectively, almost a meaningless word.

From the standpoint of biology, there is only one human race, all the same, or at least as much the same as any large set of creatures can be. The variability of genes and physical characteristics between one "race" and another is smaller than that *within* each "race." If you compare yourself against a "white" and a "black," chosen at random, you are likely to be no more different from one than the other; a white may even be more similar to the black than to the other white. Thus, the concept of "race" entails no meaningful differences among human beings; it is essentially a social construct, devoid of scientific significance.

Many past researchers tried to link characteristics and accomplishments of different societies and ethnicities to genetic differences in an effort to prove that some are biologically more advanced than others. They measured brain sizes, assessed IQs, analyzed physiological features, and endlessly so forth. Today we know that all such notions of racial superiority are bosh. There are no material genetic or biological differences among races. None.[201]

So how, then, can we explain the varying fortunes attained by dif-

---

201. See Stephen Jay Gould's *The Mismeasure of Man*.

ferent segments of humanity? Jared Diamond's book *Guns, Germs and Steel* persuasively finds the answer in accidents of geography, in the cards that different peoples were originally dealt: availability of native plants for cultivation, availability of animals suitable for domestication, differences of climate, and even geographical features (affecting the spread of ideas and innovation). Factors like these gave some cultures a crucial head start, with complex knock-on effects that have reverberated through all subsequent history. That—not biological inferiority— explains why some societies fell behind, why Africans were enslaved and colonized by Europeans and not the other way around.

This doesn't deny that there are regional physiological variations among people, that Africans tend to look different from Italians in certain predictable details such as skin tone, facial construction, hair type, and so on. But these are details, and only details. The points of similarity overwhelm them; and so insignificant are the differences that you are liable to find greater differences among Italians than between an Italian and an African. This is not obvious only because we tend to look past the *kinds* of differences that exist among Italians, when we lump them all together as Italians; whereas we tend, contrariwise, to *focus* upon those particular kinds of differences that distinguish one race from another. We do this strictly as a product of culture and not because the features we focus on are objectively any more important than those we ignore.

For example, being attuned to skin color, we might differentiate an African from an Italian based on a color difference that is quite slight; in fact, many Italians are actually darker than some Africans—in which case we look at other details to make the "diagnosis." Yet one Italian might be three times the size of another—obviously, a far more dramatic physical difference—but this we choose to overlook when we put them into the same ethnic category. Furthermore, the waters are greatly muddied by racial mixing, especially in the United States, where virtually all African Americans have some non-African ancestors, and, in many cases, the physical earmarks of African descent have nearly been blended away.

Still, differences among races are, of course, not random, as size differences (generally) are. If it were just a question of skin color and nothing else, we might never have gotten ensnarled in the briar patch of race. But different races have different histories, the story of their interrelationships is very fraught, and the existence of visible markers to differentiate among races complicates untangling it all. Those physical differences serve to perpetuate the historical and relational differences. In ancient times, slaves and their enslavers were often enthnically indistinguishable, so that once a person was freed, the social baggage of having been a slave would evaporate pretty readily, certainly within a generation or two. But here we are in America, a century and a half after slavery ended, still engaged in cleaning up the mess it left.

However, those who say that little has really changed and that America remains deeply racist are totally mistaken. This has already been discussed. But let's take a moment to actually define racism. It's a belief that blacks are inferior, less fully human, less moral, dirty, and contact with them contaminates whites. Thus, they should be disliked, disrespected, shunned, segregated, and denied equal rights. If all this sounds ridiculous to us, that only goes to show how far we've advanced, because this was, in fact, the face of racism, the common viewpoint of most white people, not just in the South but everywhere, not so many decades ago.

It's true that some people still spout doctrines of white supremacy (the stupidity of which actually proves how nonsuperior they are). But this vestigial racism is mostly confined to whites in disadvantaged circumstances who are relatively powerless—which is, indeed, a wellspring of their racial antagonism. And, in fact, such people don't matter. They have scant influence upon the larger society and no real effect upon the lives of most black people. Their racism amounts to mere fleabites that blacks can ignore.

Meantime, the great majority of whites have not only moved beyond the crude racism described above but have also accepted both that blacks are equal and that they are entitled to equal treatment. This is not to say that most whites have totally cleansed their minds of negative thinking toward blacks. Relations between the races still remain complex, fraught, and heavily burdened by history. But most whites now understand that racism is wrong, and when they do find their thoughts veering in that direction, they feel shame and remorse.

Furthermore, the *institutional* racism that one still hears so much about is largely a figment of the imagination. In today's climate, no important American institution could get away with racist conduct—not with such pervasive scrutiny targeting this subject and the inevitability of bad publicity and lawsuits at the least whiff of discrimination. In fact, today's operative institutional bias is affirmative action—reverse racism in *favor* of blacks.

Some would answer that all this overlooks the plight of the black underclass, its economic troubles, its members being jailed in much greater proportional numbers than whites, and so on. The black underclass does have a rough situation. But the key word is not "black" but "underclass." The problem confronting the black underclass today is not race and racism; it is, instead, the panoply of social pathologies associated with its economic and cultural circumstances. True, past racism had a lot to do with putting them in that predicament—but it's not racism today that's keeping them in it.

And yet, of course, we still do have a race relations problem. Half a century ago, the problem's core concerned white attitudes toward blacks; that problem has been largely solved and the core of the problem remaining today is actually the attitude of blacks toward whites. The truth is that most whites don't think all that much about blacks and the race issue and don't have much antipathy toward blacks—whereas many blacks are almost obsessed with the subject and have considerable antipathy toward whites.[202]

---

202. Thus, Debra Dickerson's book *The End of Blackness*, even while urging blacks to let go of their old racial grievances, still vents at great length the author's own bitterness over them.

That blacks and whites see the world very differently was also manifest in reactions to the O. J. Simpson acquittal. Most blacks believed Simpson was innocent and rejoiced at the verdict; whites overwhelmingly thought him guilty and considered the verdict a travesty.

Whites cannot fix this. They have done pretty much all that could reasonably be asked to make amends for past wrongs and, at this point, there is little more of significance that whites can be expected to do to ameliorate race relations. The ball is in the hands of blacks and fixing the rest of the problem must come from them. The white community has reconciled itself to living with blacks; it is the black community that seems to have trouble reconciling itself.

That said, whites should certainly continue trying to help black people with that reconciliation. This means not rising to the bait of the racism hustlers. This means keeping extended the hand that has been extended toward black people. This means affirmative action on the personal level; that is, to always be sure to interact with blacks in a way that acknowledges their humanity and our human bond.

But what it does not mean is the formal, institutional affirmative action programs that cause so much controversy. These are schemes where, for example, black (or other "minority") applicants for a job or school admission are favored over equally (or even better) qualified whites. This is cast as necessary to right past wrongs and ensure that minorities are fairly represented in universities, workforces, and so forth. But officially categorizing people by race and treating them differently based on it is wrong, counterproductive, and most definitely not the way to bridge the racial divide.

The introductory points here are particularly pertinent. We have a problem with race, in major part, because we insist on making race so visible; we focus on differences among races in spite of their objective biological meaninglessness. The ancients could erase the social effects of slave status quickly because slave background was not visible. We keep our eyes focused on it, almost like we're picking at a scab we won't let heal. Anything that intensifies this focus upon racial differences is the wrong way to go. Instead, we should be trying to *de-emphasize* such differences.

"Race" in this context is, again, really a proxy for ancestral and cultural history. We focus on it not because we think that skin color per se is important but, rather, because we think it tells us something about the person. We can't forget that blacks were once slaves and victims. And of course history is important to understand how we came to be where we are today. But that does not mean such history defines an individual. The politically correct *do* consider race and ancestral history central to defining individuals. To such a mind-set, that a person is black, descended from slaves, is his defining characteristic; indeed, he is still a slave—a slave to that past.

That is totally contrary to how I see the human condition. I believe all people make their own lives and stand on their own merits; the meaning of their lives flows from what they do and who they are, what is in their brains and in their hearts—not what happened to their ancestors generations ago. Every human being is an individual—free to make of his life whatever he will—not defined by an ancestral history over which he has no control and which need have no bearing on his own life except insofar as he himself chooses.

During the civil rights movement of the 1950s and 1960s, the goal was integration, the breaking down of barriers between races to achieve equality and a color-blind society where, as Martin Luther King said, people are judged on character and not skin color. This was wholly in keeping with America's founding ideals and most people could, with fundamental decency and goodwill, embrace it. Because this idea was so compellingly right, it enjoyed broad support and, consequently, was actually achieved to an extent that once seemed inconceivable.

But then we went off the rails. The voices preaching integration and color blindness were drowned out by more strident voices urging seemingly more advanced and radical notions, with color blindness abjured in favor of color chauvinism. And so we come to affirmative action, the antithesis of color blindness. Instead of looking at people as individuals based on character and merit, they are once more to be defined by race. And in place of equality, treating all people alike, they are once more treated differently by race.

When government and societal institutions engage in that kind of racial classification and discrimination, it is really the same wrong that the old segregationist "Jim Crow" regime committed. It violates the ideals of our open democratic society founded upon equality before the law and individual dignity.

Affirmative action is, nevertheless, defended as recompense for past wrongs. If I harm you, I should compensate you. But affirmative action gives the compensation to individuals who were never themselves injured, at the expense of others who harmed no one. That simply is not justice. And in the eyes of many (if not most) whites, no arguments for affirmative action can overcome this fundamental objection and justify the inequality and reverse discrimination. Whereas the original civil rights goals had such clear moral force that they compelled support by most whites, the opposite is true of affirmative action. It generates resentment and hostility. Instead of helping to bridge the racial divide, affirmative action aggravates it.

It also, by giving jobs or university slots to some underqualified blacks, sets up many of them for failure, which, regrettably, helps keep alive old racist stereotypes of black inferiority. Meantime, the genuine achievement of able blacks is rendered suspect by the idea that they got where they did not by merit but by reverse discrimination. None of this serves the much-invoked goal of university and workforce diversity in a healthy or positive way. It doesn't improve our society. The better path is, again, color blindness—making sure we remove barriers that keep people from rising by character and talent.

Furthermore, affirmative action might make some sense were it helping disadvantaged blacks vis-à-vis privileged whites. But too often it actually puts a middle-class black ahead of a poor white. Meantime, not blacks but Latinos are now America's largest minority; and intermixing is blurring all such categories. The notion of trying to sort all this out to somehow assist the "right" individuals grows increasingly bizarre.

Affirmative action is part of a broader retreat from the old integrationist ideal. Separateness is now in vogue. Where people once fought with great courage to integrate our universities, now black students demand resegregation into their own dorms. And we are redrawing political maps to create "majority minority districts" (i.e., herding black voters together).²⁰³ The assumptions are that white public officials can't properly represent black constituents, whites won't vote for black candidates, and blacks wouldn't vote for whites. History provides plenty of contrary examples but, in any case, these assumptions are profoundly insulting to blacks and whites alike. Instead of promoting desirable social cohesion, they promote social divisiveness.

Another aspect is the politics of racial grievance and victimhood. There is a class of black political operators and polemicists whose stock in trade is to exacerbate racial resentment.²⁰⁴ Their every other word is "racism." Blacks, instead of being encouraged to positive action to overcome problems of poverty or educational underperformance, are told to blame racism and to see themselves as aggrieved victims. This shifts their focus from things they can fix to something beyond their control as the imagined cause of their troubles. It is a disempowering message.²⁰⁵

But, in spite of everything, it is remarkable how much amity actually prevails among races in America. Racial antagonism may lurk below the surface but we do extremely well in keeping it down there. While some blacks claim to experience constant racist slights, Dr. John McWhorter, a leading black scholar, reports that he actually encounters such treatment quite rarely. He believes those others demonstrate a victimhood mentality—if you view the world through

---

203. The old word for this was "ghetto," connoting blacks being confined within boundaries. (The original ghettoes were European neighborhoods in which Jews were literally confined.)

204. This is exemplified by the movement seeking "reparations," cash payments to blacks to compensate for the injury of slavery; never mind that no living black was ever a slave, or that six hundred thousand whites died in the war to free the slaves.

205. There is also a political dimension here. The Democratic Party is crucially dependent on black votes. The politics of victimhood, and of looking to government for relief, fits with that party's ethos and serves to maintain black loyalty to it. But meantime, slavish support by blacks relieves the Democratic Party of actually having to earn it, and thereby actually disserves black interests.

lenses totally colored by an obsession about racism, you will see a racist world. Meantime, I am gratifyingly surprised at how often black strangers give me a smile. Maybe they're just amused by my fuzzy beard. But, seriously, the racial harmony we do have must not be taken for granted. Such a condition is the exception rather than the rule in human affairs. Even after living together for generations, tribes have often gone at each other's throats. I myself exist because this happened in Germany, where Jews had long lived as normal people, part of society, and then were rounded up and slaughtered. And in Bosnia, Kosovo, Nigeria, Gujarat, Rwanda, Indonesia—the list is endless—ethnic conflict has broken out far too often to imagine it can never happen here, that America is somehow uniquely exempt. We divide ourselves by race at our peril. Any program or policy that classifies people by race is playing with fire.[206]

So, what is to be done? Let me acknowledge the difficulty of a white person (comfortably affluent at that) telling blacks what to do. I understand that the powerful resentments many blacks hold against whites are not baseless. But for blacks to let these resentments over the past control their future is self-defeating. As in so many spheres (Israel and Palestine, for example), difficult though it may be, people's true self-interests are served if they overcome resentments and grievances and deal with each other, going forward, on a basis of goodwill and in recognition of their common humanity. I believe, again, that white America has gone as far in this direction as it is reasonable to expect (if anything, too far, with affirmative action). White America has held out its hand of reconciliation to black America. But black America has yet to firmly clasp that hand.

I have recognized, too, that some whites still hate blacks. But

---

206. As already acknowledged, some racial hatred certainly does persist in America. And every society, it seems, harbors alienated misanthropes who will act out their aggressions if given an opening. Thus, the likes of Hitler, Pol Pot, or Milosevic never have trouble recruiting them for atrocious deeds. Such miscreants already figure in our own history of barbaric lynchings. We must not let slip the cork on the bottle of poisonous racial antagonism.

blacks need to ignore these fleabites and see the big picture that white America, as a society, has rejected that kind of racism and condemns it. Indeed, that word "racism" should be given a rest and banned from the conversation because, in a sense, it is as offensive as the word "nigger"—because black people now are harmed not so much by racism as by the *idea*, in their own minds and psyches, that they are harmed by racism. It's a pernicious idea. Someone who sees himself primarily as a victim is not apt to achieve as happy a life as one who correctly perceives that racism does *not* actually harm him, that most white people are *not* against him, and that his fate is dependent, instead, upon his own efforts and character.

That's personal responsibility. It means that you're the captain of your own vessel and its course is up to you. Nowhere has that ever been more true than in today's America, and it's as true for blacks as for whites. Their destinies are in their own hands. Blacks who get an education, who learn to speak and think and present themselves well, who follow the rules and work hard, and who honor their family responsibilities will likely enjoy rewarding lives. A black who does none of those things will not; and there isn't much whites (or government programs) can do to alter that reality. It's up to blacks themselves.

A key issue for black America is absence of fathers. While the efforts of single mothers deserve respect, their children do miss half the adult support two-parent families provide. Two-thirds of black births are outside marriage. True, many black men are unavailable because they're in prison, but that accounts for only a fraction of the two-thirds. Mainly we have a self-perpetuating cycle, with boys lacking fatherly role models being unlikely to assume that role themselves. And racism cannot be blamed because black fatherlessness has soared in recent decades even as discrimination has plummeted. This, too, is primarily a problem blacks themselves must confront and grapple with.

It tells us something that black *immigrants* to America do better economically, on average, than native-born blacks. Immigrants don't come here to whine about racism; they come to work to improve their lives. They understand that the economic opportunities in America, for anyone willing to grasp them, far outweigh any lingering vestiges of racism. They do not expect to be held back by racism and they are not held back. The lesson for all Americans is obvious.

But positive messages may be getting heard within the black community. Bill Cosby, for example, has given some tough speeches (deplored by activist race hustlers) urging blacks to turn the mirror on themselves and tackle directly their problems of illiteracy, teen pregnancy, broken families, and so on, instead of blaming whites. Columnist William Raspberry, noting a 2005 Urban League report showing that a fourth of American blacks remain poor, queried how come, if racism is the problem, three-fourths *escaped* poverty into what the Urban League itself said is a "larger, stronger black middle class." Raspberry added that, instead of focusing "on what white people have done (or failed to do), wouldn't it be interesting to examine what the members of that growing black middle class have done and are doing?" And Debra Dickerson's *The End of Blackness* makes many points similar to my own.

We have long wandered in the desert. But we can see the promised land ahead, and we can reach it.

Pro-Life and Pro-Choice

Ancient Sparta had a simple answer for unwanted children. At birth all babies were judged for fitness. Those not passing were put out on a mountaintop to die.

My college embryology class studied fertilized chicken eggs. We started with day-old eggs, which, when opened, looked just like those we eat. Indeed, we made omelettes of them with no twinge of remorse. But as we worked sequentially through the eggs, we soon found a tiny blob of protoplasm and then a beating heart and, at the end, a fully formed chick, wrigglingly alive.

I remember no fine points of embryology from that course four decades past. But the lesson that does remain vivid to me is how differently we students felt about the starting and ending eggs. The first, when opened, put mere goop in our hands; the last ones, sentient living creatures. At what point, exactly, could we say the changeover had occurred? We couldn't. It was impossible to point to any stage of the process and declare that *here* life began.

But this debate in America—centered upon abortion, but spilling beyond—is dominated by zealots who believe themselves in possession of absolute moral truth. And they feel that to yield even an inch, no matter how reasonable it might seem, opens the door to the abyss. So pro-choice extremists refuse to accept any restrictions whatsoever on the right to abort, not even parental notification requirements for underage girls or banning dismemberment of fully developed infants. They reject anything that even hints at discouraging abortion. Extreme pro-lifers refuse to accept that any circumstances might justify ending a pregnancy, not even in cases of rape, or deformed fetuses, or where the mother's health is threatened; and they oppose medical use of laboratory embryos that otherwise would be thrown away, even if it holds great promise to aid living human beings.

Both sides frame these issues in the starkest moral terms. Yet, if ever there was a tough moral dilemma, a zone not black or white but gray, it is here.

The pro-life side is right that a human fetus is a living being entitled to society's protection. While their opponents argue against according personhood to fetuses, based on their maternal dependency and lack of various functional characteristics, in fact, a newborn child is likewise functionally limited and utterly dependent on parental care. So whether an infant is inside or outside the womb really makes scant substantive difference. Furthermore, we recognize the personhood rights of impaired adults who sometimes actually lack the functional capabilities of a late-term fetus; we'd be horrified at killing such people just because their existence is inconvenient. The idea that society can decide who is or isn't fully human, allowing some to be dispensed with, has led to monstrous consequences, as we all know.

Nowadays, a five-month prematurely born infant can (with a little help) live and grow to adulthood. Given that fact, it's not a stretch to call the destruction of such a five-month infant murder. A person who smothered that baby in the incubator would be punished. Yet, we permit babies like that, and even older, to be killed in abortions. How different is that from Spartan practice?[207]

---

207. Simply removing an early term fetus from the womb insures immediate death; but, for a viable fetus, separating it from the mother isn't enough. Further action must be taken to stop its wriggling and screaming. In other words, it must be killed.

It is no surprise that we have pangs of conscience over abortions and that a woman who aborts a child is often haunted by it for the rest of her life. Certainly, women should not be encouraged to imagine that abortion is just another antiseptic medical procedure.

To hold that life begins at conception has some undeniable logic. Conception sets the process in motion and sets the genetic blueprint for the person-to-be. While conception is thus a definitive moment, there is no other such moment between conception and birth, as my college egg study demonstrated. After conception, development is seamlessly gradual.

Yet there is a difference between a human life and what merely has the potential to become one. It's true that a fertilized egg has all the information to make a person. A blueprint has all the information to build a house. We understand that burning blueprints is not the same as burning down a house.[208] While it is impossible to pinpoint just when during fetal development the potentiality jells into an actuality, we must recognize that the end product differs crucially from what existed at the beginning. In the midst of the process, there are no clear demarcation points; yet, between start and finish, there is not just a difference of degree but also a difference of kind.

That difference makes for different moral standings and should change abortion's acceptability over the nine months. To kill a seven-month fetus is to kill something quite human, a real baby, and is very hard to justify. That fetus weighs heavier on the moral scale than one at two months with no self-awareness or viability outside the womb, and, in balancing the latter's rights against those of the mother, it may be reasonable to allow ending an early pregnancy if there are sufficient reasons.

But, even if you disagree and insist that the potentiality for human life embodied in a microscopic embryo inside a womb somehow deserves as much respect as a grown person, with as much right to live, you really cannot hold likewise about an embryo in a petri dish produced by in vitro fertilization. Thus, the argument that an embryo

---

208. This analogy is admittedly imperfect; an embryo is a dynamic living thing, whereas a blueprint cannot *become* a house.

is potential life is a double-edged sword. If in the uterus, the embryo is a human being in gestation, in a petri dish or test tube it is not. This is because it cannot continue to develop unless someone chooses to implant it in a woman's womb. Yet even this some extremists seek to treat as equivalent to human life.

Hence, they oppose all medical use of human embryos, even ones created in the laboratory with no intent ever to implant them—so that even their character as inchoate life is entirely theoretical. How can an embryo be considered a potential life when the probability of its becoming a person is never above zero? And some pro-lifers not only object to creating such embryos in the laboratory for medical use, they even oppose using embryos already made during fertility procedures—embryos that would otherwise simply be thrown away.

Whether or not you believe an embryo is a life, the act of reproduction, creating it in a woman's womb—the nearest thing to a miracle in our experience—must be held in reverence. But an embryo created artificially in a lab for wholly different purposes is not at all the same thing. Though it should be treated respectfully as something meaningful and precious, it should not inspire the same considerations as for one growing in a uterus. While we shouldn't handle it frivolously or wantonly, to use such an embryo in legitimate scientific research or in treating disease entails sufficient seriousness of purpose to overcome ethical misgivings.

Such medical use of embryos holds great promise for combating illnesses that are a scourge of humanity. No serious scientific researcher proposes to clone complete human beings, the bugaboo of cloning's opponents. Nor is anyone "creating life to destroy it," as some have argued. But cloning and other techniques could potentially produce embryonic stem cells that can, for example, give someone a bone marrow transplant compatible with his own tissue—thereby saving his life. That's the kind of thing we're really talking about here; if it is creating life, then it's doing so not to destroy but to save lives and promote life. And if thusly harvesting stem cells from embryos or therapeutic cloning is "playing God" or "tampering with nature," so is a heart transplant and so is most of modern medicine. We recognize the moral acceptability of harvesting organs from the dead. In this way, the nonliving help the living. The same should apply to taking stem cells from an embryo that never was and never will be a person: the nonliving help the living. That doesn't disrespect life, but honors it.

Living people with terrible diseases wait, suffer, and die because of misplaced moral cavils about specks of protoplasm that can never live at all. Extremists would apparently rather see embryos thrown away than used to cure disease and help people. How is this pro-life?[209]

The pro-choice side is right that a woman is entitled to control over her reproductive fate. She is not a baby-making machine but a human being with her own needs, interests, and desires and a right to govern her own life in accordance with them. Nothing is more fundamental in the realm of human rights than such biological autonomy. Inability to limit the number of her children was, from time immemorial, a bane of women's existence, a cause of impoverishment, exhaustion, and early death. Other reasons for abortions, at least arguably defensible, include cases of rape or incest, babies with serious developmental problems, and where completing a pregnancy could be physically injurious to the mother. Anyhow, it's an unalterable reality that women will sometimes be driven to abortion. If there is no legal option, the alternatives are nasty, often unaffordable, and certainly very dangerous. Thus, once more, when balancing the rights and needs of a living, breathing woman against those of an embryo not yet grown to personhood, it may, in some circumstances, be reasonable to sacrifice the latter for the sake of the former by allowing abortion.

All this is true. Yet it's too simplistic to preach a "woman's right to choose what to do with her own body." We're never wholly free to do as we please with our bodies. In the classical formulation, my right to swing

---

209. The moral fervor lavished upon such embryos seems further misdirected considering that millions of dying children in poor countries could be saved at modest cost; with those lives (and so many others), the "pro-life" movement does not seem to concern itself.

my fist ends at your nose.[210] Conceiving a child brings another "nose" into the picture and responsibility for someone other than oneself. It's no longer just the woman's body. We can, again, debate endlessly over just when life really begins but, at some point, an embryo does become a child, and surely no parent has a "right to choose" to end a child's life.

It has also been argued (e.g., by abortion defender Judith Thomson) that even if a fetus does have a right to life, it doesn't have a right against the woman to provide use of her body to sustain it. This gets back to the idea we've discussed that one is not obligated to be a good Samaritan; hence, the woman would have no duty to go out of her way to help the fetus. But if, indeed, one has no obligation to strangers, we are talking here about the child's *mother*; and certainly our society recognizes, as fundamental and natural, a parent's duty to support her offspring. Parents are prosecuted for child neglect.

Pro-abortion arguments invoking bodily rights and lack of duty might make more sense if pregnancy were some random thing that befalls women. Of course, that's not the case; and the time for a woman to choose what happens to and in her body is when she's having sex. Once she is pregnant, this is a consequence of her own actions, not some sort of servitude society arbitrarily imposes on her.

We have previously addressed personal responsibility, the need to face up to the consequences of one's actions. Creating a human life is a highly consequential action, taking upon oneself the gravest responsibility. Society should not condone people shucking this responsibility at will, destroying the life they've created, for any but the most serious considerations. And, in truth, too many abortions occur because the parent or parents simply feel unprepared to raise a child or just don't care to.[211]

---

210. Women's bodily autonomy is also analogized to property rights; but here again, while you have rights over your property, this doesn't mean you may kill innocent people you happen to find there.

211. While "health of the mother" figures large in abortion polemics, this is really something of a red herring because, given modern medical techniques, it is now very rare for a pregnancy to physically endanger a mother.

Of course, getting into such a fix is usually a result of irresponsibility to begin with. Today, contraception is widely available. There is scant excuse for engaging in unprotected sex with no willingness to be responsible for the child that may result. Condoms, diaphragms, or birth control pills are appropriate family planning tools.[212] Abortion, barring exceptional circumstances, should not be one.

Our discussion has suggested that it may be acceptable to allow some early term abortions, where the fetus is more like a blob than a baby, but rarely late abortions where "baby killing" is no misnomer. In the latter situation it may be fair to ask, "why did you wait?" Given that an abortion is less morally repugnant the earlier it occurs, it is a further form of irresponsibility to procrastinate. How tolerant should society be toward a person who conceived an unwanted child, then waited long enough for it to become a real child, and now wants to kill it? Or should we be really liberal, go the Spartans one better, and allow parents to kill unwanted children at any stage of development—say, up to age eighteen?

Of course, the Spartan approach is not the only option for dealing with unwanted children. And while it is certainly better for a child to be wanted, shall we assume the godlike omniscience of deciding that a child is better off not living at all than living unwanted? In our humane non-Spartan society, many cast-off children, even "defective" ones, find loving adoptive parents and live rewarding lives. If people irresponsibly conceive an unwanted child, maybe they should not be forced to raise it, but perhaps it is reasonable to at least require the woman to accept some of the responsibility by carrying that child through to birth so that it may have a life. Such a burden upon a woman is certainly outweighed and justified by the benefit to the child (and to its potential adoptive parents). In a society that values every human life, the adoption option should, wherever possible, be preferred to abortion.

---

212. But they are not infallible; and, because even protected sex can occasionally result in conception, one should not engage in this behavior without considering the potential responsibility for a child.

*   *   *

Everything in this book is an affirmation of the worth of human life. Promoting life is central to any morality. And consonant with that is giving every person the widest possible choices in life, including a woman's right to choose her reproductive fate. Now we see how these two fundamental values of life and choice can clash. We must strive to reconcile them. We must recognize that neither value can hold unbridled sway, that application of each must be tempered by application of the other.

Be pro-life *and* pro-choice.

Animal Rights

After critiquing government-created rights not just for animals but for many humans, it may seem odd to now present this chapter about animal rights. Yet, regardless of whether government should legislate about it, the matter has to be taken seriously because our interactions with other creatures are a big part of what happens on this planet, and it is indeed a significant moral issue. Some vegetarians consider it wrong to eat meat. If you don't agree, you should at least have a thought as to why. Are we entitled to make other creatures suffer and die for human benefit?

Any reason-based morality must, once more, be grounded in the fundamental facts of existence. And nothing is more fundamental to nature's reality than the food chain. Evolution populated the world with things that live by converting matter to energy (it is hard to imagine any alternative) and the almost universal source of such matter to convert (i.e., food) is other living things. Some creatures eat plants, but nature is not fastidious and her guiding principle is "whatever works." If what works best for one animal is to eat another, then so be it, with no qualms about the suffering and death. Such carnivorousness is, of course, pervasive in nature, "red in tooth and claw."

Humans evolved to eat that way as well, for at least a major part of our diet. So, if we continue doing it, we could say we are merely acting in accord with nature and with the facts of our existence. Yet we are reasoning beings, concerned with morality, which nature is not. So we cannot simply say that it's our nature to eat meat and leave it there.

We have seen that reason tells us, as a first principle, to value human life above all else. And since all people stand equally, we may not sacrifice one for the benefit of another. It is the basic equivalence of all humans in consciousness and capacity for pleasure or pain that gives us those equal rights. That is why we ethically reject cannibalism, just as we reject any exploitation that forces one person to suffer for another's gain. This isn't anthropocentrism, setting humans apart just because they are humans; rather, it is because of the characteristics we all exhibit. The same principles should apply to any nonhuman that shares our quality of consciousness. To eat him would be the moral equivalent of cannibalism.

So, the degree of deference we give other life-forms, how we behave toward them, should reflect the degree to which they possess such consciousness. At the lower end of the animal kingdom, creatures do not have much, if any, self-awareness or mental capacity for pleasure or suffering; they stand little different from machines. We need have scarcely more qualms about harvesting clams than harvesting corn. But higher animals—like cows—do have an "inner life" with feelings and emotions, even if not nearly as developed as our own. And a few—great apes, elephants, and perhaps some sea mammals—do appear to have a level of consciousness that approaches ours.

Those latter few creatures should, at least, not be eaten or otherwise unnecessarily harmed. Animals lower on the scale, like cows, are sufficiently unequal to humans in their mental life that it's arguably reasonable to continue to treat them as part of our food chain. Because of the difference in quality of consciousness, a cow does not understand or appreciate its life as does a human. Such animals probably do not grasp the concept of having a future. Hence, taking away that future should not offend our conscience in the way that depriving a human of his future does.

But this does not mean animals like cows can be treated any way one likes. As Jeremy Bentham said two centuries ago, what matters is not whether they think or talk, but whether they suffer. And, obviously, they do. This requires us to refrain from unnecessary cruelty toward them. Indeed, most advanced societies already do legally prohibit undue animal cruelty.

However, the word "rights" is problematical when applied to animals. It is true that people form a sort of ecological whole with other living things but it isn't really a *community*, which is characterized by mutuality of interests and obligations. Human rights are grounded in the reciprocity of the social contract. Our duty to respect the rights of others is integral to our own possession of rights they must respect. Obviously, there is no such reciprocity or mutuality when it comes to nonhuman beings. But even if we, therefore, cannot properly say that animals have *rights*, perhaps it is proper to say that they do have *interests*, which we cannot morally disregard. Indifference to suffering is wrong.

Another notion that arises here is "reverence for life." All creation is, indeed, wondrous; nature has to work pretty hard to make even the merest dust mite. But using the word "reverence" should not imply supernatural or religious sacredness. Certainly, animals are not objects of worship. Rather, the reverence we should feel toward life is akin to that for a great achievement or work of art—more like respect or awe, really, than reverence. Further, our general moral repugnance toward wanton destruction of all kinds should encompass animals.

So, if we kill animals, we are obliged to make an effort to minimize the pain. And, since their lives do have some value to them, they should not be sacrificed unless doing so provides humans with at least an equivalent value. A hunter must examine his conscience to judge whether the pleasure he gets in killing can justify the suffering and death of the prey. The food we get from slaughtering a cow may reasonably be considered sufficient value to justify the deed, while most of us recoil at the waste when a rhino is killed just for his horn, which is dubiously considered an aphrodisiac.

The same principles apply to scientific experimentation. Here again, a utilitarian concept—the greatest good for the greatest number

—can apply. While it is wrong to sacrifice animals or make them suffer for trivial purposes, it would also be wrong to forgo the great benefits for humankind that can flow from research using animals. A scientist is obligated to judge whether the potential benefit from an experiment is great enough to justify the animal's pain or death and must do what can reasonably be done to minimize the suffering.

Some might respond that the foregoing utilitarian argument for animal exploitation in certain circumstances could also support human exploitation. Obviously, the food value of a human could never be high enough to justify cannibalism (let's not talk about lifeboats). But should we allow scientific experimentation on people if the potential benefits are great enough? People do sometimes submit to being guinea pigs voluntarily. But absent such consent, because of the fundamentally equal rights of all humans, we do not allow the sacrifice of one person for another or others. This is because we understand that if Joe can be sacrificed for you then you can be sacrificed for Joe, and no one wants to live in such a society. Further, we're rightly unwilling to entrust any fallible human with power to make decisions of that kind. Animals, once more, stand differently because they are not our equals, do not have our level of consciousness, and are not in a reciprocal social relation with us.

The foregoing shows that the whole issue of how we treat animals is not altogether simple, and does, again, require serious moral consideration. In the worldwide happiness-versus-pain score, animals do count, even if they count for fewer points than humans. A world in which a cow does not suffer is, all else equal, better than one in which she does. It is ethical for humans to be considerate of animals, to avoid unnecessary harm to them, and even to act for their benefit.

Unfortunately, these precepts are not widely honored. Few people give much thought to animal pain or suffering; and animals do suffer more than is necessary, especially in the food industry, where economics tend to override any tender sensitivities, resulting in many animals being subjected to cruelty. The free-market system, as such, is a moral one, but that certainly doesn't imply that each and every business model is ethical. Everyone has the choice of the business or industry in which to make his living or profits, and there are plenty of choices available that don't entail the infliction of suffering.

And what about consumers—to what extent are we complicit in that suffering? This, too, is no simple question. It is recognized that becoming a vegetarian society would be highly disruptive, both economically and culturally. The animals we eat owe their very existence to our breeding them for food; vegetarianism would eliminate the cruelty, and most of the animals themselves, at the same time. Meanwhile, it is impractical for us to consider whether or not there is some wrong involved at every stage of the production and marketing of each of the many things we consume. Ethically perfect consumers would probably be nonconsumers. We make compromises; we cannot give up modern life. And those who eat meat aren't asking the meat industry to treat animals the way it does. More humane production methods are entirely feasible; they would just mean higher prices. Are we willing to pay them? There are no easy answers.

In the past, certain people were considered less than human; enslaving them was deemed acceptable—some were even exhibited in zoos. Most of us have grown beyond that, extending the concept of human rights to our entire species. This required radical rethinking. Recognizing some interests of animals is a logical next step; this too requires rethinking, but surely we are capable of it.

After all, we're so much smarter than animals. When our cat scratches my daughter, I tell her, "Don't blame him, he's an animal, he doesn't know better." We humans don't have that excuse. We know better.

Crime and Punishment

Society's main job is to protect us from harm; this is what makes all its further benefits possible. Law is the mechanism. And if people all were angels who obeyed laws without fail, there would be no occasion for punishment. Most people do obey laws willingly, but society must have a way to deal with those who don't. Punishment is needed to deter such people; its purpose is to protect us from them. (Prison also physically prevents crime by isolating wrongdoers from society.)

But punishment for crime additionally serves the interest of justice. This is a fundamental moral value, the idea that people should get what they deserve, whether it be reward for good or penalty for wrongful behavior. Society has a legitimate interest in promoting justice. It is a social good. Allowing wrongdoers to "get away with it" offends against our notions of what is fair and right and undermines allegiance to society.

For these reasons, we give up our private freedom to use violence and, instead, give the state a monopoly to use it on our behalf, to deal with wrongdoers and thereby both protect us and provide justice.

There is a basic truism about crime that, though fairly obvious, isn't pondered much. Crime is not a zero-sum game in which one's loss is another's gain. Indeed, the harm to the victim tends to vastly exceed any benefit to the perpetrator. This is certainly true where there is bodily injury. And far outweighing a crime's physical or monetary effects, victims often suffer psychologically, with a sense of violation and heightened feelings of vulnerability and fear that can leave lasting scars. This is true in spades for sex crimes, which can really mess up a victim's life, a consequence vastly disproportionate to whatever momentary gratification the perpetrator experiences. And, of course, crime often hurts not just the immediate victim but also others around him. A whole family can be devastated and blighted by a murder or a sex crime; the total societal wreckage can be enormous. That's why we must take a hard line against such crimes and apply policies that serve to minimize their occurrence.

It's true that such violators may have their own psychological problems that elicit some sympathy; they may even be victims of a sort themselves. Yet, whatever compassion we may feel toward them, it has to be trumped by our concern for their victims; crimes may be understandable but not excusable. We must not take our eye off the ball of protecting the innocent from violation, which is, after all, society's paramount mission. Where a crime does great harm to the victim, severe punishment is just and also serves society by deterring would-be perpetrators.

Note, however, that while we shouldn't, therefore, shrink from applying serious punishments for serious crimes, it is neither justice nor necessary for safeguarding society to severely punish trivial crimes. Justice and society's interests lie instead with punishment fitted to the crime.

Most of us intuitively understand all this. But one area of intense and emotional controversy is punishment by death.

Whether capital punishment actually deters murder is a part of the debate too familiar to be worthy of rehashing here. The deterrence, over and above that supplied by the threat of prison, is almost certainly negligible. But capital punishment is not just an issue of pragmatism; it is mainly a moral issue. If we grant society's legitimate purpose to advance justice through punishment, then the real issue is, again, whether any particular punishment fits the crime.

Capital punishment's opponents say that two wrongs don't make a right—if it is wrong for an individual to kill, then it's wrong for the state; and killing a murderer doesn't undo his wrong but rather compounds it. Some even say that executing a murderer makes the state "just as bad" as he is.

This kind of argument has one key problem: it can apply to all punishment of lawbreakers. If two wrongs don't make a right, so the state cannot kill a murderer, then why is it okay to inflict long imprisonment? Isn't that also a "wrong" done to the prisoner?

Death penalty opponents might answer that, unlike prison, killing is *violent*, and, for that reason, morally illegitimate. But prison is not "nonviolent." If a man is kidnapped and confined for years, obviously this is a horrible crime. Of course it is violent; it entails force. While it does not take away all of the victim's life, it takes away a big part of it and causes suffering. So, too, prison is not somehow nonviolent in distinction from capital punishment. Imprisonment is violence, just of a different type. It too employs force. It doesn't take away a person's life, but takes a big part of it and inflicts suffering.

We don't allow individuals to imprison others but give the state the right to use this kind of violence, as explained, in order to protect society. And if government can do that, can take away part of a person's life, acting lawfully and morally on behalf of society, then it can likewise properly take away an entire life by execution.

Opponents also decry capital punishment as "vengeance," saying that the old biblical notion of "an eye for an eye" will "make the world blind." Another seductive but facile bit of rhetoric. The biblical prescription did concern vengeance, one person wronged by another seeking to even the score, but we needn't explore the morality of *that* since it has nothing to do with the state's role in punishing crimes. The state doesn't do so for vengeance. Rather, again, it punishes crimes to protect us against criminality and to promote justice.

Death penalty critics also invoke the sanctity of life.[213] But it is

---

213. Yet, many of them are less concerned over the sanctity of life when it comes to abortion. One might even say they are willing to kill the innocent but not the guilty.

precisely our high valuation of human life that makes capital punishment consonant with justice. Murder victims are not abstractions; they are real people whose lives are as valuable to them as yours is to you. To murder someone, depriving him of the entire rest of his life, is so great a crime we cannot really fathom it—just as one cannot really grasp nonexistence after one's own death. If a man deliberately robs another of life, then it can be a just and fitting punishment to deprive that murderer of something of equal value—his own life. To do otherwise devalues the life of the victim.

And there is no moral equivalence between murder, taking an innocent life contrary to law, and the state lawfully taking a murderer's life. Again, we all recognize that anyone committing a crime may thereby forfeit his right to freedom and that imprisonment, confiscating his freedom, is legitimate. Likewise, one who commits murder, the ultimate breach of society's law, can be deemed to forfeit his membership in society, and not only his right to live freely, but his right to live at all. In consequence of his crime, the state's confiscation of his life is legitimate and proper. It is a punishment that fits the crime.

Remember once more the social contract. We all have natural human rights that society protects—so long as we respect the rights of others. That's the deal. If you violate the deal, you lose your rights under it. If you steal, you can lose your right to liberty. Thus, no rights are absolute and unqualified, not even one's right to life itself. Violate another person's right to life and you lose your own such right.

All of the foregoing constitutes the moral case for capital punishment. But one must acknowledge that its implementation is highly fraught. This is because the justice system is a human institution and, hence, fallible and imperfect. The seriousness of capital punishment demands fairness in applying it, but perfect fairness is unattainable in any human endeavor. Further, we obviously must avoid executing the innocent, and here, too, this human system is fallible.[214]

---

214. Meantime, while great care must be taken before executing anyone, that should not mean decades of interminable process. In some states, the mortality rate for death row inmates is lower than in the general

In fact, too many prosecutors see their job as getting convictions, not necessarily convicting *the guilty*. Actual guilt often seems a secondary consideration, and prosecutors are, furthermore, humanly recalcitrant about admitting and rectifying their mistakes. Juries are equally culpable, frequently failing to understand the state's burden of proving guilt beyond a reasonable doubt, and, hence, they convict defendants on flimsy evidence far too often. We have to do better—and not just in capital cases. If a wrongful execution does irreparable harm, so does a wrongful imprisonment; and monetary compensation cannot really make good the loss of years of life or undo the pain. It is hard to see why a mistaken imprisonment is deemed somehow tolerable in a way that a wrongful execution is not. Nevertheless, recognizing the inevitable imperfection of all human institutions, we do tolerate imprisoning some innocent people on the defensible basis that this is a price worth paying for the benefits the criminal justice system provides for society.[215]

Further, the wrongful execution problem has a fairly obvious solution, at least in theory: to require, for capital punishment, a standard of proof higher than the normal "beyond reasonable doubt" criterion for criminal conviction. Certainly, there are many murders where the perpetrator's identity is not an issue or is provable by ironclad forensic evidence. It does not make sense to bar capital punishment in such a case only because in some other case guilt might be less certain.

Its opponents often do argue in effect that because the death penalty is wrong in some cases, it is always wrong, in all cases. Such absolutism seems neither logical nor moral. Capital punishment is, indeed, sometimes wrong; but for heinous crimes, where guilt is not in question, it can be right.

---

population. One confessed serial killer actually hired a lawyer to get Connecticut to finally carry out the death sentence it had decreed twenty years earlier. This undermines respect for the law and our justice system.

215. And there's another side to this coin: countless murderers are not convicted, or serve relatively short sentences, and go on to kill others—who are also innocent victims of what might be considered mistakes by the criminal justice system.

* * *

All the preceding discussion of crime and punishment centers upon protecting us from others. Yet many laws don't actually do that; some aim to protect people from *themselves* or from behavior by others that may offend but doesn't really harm them. These are *victimless crimes*.

If the true goal is an environment for maximum freedom, then any law restricting anyone's liberty must pass a key test: is this really necessary to promote society's interests and protect its members? Does it ultimately make us more free, or less? Again, we don't join society to be told what we can't do—we join it to be empowered for the things we want to do.

This basic concept should always be kept in mind regarding victimless crimes. Take prostitution. I can pay a woman to mow my lawn, to clean my toilet, to sing, to dance, to nurse me, to teach me, even to massage me; all of this is legal. And I can even have sex with her; that's legal too. But I can't *pay* her for sex because that's illegal.

Why? Because it's "immoral"? Many folks do think so.[216] If they do, they have the right to abstain. But is it wrong to pay someone to provide pleasure or wrong to be paid for giving pleasure? Neither person is harmed; to the contrary, like any free-market transaction between a willing buyer and a willing seller, both benefit; indeed, this is actually value creation for society as a whole. Why should it be banned?

Some might say a woman is degraded by having sex for money. Some might say she is degraded by cleaning toilets for money. Others would see that as merely honest employment. Shouldn't a woman be allowed to decide for herself whether she feels degraded to clean a toilet—or copulate with a stranger—and whether she nevertheless wants to do either for sufficient pay?

---

216. As *The End of Faith* notes, while sometimes such prohibitions are premised on a notion of preventing societal harm (even if indirect), some of them cannot be justified on any such pretext. They reflect, instead, a religious concept of "sin," where the putative offense is not against people or society, but against God. Such matters are best left to private consciences.

Concededly, prostitution can be a nasty business, and sellers of sex are not always really willing sellers. If a woman is coerced into prostitution, this is certainly a crime against her that should be punished. Some maintain that prostitution lends itself to such abuses.[217] This is a common argument when it comes to otherwise victimless crimes: they lead to this or that bad thing or they have bad side effects. But the right answer is simply to criminalize the behavior that actually does harm people. If prostitution is sometimes associated with human trafficking, then punish the trafficking. If a drug user feeds his habit by robbery, then punish the robbery.

But if people are not harming others, then leave them alone.

In America, after a long social crusade, alcoholic drink was prohibited in 1920. This spawned a huge and violent criminal industry supplying booze to people who did not stop drinking. Widely seen as a failed experiment, Prohibition was repealed in 1933. We still recognized alcohol's great harm, but also recognized that Prohibition, instead of solving the problem, compounded it. Today we're repeating that same mistake with the "war on drugs."

Drugs do cause great harm. But freedom means making one's own choices, for good or ill. Drug use isn't a freedom I want for myself, but that isn't the point. If you value the freedom to do things you want, you must honor the freedom of others to do likewise, even if they make bad choices.

Anyhow, the moral argument here rings hollow because, just as Prohibition didn't curb drinking, neither does the drug war impede drug use. Is there anyone actually deterred by drugs' illegality who would want to use them if legal? And while legalization would cut the price, which theoretically should stimulate demand, clearly drug demand is extremely price-inelastic, meaning that price has little bearing on how much drug consumption a person chooses. Meantime, legalizing drugs might actually dampen usage by removing some of the "forbidden fruit" mystique.

---

217. On the other hand, it can be argued that such abuses go hand-in-hand not with prostitution per se but with its being illegal, and that with legal prostitution the abuses would be less prevalent and easier for society to control.

Stopping the supply has proven wholly futile too. As long as the demand persists and huge profits can be made, the supply will come. Drugs are easily smuggled from poor countries, with a street value a hundred times the production cost. For every coca field destroyed, growers start another. For every dealer jailed, another pops up. Incarceration for drug offenses actually rose by 900 percent between 1980 and 2003, but even that didn't dent the drug trade; in fact, over that same period, real-dollar prices for hard drugs actually fell by half (indicative of supply outrunning demand). Why imagine we can somehow keep drugs out of America when we can't even manage to keep them out of *prisons*? It's like trying to stop the tide with a teaspoon.

And the drug war actually undermines public order and safety. Just like Prohibition did, the illegality of drugs engenders violent criminality. The drug trade is so profitable that murder among competitors fighting over turf is commonplace, with innocents often caught in the crossfire. Some neighborhoods have become virtual war zones wherein the successful role models seem to be the drug dealers. Many are sucked into the trade who might otherwise go into socially beneficial careers. Furthermore, the huge amounts of money at stake in drugs corrupt our police forces and justice system.

Also, since illegality greatly raises the street price of drugs, many users resort to crime to feed their habits. That accounts for a high proportion of muggings, robberies, burglaries, and more. Much of that crime would disappear if drugs were legal and, hence, less costly. And obviously, all the police resources now spent chasing those petty addict criminals—and being squandered on the drug war itself—could be redirected against other types of criminality. Legalizing drugs would be a quantum leap toward reducing crime. (It would help fight terrorism too, since a key source of its financing is the drug trade, once again, made incredibly profitable by illegality.)

Furthermore, this crusade seems as much a war on civil liberties as it is a war on drugs, with our rights being sacrificed in countless ways in the name of fighting drugs. For example, the Constitution's Fourth Amendment protection against "unreasonable searches and seizures" and the Fourteenth Amendment provision that no one can be deprived of property without "due process of law" have become practically dead letters whenever the drug war is invoked, with police allowed broad powers to confiscate any property alleged to have some drug connection without necessarily even having to prove it. People have lost their homes because a relative was caught with marijuana. And the justice system is so overwhelmed by drug cases that, in trying to cope with them all, meaningful respect for defendants' rights goes by the boards.

But the chief victims are the multitudes imprisoned (and their families). Much of our prison population is there because of drugs; that's why America has the world's highest incarceration rate relative to population. Some of those prisoners are bad people who deserve to be there; but too many are basically just ordinary people who are simply unfortunate and unlucky. The cost is huge—not just the costs of running the prison system, but the human cost, the loss to society, and the ruined lives, many of which might otherwise be productive.

I don't share the mind-set of blaming society for criminal behavior. I want crimes punished—to deter them, to promote justice, and to keep us safe. This is government's key mission. But that simply does not apply to drug use. Addiction is a problem for the addict, not a crime against society. Addicts should be helped, not punished.

If a tenth of the money thrown down the drug war toilet were instead spent on treatment for users, it would reduce drug use far more. Many lives would be saved instead of wrecked, billions of dollars would be available for better uses, civil liberties would be enhanced, crime would plummet, and society would be richer, happier, safer, and freer.

Of course, we don't criminalize all drugs. Indeed, we're very inconsistent. We gave up trying to ban alcohol. We permit tobacco, a powerfully addictive drug that knocks ten years off the average smoker's life, but outlaw marijuana, which is only mildly addictive, with generally minor health effects (and, indeed, some valid medical uses). This is the real "reefer madness."

And while we permit smokers to commit slow suicide, we don't allow people in pain the option of ending their lives. If freedom to live as one chooses means anything, surely it ought to mean deciding for oneself whether to live at all.

This is a troubling and complex topic, often presenting thorny dilemmas for individuals and their loved ones. This book has stressed the value of human life and how people can find meaning even under terrible conditions. Certainly, society should be fundamentally pro-life, giving its members support and encouragement to see meaning in life even in adversity. For lack of such support, and of life-affirming answers, some people tragically commit suicide. But others make messy ends of their lives because society does not allow for an orderly humane departure. For all the value we place on life, we must recognize that a decision to end one can be rational and reasonable and, in such cases, respect for human dignity demands that we honor that choice. The existential meaning of life and of freedom consists in making consequential choices, and there is none more consequential than whether to live or die. Bowing to such a choice is the highest homage we can pay to the sanctity of every individual's life.

Certainly, there should be safeguards to ensure that an assisted suicide is truly voluntary and chosen with due deliberation.[218] As in all spheres, abuses are possible, and society can and should make laws to prevent them. Unjustly harming others should always be unlawful. But otherwise, making choices for oneself ought to be lawful.

That is the essence of a free society.

---

218. Some say this would violate a doctor's Hippocratic Oath. But a lot has changed in 2,400 years, and perhaps we should amend the oath to recognize that occasionally dying can help, not harm, a patient.

Homosexuality

Homosexuality is disturbing to many people. But this wasn't always so. The ancient Greeks and Romans, among others, had rather more relaxed views toward sexuality in general, including homosexuality; and a man's lust for a pretty boy was considered normal. The subsequent change in attitudes is at least partly attributable to religious doctrines stressing sex for procreation and not recreation.

This leads many to regard homosexual acts as sinful—and further, whereas the temptations of most sins are understandable, many people are baffled by same-sex attraction and see gay sexual practices as repellent, unnatural, and perverted. That gays actually prefer and enjoy such doings makes them seem virtually an alien species. And straight people who are not totally secure about their own sexuality may feel somehow threatened and unsettled by the phenomenon of gay sex. All of this creates animosity toward homosexuals.

Gays would respond that homosexuality is not unnatural at all, that it is, indeed, a part of nature. Now, it is, obviously, "natural" in the sense that homosexuals are produced by natural processes. One can even deem them "normal" inasmuch as, out of any random thousand people, a certain predictable percentage will be gay. Thus, it's simply a normal variation—just as blue eyes are not abnormal and, in every population, a certain percentage will have blue eyes.

However, a certain (small) percentage of humans is also born with two heads. While that is likewise "natural," it can hardly be termed normal. Clearly, in such a case something has gone awry in the procreation process. The standard blueprint for making a human being was not followed.

Can something similar be said of homosexuality? Gayness is certainly far less aberrational than two-headedness, being, instead, a rather common variant. From this one might infer that the workings of evolution have incorporated some homosexuality into the human blueprint. Yet this seems to be a highly nonadaptive trait from an evolutionary standpoint; it positively subverts, rather than promotes, DNA propagation. That's contrary to nature's game plan. And, of course, if there ever were gayness genes, they would tend to get weeded out from the gene pool because their bearers would sire few children.

How, then, can we account for the commonness of homosexuality? Gender *is* governed by genes; males and females have different chromosomes. But every fetus starts out physiologically gender neutral, able to become either male or female, until the genes duly trigger the production of hormones that decide the issue. This is a complex stepwise process, and if the right hormones don't kick in at just the right times—if the instruction sheet is not followed perfectly—this will affect the person's resulting sexuality. Serious deviations from the blueprint cause such rare major abnormalities as hermaphrodites and ambiguous gender. A lesser and fairly common variation from the standard blueprint, it would seem, produces homosexuality. In other words, there probably aren't gayness genes, and homosexuality is not inherited; but it is, nonetheless, biological, resulting from variations in how genetic instructions are carried out in developing fetuses.

Gays themselves mostly do insist that they are born that way, that homosexuality is not a choice. Of course, there may be exceptions—the human psyche is very complex and variable—but, in general, we should believe gays who say that, with all its social stigma, "why would we choose this?" That notion certainly seems consistent with the preceding paragraph. While science has not yet fully untangled this story, what we do know does suggest a biological explanation for homosexuality. There have even been studies finding physiological brain differences between most gays and straights. And, on the other hand, there has never been any valid evidence tracing homosexuality to "nurture" rather than nature. The commonplace idea that gayness has something to do with a child's upbringing or sexual role models, or is otherwise a psychological phenomenon, seems to be baseless. The parents of gays need not ask themselves what they did wrong. This is confirmed by the virtual impossibility of "curing" homosexuality. Such sexual orientation instead seems to be a built-in feature that is unavoidable and unchangeable for anyone born with it.[219]

So gays are indeed different. But let's not forget that everybody is, after all, different from everybody else. One can even say that being different is normal; variation among individuals within a species is the rule throughout all nature. Differences are the spice of life and should be celebrated. It would be a dull world if all people were identical. And people certainly exhibit great variation when it comes to sexual behavior and preferences. Furthermore, though 100 percent gays are a small minority, many others are not 100 percent heterosexual, with some degree of same-sex attraction being quite widespread.

All the foregoing makes clear that stigmatizing homosexuality is irrational. Gays do what they do not because they are willful transgressors of societal norms but because of how they were made.

Recall now the discussion of personal responsibility and how civilization requires us to control our behavior. The impulses to be

---

219. It may be noted that the biological mechanisms involved with male and female homosexuality apparently differ. And some believe that women, in particular, sometimes turn to lesbianism as an emotional response to life experiences. Again, one can't say this *never* happens; but most such cases are probably the surfacing of a biological predisposition. Certainly many gays of both genders try to repress and deny their true inclinations, often for many years; if this ultimately fails, it doesn't mean they have turned to homosexuality as a free choice.

restrained are those that harm others or society. Pedophiles must refrain from raping boys. But, on the other hand, society has no legitimate concern with the private sexual conduct of consenting adults. If they do not harm anyone, or society, they should be left alone.

As noted, much hostility toward homosexuality is traceable to religious dictum condemning *any* sexual activity not geared toward procreation. However, most of us have moved some distance away from that latter notion, accepting, instead, that nature has made us to enjoy sex. Here again, nature's purpose is merely to promote DNA replication, but we need not enslave ourselves to that narrow remit, being, instead, free to use this gift from nature to enrich our lives however we can, just as we can use our other gifts. That means using sex not just for reproduction but for physical and psychic pleasure and to enhance our bonds with loved ones. And if that is okay for heterosexuals, it should be equally okay for gays. They, too, have a fundamental human entitlement to enjoy sex.

But even if you still see gay sex as somehow wrong, you should then view homosexuality as an affliction rather than a sin, inspiring compassion and not condemnation. This should certainly apply to gays who wish they had been born straight. Meantime, many gays do not regret their situation and would not change it if they could; and if they are happy, we ought to be happy for them.

In other words, the basic principle should be—guess what?—live and let live.

We have indeed grown more tolerant of homosexuality, at least no longer punishing gay sex itself (in most places). Yet we still struggle over issues of discrimination against gays. Many of the arguments are couched in terms of seemingly legitimate societal interests. But what really lies behind them is psychological hostility toward homosexuality.

Take gays in the military. The main argument has always been that gay soldiers would disrupt good order among the troops and undermine morale—how could a gay man be expected to control his impulses in a barracks full of young men? Yet we have integrated *women* into today's American military. Has this caused problems of sexual misbehavior? You bet! Plenty! Remember Tailhook? But we live with problems like that because we now realize it would be wrong to bar female participation. Sexual misbehavior is handled, appropriately, by punishing actual misconduct when it happens. Why shouldn't the same apply to gays? Of course, the real animus against gay soldiering is that, whereas many macho military men don't mind having women around, they just don't like gays and don't want to be forced to mix with them. But most nations, including Britain (which actively recruits them), accommodate gays in their armies without undue problems—and so, in fact, does America itself, with many thousands of closet gays undoubtedly serving. So all the arguments against it are really just a smoke screen.

The big issue is gay marriage. It does offend against deeply ingrained cultural tradition, which is a consideration that merits some serious respect and weight. We shouldn't just toss our traditions in the trash. However, culture evolves. Not so long ago, firmly established cultural tradition barred interracial marriage—and sanctioned numerous other forms of racial discrimination, including slavery. Our culture has changed, and for the better, broadening our concepts of human dignity and rights.

At the outset, we must differentiate between religious and civil marriages. Whether a religious rite of marriage should be available to same-sex couples is something for congregants to work out among themselves; consonant with religious freedom, government or society should have no say about that. But, when it comes to civil marriage, with all its legal ramifications, including income tax status, inheritance rights, child custody, and so on, the guiding principle ought to be equality before the law.

And here again, the contrary arguments seem less like rationales than rationalizations, covering for what is more truly a prejudice or an inarticulate fear.

The chief claim is that same-sex weddings undermine the institution of marriage. Yet, obviously, the immediate result is more, not fewer, marriages. If marriage is a good thing, and it's better for men and women to be married than not, or better than cohabiting informally, why isn't the same true for gay couples? In fact, one thing about the "gay lifestyle" that particularly troubles straight people is frequent sexual promiscuity—and, certainly, gay marriage would work against such behavior. (It would also thereby help curb sexually transmitted diseases such as AIDS.)

Further, it is fanciful to imagine that heterosexual marriage would decline if people could now choose a same-sex marriage instead. Again, sexual orientation is not a choice, but an inborn trait; people do not generally opt for homosexuality on a whim. As a straight person, I can attest that the opportunity to marry another man would be no temptation! Of course, concededly, some people are bisexual or confused about their sexuality, and many gays do enter conventional marriages in an effort at conformity. But such marriages are clearly not made in heaven; they tend to be problem-ridden and failure-prone. So it hardly constitutes sound social policy to favor them—in contrast to allowing people to be who they really are and to make marriages that fit them better. If you truly care about the institution of marriage, you should prefer to see a lesbian successfully married to another lesbian rather than being unsatisfactorily married to a man.

Child rearing is also a concern. Some say that a child is best raised by a father and a mother and that every child is entitled to have both. That is a fine sentiment, and such dual parenthood should be encouraged. But society does not insist upon it—does not prohibit single parenthood. Though we do take children away from parents who are proven unfit in specific ways, parenthood is otherwise a universal right. A teenaged unwed mother is allowed to raise her child. And if we let that single mother raise a child, why shouldn't we let *two* mothers (or fathers) do so? Aren't two parents better than one? Moreover, being unable to have children the usual way, gay couples often get them through adoption. And surely *those* children are better off having two same-sex parents than having *no parents* at all![220]

---

220. Incidentally, many opponents of abortion also oppose gay marriage; but gay couples almost never have abortions.

Some might still object that a gay couple would raise a gay child. Even if this were so, would it harm society? Gays will never be anything but a small minority; there will always be enough heterosexual activity to ensure human continuity. But, again, the truth is that sexual orientation has nothing to do with upbringing, it is inborn; so a child raised by gays is no more likely to turn out gay than one raised by straights (though if he does happen to be gay, he is likely to be more comfortable with it).

And let us not forget that gays can (in most states) legally adopt and raise children even *without* being married. So barring their marriages does nothing for the children. Allowing such couples to marry should, in fact, provide a more stable and nurturing family environment.

In the end, the issue is really all about love and joy and happiness. Even if you do see valid social policy points against gay marriage, surely those rationales must yield to the more fundamental human right at stake. What can be more crucial to the pursuit of happiness than to marry the person you love? Gays are human beings, entitled to seek fulfillment in whatever ways work for them. If same-sex marriage is a vehicle for pleasure, love, and self-realization—if it raises the worldwide human happiness score—we should welcome it.

The War with Islamic Extremism

This is a very big war that we are in. Calling it the "War on Terror" is something of a misnomer. Terrorism is merely the tactic used by the Islamic fundamentalists (or "Islamists") making war on us. However, it is a good idea to avoid the word "Islam" in naming this conflict because too many people already believe (wrongly) that the United States wars against the entire Muslim world.

Historian Samuel Huntington, in 1993, foresaw "the clash of civilizations." But we are not doomed to play this out. Some, in contrast, actually see convergence toward a global civilization and believe that what those still outside it most want is to get in—caring less about culture than about democracy, personal freedom, and their by-product of economic advancement. This is a powerful force in the world that, of course, provokes a reaction. Islamic fundamentalism is just such a reaction, warring against those modernizing and liberating trends. It seems tragic that, just when masses of people finally have an opportunity for freer and richer lives, some Muslims are violently fighting it.

The "blame America first" crowd (to use Jeane Kirkpatrick's phrase) believes this conflict is somehow our fault, that we brought it on ourselves, even that we deserve what we're getting. They ascribe anti-Americanism to our alleged foreign policy sins. We have indeed made a lot of mistakes and done a lot wrong. But, as already discussed, in the big picture, American foreign policy is hardly the evil misguided thing so many detractors claim to see. No other nation has done more than America to advance the causes of human rights, freedom, democracy, national self-determination, and better lives for people everywhere. America is not perfect, but to cast it as a bullying villain is grotesquely myopic.

With respect to the Muslim world in particular, America's record is actually admirable. Time and again we have sided with Muslims. In 1956 we opposed Israel, France, and Britain, our own allies, when they tried to seize Egypt's Suez Canal. In Afghanistan, in the 1980s, America assisted Muslims fighting the Soviet invasion. (One of them was Osama bin Laden. A lot of thanks we got.) In 1999 we intervened in Kosovo to save Muslim lives that were threatened by their Christian Serb enemies, solely because it was the right thing to do, and not to serve any self-interest—other than, of course, America's permanent national interest in making the world as free, just, and safe as possible, for all people, including Muslims.

And, within our own borders, we do not persecute Muslims. Instead, we share with them the blessings of freedom, allowing them greater liberty to practice their religion than exists in many Muslim countries. Countless Muslims have come to America as a sanctuary from repression in their own homelands.

It is true that America has propped up some undemocratic Arab regimes. This is largely because there are *no democratic Arab regimes*, and that's where the problem lies. It is not America's fault that there are no Arab democrats to support and that the potential alternatives in many Islamic countries are even less palatable than the existing regimes. We backed the shah of Iran, admittedly no democrat, but he presided over a far more open society than has the brutal Islamic tyranny that overthrew him. Likewise, we assist Egypt's authoritarian regime because that nation has yet to develop any reasonable democratic alternative. But we do criticize Egypt and other such countries for their human rights abuses and, as a matter of policy, push them toward democratization.

Of course, this is controversial too. The very people most vocal in criticizing America for tolerating undemocratic regimes at the same time vilify America as "arrogant" and "imperialist" for seeking to "impose" its democratic values on other nations. I guess we are damned if we do and damned if we don't.

America is also criticized for being too pro-Israel and failing to force Israel to make concessions to the Palestinians. Arguably, at various points, America should have been tougher on Israel. But America cannot control Israel's policy or force it to do things it considers against its interests. Further, Israel is the only Middle East nation that upholds, to any degree, our own core values of democracy, freedom, and openness. We owe no apologies for supporting Israel against enemies that seek its destruction.

Yet our policy has not been one-sided. We have consistently supported an independent Palestinian state and have taken the lead in working toward that goal. In negotiations in 2000, the United States labored mightily to broker a settlement creating a Palestinian state, with Israel offering to give up over 90 percent of the disputed land. But Palestinians would not take yes for an answer.

When Europe was in the Dark Ages, Muslims were the vanguard of civilization, excelling in science, mathematics, engineering, arts and literature, and at the art of life itself—a burst of vitality by a new culture. Then Europe came out of the darkness and experienced a great rebirth. The Enlightenment was a welcome revolution in thought that ultimately brought forth the tremendous advancements whose fruits we in the West now enjoy. Muslims, meanwhile, retrogressed as their initial vibrancy dissipated under the ascendancy of a conservative religious orthodoxy. Historian Bernard Lewis considers secularization to be a key factor in the West's technological, cultural, and political advancement, while the Muslim world has been held back by its failure to separate mosque and state.

Politically correct cultural relativism frowns on deeming one civilization better than another. But one can't deny that the Arab realms have suffered an intellectual, economic, and spiritual stagnation. Their economies are dead in the water; only the fortuity of oil wealth keeps them from abject poverty. There are far too few jobs for their exploding youth populations; there is scant entrepreneurialism, development of science, technology, or innovation; and their schools churn out graduates who have learned little but to recite Koranic verses by heart. They toss away half their human potential through medieval treatment of women. And, when even most African nations have been stumbling toward democracy, the Arab world remains stuck in the grip of unaccountable, unresponsive authoritarian regimes.

It is hardly surprising that this deep systemic Arab sickness has given rise to movements aiming at a cure. A number of different Muslim regeneration movements began to pop up around the middle of the twentieth century. Some of this thought has been more or less sensible, positive, even modernist; but much has not, and, unfortunately, the most robust of such movements today seems to be the Islamic fundamentalism spearheaded by al Qaeda.

Its followers ascribe Arab malaise to apostasy, or deviation from the pure Islam embodied within the pages of the Koran. They read the Koran as requiring a unified community of people (the "Umma," rather than nation-states) ruled by God through his instrument, the caliph, a sort of priest-king. They believe this was the model followed in Islam's infancy, and that it needs to be restored. (Return to original purity is a common theme among fundamentalist religious movements.)

Their belief in following strictly the laws of God alone means that they condemn all man-made laws. Most important, this means that they reject democracy, where laws are made by people, in opposition (as they see it) to the laws of God.

Naturally, these Islamic fundamentalists regard Western nations as offensive to God, not only thumbing our noses at God by democratically governing ourselves, but mired in licentiousness too. And we certainly have dramatically different views of women and sexuality.

It is worth noting that there isn't even a single Muslim nation that satisfies the fundamentalists' standards of Islamic purity. And so they are at war with all, at war against every nation. And, from their perspective, "war" is not just a metaphor. The Koran's word "jihad" means "holy war." There is debate as to jihad's true meaning. Some say it refers merely to personal struggle against one's own failings. But most Islamists read jihad to mean literal war against everything not Koranically pure and, further, they see a positive duty to wage that war. Thus, they have truly declared war against infidels and apostates and, for them, it is an all-out war, with the very soul of mankind at stake.

As for the war's casualties, in their view, most victims are sinners who deserve death and damnation. And, even if some good people die, they will go to heaven, so no real harm is done! Accordingly, not only do they not quail from killing, it is really the only tactic they can come up with that they deem effective. They encourage their followers to willingly sacrifice their own lives just for the sake of killing infidels. Unable to achieve anything positive, they have created a cult of death and have made suicidal violence a sacrament.

But as David Brooks reminds us, Islamic terrorists are not all, or even mainly, products of Arab dysfunction. Most are actually college-educated professionals from the middle and upper classes. They are basically rebels, embracing a simplistic utopian vision as a way to cut through the confusing fog of modern life's complex challenges, to somehow strike a blow against a dominant society, and to give their lives meaning. And this sort of thing has a long history, in many respects harking back to the leftist radicalism of earlier decades, perhaps even the bomb-throwing anarchists of the nineteenth century.

Meantime, we must also recognize that Islam is not really a benignly peaceful religion that, apart from a few fanatics, can coexist comfortably with the Western way of life. The problem is deeper and larger. As Sam Harris observes in *The End of Faith*, the Koran is saturated with venom against "infidels" (all non-Muslims) whom it insistently condemns to death; Harris quotes a numbingly long list of such passages. Because this reading of the Koran is not "extreme" or "radical" but, unfortunately, hard to avoid, it is no surprise that what we regard as Islamic extremism actually finds wide support throughout the Muslim world.

The foregoing discussion about our enemies should highlight a few key points.

First, their war against us was not somehow triggered by anything we've done to them, by any aspect of the much-maligned "US foreign policy." They do spout a lot about this, but that's because it provides a handy whipping boy, gets attention, and has demagogic value. It is always useful to have a clear enemy to set yourself against, especially if it is a "foreign devil." However, it is a mistake to read all this as indicating that the war is truly about US foreign policy.

Our enemies are not fighting to get our troops out of the Middle East or even for Palestinian independence. They have a bigger mission: restoration of the caliphate. And, to the extent they do hate us, it is not so much for anything specific we've done but, instead, because they have totally different visions for human society and consider our way of life an affront to God.

Thus, it should be obvious that there is nothing we can do to somehow mollify these enemies and make them desist. Calls to reach out to them, to listen to their grievances, to meet their hostility with understanding, to dialog with them, to try to resolve our differences—all that warm and fuzzy stuff—all reflects our humanistic vision, but not theirs. People who say we should listen to and understand our enemies seem to have done no such listening and to possess no such understanding. If they did, they would know that our enemies inhabit a wholly different universe wherein we are offenders against God and the only possible response is to kill us. There is no space for dialog with that.

This is highlighted by posing the question: what do the Islamists actually want from us? What, indeed, is their war aim? What would they perceive as victory? The answer has already been given. They want a restored caliphate ruling the world and imposing God's law. They seek our surrender to that vision.

Of course they can't win. But religion can blind people to reality.

At any rate, we clearly cannot give them what they seek. So how, then, are we to approach the challenge of this war?[221]

First, we have no choice but to tough it out. We must, of course, do everything possible to defeat these enemies and thwart their plots against us. But, at the same time, we must recognize the limits on our capabilities. We will never be able to keep out every terrorist or foil all their plans; some will get through, and they will hurt us. We have to steel ourselves and take the punches, knowing that, no matter how much pain this enemy inflicts, it can never defeat us. They think our society is weak, but they are wrong.

This is realistic, not hubristic. For all the damage of 9/11, in the big picture, it was a pinprick and not a body blow. A few buildings out of many thousands were knocked down; 0.001 percent of our people died. That kind of thing is horrible, but it will not destroy America. If our enemies strive this way to terrorize us, to defeat them we must refuse to be terror-stricken. Even if worse is yet to come, even if it's a biological or a nuclear attack, it will not demolish our way of life either. As in New York, we will dust ourselves off, mourn our losses, rebuild, and continue.

---

221. A word about our "allies." We grew accustomed to solidarity with many nations through the Cold War, and some blame America for undermining these relationships. But it has been said that nations have permanent interests, not permanent allies. France and Germany opposed America on Iraq not because it was doing something wrong, or failing to play nicely, but mainly because they no longer saw their own interests as coinciding with ours. Unlike in the Cold War, France, in particular, now views US power as a key problem, which its foreign policy is directed against.

These "old" Europeans also increasingly see themselves as culturally opposed to America, which they consider too religious, too vulgar, and too brash, and they deem their social welfare mind-set morally superior to American "harshness." They take a cynical view of America's emphasis on pushing freedom and democracy (a bit odd given that those very ideals impelled America to liberate those same European nations in WWII). But, despite all this, America and Europe still share many key values and are surely on the same side in the war launched by Islamic extremism.

We can be morally strong, knowing that we are defending a society worthy of defense, because its values are grounded in empowering every person to live the best life possible. We must remain steadfast in our adherence to our fundamental human values, not only for our own society, but for the Muslim world as well.

Some, again, deem it misguided to want Muslim societies to be more like ours. But Western societies do not produce legions of people who see no better use for their lives than to destroy them for the sake of taking others down with them. If this is to stop, Muslims must see opportunities to hope and dream and achieve. This *does* mean Muslim societies more like ours and less like they are now. We must reject the canard that this is "imposing" our values on them. It is not "arrogant" to think that what Muslim nations need is more freedom and opportunity for their citizens and more toleration toward religious and other cultural differences among people.

Thus, critics are correct in pointing out that our own war plan must go beyond efforts to stymie terrorist attacks and must address their root causes as well. But changing our foreign policy is not the way; that is not the root cause. Instead, we must do a far better job of defending and promoting our ideals and values throughout the world, persuading people that our vision is consonant with their own true self-interest. We won the Cold War chiefly because our values rather than communism won the war of ideas.

This one, too, is a war of ideas between two radically different visions of humanity and society. The war was sparked by a failure of ideas in the Muslim world. As Thomas Friedman points out, that Islamic fundamentalists and autocrats have had to resort to despicable violence shows their failure in the war of ideas.

In the long view, curing Muslim malaise is the key to ending the war. Of course, we in the West cannot render that cure; the war's front line is inside the Islamic community. Our task is to help, support, and encourage the decent, thoughtful, humanist individuals in that world to overcome the negative forces with which they must contend. The answer lies not with the antimodern, antidemocratic, and antihuman vision of Islamism, but rather with the true human vision and values that we share, those of the Enlightenment, of freedom and democracy, and the right of all people to seek their own bliss.

We cannot lose.

Coda

This book began with the familiar indictment of mankind: cruelty, greed, profligacy, and so forth—all the evils of civilization.

It's all true. Yet it overlooks a larger reality. Human life presents no simplistic monochrome picture. Instead, the story is, of course, extraordinarily complex and richly textured. There are surely nasty parts—we're not angels, we're human. Indeed, we are animals, and some pessimists actually compare us unfavorably against other, "innocent" creatures. But we arose out of a natural world in which the concept of morality did not even exist. And, considering that's where we came from, we have not done badly. In fact, we have risen from our amoral brutish origins to build a world in which there is at least *some*—many would say there's much—morality, justice, nobility, and virtue.

What does it all mean for me or you? How are we to think of and live our lives?

That we exist at all is nothing but a cosmic accident; and this absence of higher meaning leaves us free to make our lives mean, for each of us, whatever we choose. This means we have the opportunity to be happy and the right to be happy.

And we also have a most powerful tool for getting there: *reason*. It is by use of reason that we have ascended from living as animals to something better. Reason gives us all the gifts of knowledge and technology that enable us to surmount so much of the pain and suffering that nature inflicts upon her progeny. And reason provides to us something even more precious that no other creature has: our moral sense. While we are not angels, not perfect, and too often fail that moral sense by doing wrong, we are unique among species in *knowing* when we've done wrong and in *striving* to do better.

This is at the heart of our humanity. And it's not just some superficial gloss that reason has painted upon our animalistic nature. While evolution did instill us with aggression, competitiveness, selfishness, and so on, all those traits pessimists harp on, the fact is that survival for our ancestors also crucially required social cooperation and altruism within the tribe. That basic ingrained social sense was the foundation upon which, with our reason, we built our morality and civilization. Thus, both our nature and our reason tell us to value and promote, above all else, human life, and not just our own, but the lives of our fellows. This, in turn, leads us to understand that every person is equally entitled to enjoyment of life and freedom to seek it in his own way, and that justice means treating people fairly according to what they deserve.

This moral sense resides in every normal human being. It is why, notwithstanding whatever ugly qualities we may harbor, most people are good most of the time. That all of us may be capable of evil is not what matters. What really matters is what we actually do, how we behave, day in and day out, in the ordinary business of living among others. And the reality is that, in those normal everyday circumstances, *most* people, because they do have a moral sense built in by evolution and enhanced by reason, are decent, honest, kind, and just.

And we are entitled to happiness, as long as we seek it in ways that are consonant with our moral sense. If you do that, you can deservedly be happy, without laboring under a burden of unearned guilt for all the wrongs and sufferings that exist in the world. You don't *owe* it to everyone on Earth to sacrifice yourself for them; however, doing good deeds for others, not from duty but from free choice, is one way to enhance your own life. And, regardless of whether you gain personal fulfillment in that way or by some other means, your own happiness augments the global happiness quotient and thereby also makes the world a better place.

So we are free to be happy even in an imperfect world. We can see the glass as half full rather than half empty. We can find meaning in our lives through doing good, through love, or by using our creative talents to accomplish worthwhile things. In all these ways, we use our rational minds. That is how we live truly. This means taking responsibility for ourselves and our actions. And it means making judgments: between truth and falsity, good and bad, right and wrong. By making such judgments and choices we live that moral sense that elevates us above the other beasts.

This is what freedom is ultimately all about. The word is so commonplace that perhaps we lose touch with what it really signifies. That we are, again, moral beings with the power to choose is what ennobles our lives; take that away and we might as well be machines or insects. They cannot make free choices; to them, freedom is a meaningless concept. Our ability to make moral decisions for ourselves—the essence of freedom—is, again, what defines our humanity.

Our biologically wired and reason-based moral sense leads us into society, where we broaden our opportunity to live rewarding lives. Society's foundation is the social contract. In exchange for the law's protection, we give up some freedom, mainly the use of violence. In doing this, though, we actually seek to maximize our true freedom, our humanness. Society's purpose is to provide the environment in which all people can flourish in their own ways.

But we must constantly struggle over this balancing act of giving up some liberties in order to gain the most true freedom. To that end we created government, but must battle mightily to keep it our servant and not our master. The great political debate is always over how much liberty we must give up for the sake of serving our human needs.

Some are all too eager to deprive people of freedom in order to promote other social values. Implicitly believing we are basically selfish, they want government to regiment us into acting for the common good.

But trying to achieve social cohesion by force can only serve to undermine it; attempts to improve the species by coercive means have always been doomed to fail. The truth is that people are naturally socially cooperative and, if left to their own devices, they tend to show it. Thus, freedom is not incompatible with social values; it is itself the most fundamental of social values. And because we do have a moral sense and do usually behave decently without compulsion, we are rightly entitled to enjoy freedom rather than being told what we must do.

This freedom of every person to seek his own bliss in his own way is the moral idea at the heart of market economics as well. Participating in the economy is a key way by which we strive to realize our dreams. In a sense, this is self-serving. But, as we've seen, commerce is no zero-sum game with a winner and a loser in every transaction. Instead, everybody is made better off; goods become available at prices people are willing to pay and resources are utilized more efficiently. That's how leaving people free to act in their own interests ends up enriching all of society.

Of course there is inequality. A lot of it is just luck. But the rich don't get their wealth at the expense of the poor; profit and wealth are not immoral but are generated through creating value that others willingly pay for; and much inequality is a consequence of peoples' differing talents, skills, and efforts, and what value they create. True justice means rewarding that. Such inequality can be eliminated only by destroying the free market's incentives for productive effort. Instead of having rich and poor, we'd all be poor. Moreover, while the market economy serves society by means of empowering people to seek their happiness, in contrast, the alternative models all operate by coercion, by taking away from people what they've rightfully earned. That is no justice, it is not moral, and it never works.

So schemes for more "justly" carving up the economic pie only make it smaller. We make it bigger by letting people run their own lives, keep what they earn, and spend it as they choose. A society's true virtue is best measured by how well it does this—how free it is and how successful at empowering people to attain their happiness.

No country has ever been better at this than the United States of America. We say "God bless America"—but its true blessing comes from the human beings who worked to build this wonderful nation and who continue working at it every day.

As pessimists keep reminding us, the past century was full of horrors. Yet its far bigger story was of unparalleled human gains. Worldwide average life spans almost doubled and incomes grew fivefold. People are living longer, healthier, and better. And this all occurred while population rose at unprecedented rates. The explanation is that adding people doesn't add just mouths to feed, but also hands to work, and most people produce more than they consume.

Knowledge and technology are key factors here. Population has not outrun the food supply because farming advances made the opposite occur. Our working hands and minds become ever more productive. That spreads wealth and raises living standards, widening our choices and ability to control our lives.

Francis Fukuyama has written of "the end of history." What he means by this curious phrase is that the societal model encompassing democratic politics, free-market economics, and individual rights has achieved a triumph that is final, because that model at last gives us the means to gain what we have always wanted, materially and spiritually. Much of that, Fukuyama contends, boils down to a hunger for recognition as human beings of dignity and worth. This has been a prime source of past conflict. But democracy and economic freedom enable people to satisfy their craving for recognition and self-realization through cooperation rather than conflict.

Thus, the biggest fact of modern history is that the world, taken as a whole, has experienced a democratic revolution. The blight of war and violence has been receding while freedom and human rights are spreading. At the same time, our society grows not only richer, but more open, tolerant, humane, and fair.

All this I call progress. Today's world is the best ever; and tomorrow's will be better still.

It is true that all our gains have a cost; nothing comes free. So we do have some environmental problems. But never forget that they are the unavoidable price for living the lives we enjoy. We could never have risen from the caves while leaving the planet unspoiled. Surely the trade-off has been well worth it.

And, just as increasing knowledge is a force for improving our lives, so, too, does it equip us to cope with environmental challenges. Our planet, though beautiful and lush, is not hospitable for anything but a hardscrabble existence. The central story of humankind is our battle with that environment, to overcome those challenges and carve out decent lives. Our achievement in doing so has been stupendous. Be proud of what we've done.

I have quoted Newton saying he stood upon the shoulders of giants. I, too, in living my life, in raising my child, and in writing this book, feel that I stand on such shoulders: of Aristotle, Jefferson, Darwin, Mill, Frankl, Adam Smith, Rosa Parks, Milton Friedman, Newton himself, and others beyond counting—my own parents too—and, indeed, all the nameless billions of men and women through the ages who, in their own countless special ways, were giants.

We arrived on this Earth as naked animals, starting with nothing, daring to quest for the great prize of knowledge and, through titanic struggle, we grasped hold of it. And we have used that knowledge to make a better world, with lives far finer than what nature handed us.

Yes, her sea is vast indeed, and our boats are very small. But with our reason, our courage, our grit, we set out upon our journey.

And we *shall* reach the stars.

Index

AARP, 240
abortion issue, 154, 154n102, 180, 298–305, 313n213, 326n220
academic freedom, 284
action vs. thought, 65, 67, 67n42
ADA. *See* Americans with Disabilities Act
Adams, John, 195
"adaptation" effect, 55
adoption, 304, 327
Adventures of Huckleberry Finn, The (Twain), 26–27
advertising, 238
affirmative action, 291–94
affluence, 51–52, 55, 157–58n107, 192, 248–49, 267
   See also rich; wealth
affordable housing, 142
Afghanistan, 92, 197, 198, 201, 329
Africa, 218, 256, 288
African Americans. *See* blacks
aging, 19n9, 248–49, 267
AIDS, 326
Airbus (company), 224n151

air pollution. *See* pollution
air travel, 275–76, 276n188
Alaskan oil spill, 176n118, 232
Albany, New York, 277, 277n189, 278
alcohol, 317, 319
Alger, Horatio, 193
Allen, Woody, 61, 70n44
allies in war on terror, 334n221
al Qaeda, 71–72, 331
altruism, 35, 36–38, 36n25, 41, 246, 338
American Crisis, The (Paine), 184n122
Americans with Disabilities Act, 175–76, 175n117, 176n118, 180
amnesia, 272
Amnesty International, 200
Amoco (company), 139, 141
Amtrak, 203n141
animal rights, 26n14, 306–10
anthropocentrism, 307
anti-Americanism, 125, 187, 187n126, 194, 196–97,

197nn134-136, 199n139, 284, 328–29
antibiotics, 96n60
anticommunism, 123, 124, 284n196, 285–86
Apollo 13 (moon ship), 270
Arabs. *See* Islamic extremism
Aristotle, 23, 24, 30, 342
Armenian genocide, 275
Arnold, Matthew, 245n168
arsenic reduction, 75–76
art, evaluating, 83, 83–84nn50-51
artificial intelligence, 60n38, 266
Asimov, Isaac, 266n183
assembly lines, 205
assisted suicide, 320, 320n218
AT&T (company), 240, 240n164
Athens, 183
atomic bomb, 155n103
"atomism," 134
Auschwitz, 92
autarky, 220
authoritarianism, 329, 331
autism, 37n26
autocracy, 183, 335
auto death statistics, 106, 107, 107n72
automation, 267
aviation death statistics, 105–106, 106nn70-71
Ayer, A. J., 87

baby boomers, 162
bacteria, 103, 107
Balkans, 189
Baltic states, 274
Bangladesh, 225n152

bankruptcy, 146
bartering, 214
"Beast in the Jungle, The" (James), 45n30
Beethoven, Ludwig van, 117
beliefs vs. knowledge, 21–22, 24
Bell, Derek, 150
bell-shaped curve, 78, 114n75
Bentham, Jeremy, 39–40, 308
benzene, 139, 141
Berle, Adolf, 210–11
Berlin Airlift, 200
Berlin Wall, 256
Berra, Yogi, 81n49, 113n74
Bhopal tragedy, 236
"big bang," 97–99, 97n62
"big box" store, 190n128
Bill of Rights. *See* Constitution
bin Laden, Osama, 80, 329
biosphere, 134–35
birthrates, 248
bisexuality, 326
black hole, 99n65
blacklisting, 285–86
blacks, 69, 91, 184, 188, 188n127, 273, 287–97
"blank slates," 62
Boeing (company), 224n151
Bohm, David, 61
Bolingbroke, Lord, 273
Book of Mormon, 80
Borg (fictional characters), 121
Bosnia, 200, 242, 295
Bowling Alone (Putnam), 166n114
Bradley, F. H., 15n3
brain, 59–61, 60n37, 70
    See also mind

brain imaging, 36, 59, 79
Britain, Great, 245n168
"British Disease," 165
Brockovich, Erin, 231, 231n156
"bronze rule," 29, 29–30n17, 31, 86
Brooks, David, 91, 163, 242, 243, 282, 332
Brussels, 241
BSE. *See* mad cow disease
budget deficit, 158n108, 217n147
Bulgaria, 254–55n173
bureaucracy, 153, 154, 171, 228, 232n157
Bush, George W., 75, 161, 222
Byzantine Empire, 273n186

Calvinism, 39
Cambodia, 199n139
campaign finance reform, 140, 148, 149n98, 150
Camus, Albert, 15
Canada, 225n152
Candide (fictional character), 54
cannibalism, 307, 309
capitalism, 121, 202–16, 204n142, 222, 238
Capitalism and Freedom (Friedman), 164
capital punishment, 312–15, 314–15nn214-215
"Captive Nations Day," 256
Carlson, Richard, 115
Carnegie Endowment, 223
Carroll, Lewis, 284n199
Carter, Jimmy, 67n42
censorship, 286
CEO. *See* chief executive officers

Cervantes, Miguel de, 78n48
charity, 35, 53n34, 156, 171–72, 180, 230
charter schools, 77
Chase, Stuart, 267
Chavez, Hugo, 227n153
Chechnya, 244, 246
Chevron (company), 236
Chicago, 145, 180
chief executive officers, 232, 235–36, 235n160
child pornography, 286n200
China, 105n69, 120, 134, 200, 244–45, 245n167, 256, 259, 276–77
  economy of, 165, 218, 223n150, 224–25, 226, 257
Chomsky, Noam, 196
Christianity, 22, 131, 329
Churchill, Winston, 182, 262
Civilization and Its Discontents (Freud), 68
civil liberties, 150, 152, 152n99, 195, 318, 319
civil marriage, 325–26
Civil Rights Act (1964), 153n101
Civil War (US), 74, 188n127, 195, 272, 273
class action suits, 178–79n120
climate, 261, 262, 288
Clinton, Bill, 71–72, 137, 150, 159
cloning, 301–302
coin selling business, 31n19, 204, 206n144
Cold War, 272, 278n191, 334n221, 335
Collapse (Diamond), 236, 260

collectives and collectivism, 121, 134, 209
colleges and universities, 283–85, 284nn197-199, 285–86
color-blind society, 292
communism, 121, 122, 122n82, 134, 156, 159, 335
　anticommunism, 123, 124, 284n196, 285–86
　in Asia, 199, 199n139, 245
　economics and, 161, 164, 202n140, 214
"communist chic," 283
"comparative advantage," 219
competition, 203n141, 210–11, 220–22, 239
computers, 60, 60n37, 61, 105, 112, 113, 267
concentration camp, 43, 92
conception, 300, 304n212
Confucius, 29n16
Congress, 140, 141–42, 147, 162n112, 177, 177n119
Congressional Budget Office, 162
consciousness, 17–18, 27, 271, 307
　individual consciousness, 46, 59–68, 132
　social consciousness, 134, 166
conservatives, 120, 123–25, 163, 215
　See also Right (political)
"conspicuous consumption," 52
Constantinople, 273n186
Constitution, 128, 154, 179
　Bill of Rights, 128n87, 157n105
　First Amendment, 280, 284n198, 285

Fourteenth Amendment, 319
Fourth Amendment, 318
consumerism, 34, 143–44, 144n94, 211, 237–40
contraception, 304
cooperation, 134, 209n146, 243
　social cooperation, 31, 31n18, 36–37, 246, 308, 338
corporations, 210, 218, 224, 231–40, 235n160, 239–40
　corporate welfare, 150, 170
　demonizing of business, 9, 93n58, 144n95, 231, 235, 238, 239
　and social responsibility, 236, 236n162
corporatist, 122n82
Cosby, Bill, 297
cosmology, 95–100
cost-benefit analysis, 75, 212
cover-ups, 66, 66n40, 71
"creative destruction," 211, 223
credit cards, 53, 193
crime, 311–20
Crook, Clive, 234n159
Crumbley-Snoot bill, 147
Crusoe, Robinson (fictional character), 133
"cultural imperialism," 196
cultural relativism, 89–91, 330–31
Cuomo, Mario, 187
currency exchange rates, 223n150

Danish newspaper cartoon, 282–83
Danko, William D., 53
Dante, 89
Darfur, 242
"dark matter," 97

Darwin, Charles, 24, 97, 211, 342
David (Michelangelo), 117
daycare centers, 142
DDT, 76, 104n68, 268
"dead white males" ideology, 89, 90
Dean, Howard, 71n45
death, 19–20, 19n9, 26n13, 45–46, 48, 271, 302n209
   death sentence, 45, 312–15, 314–15nn214-215
   euthanasia, 319–20, 320n218
   statistics on, 105–106, 106nn70-71, 107, 107n72, 248–49, 253, 262n179
Death of Common Sense, The (Howard), 141, 180
Declaration of Independence, 51, 127, 128, 129, 175, 179, 188, 199
deconstruction, 84n53
deferred gratification, 56–57
deficit, 158n108, 217n147
Delaware River, crossing of, 184–85, 185n123, 186
Dell (company), 220
democracy, 27, 119–20, 128, 148, 182–201, 242, 341
Democratic party, 123, 294n205
Dennett, Daniel, 61
descent with modification, 96
determinism, 64
Diamond, Jared, 236, 260, 260n176, 288
Dickens, Charles, 53, 57
Dickerson, Debra, 290n202, 297
dictatorships, 93n58, 199, 256, 278n191

Diogenes, 265n181
disabled, 175–77, 175n117, 180
discrimination, 153n101, 176n118, 290, 292, 293, 296, 324–25
Disraeli, Benjamin, 76
divine right, 126, 128n87
DNA, 16–18, 17n5, 31, 36, 47, 78, 322, 324
Dobzhansky, Theodosius, 97
Doctors Without Borders, 156
Dolphins (football team), 278
domestic violence, 102–103, 103n66
"domino effect," 199n139
Donne, John, 112
Don't Believe Everything You Think (Kida), 80
Don't Sweat the Small Stuff, and It's All Small Stuff (Carlson), 115
drugs, 143–44, 317–19
"due process," 319
dust bowl, 262

East Timor, 244, 246
eBay, 31n19
economics, 28, 41n29, 119, 164, 165, 171, 206, 218–19n149, 230
   "economic hypochondria," 192
   economic incentives, 56n36, 160, 164, 207, 212, 214, 236, 240
   economic inequality, 190, 191, 192, 193, 202, 207–208, 209
   economic injustice, 202, 217, 219, 223, 224
   supply side economics, 160–61n110

See also capitalism; communism; free market; laissez-faire

Economist, The (magazine), 166, 191, 234n159, 236n162

Edsel car, 239

education, 10–11, 77, 177, 192, 194n133, 211–12, 296
and global economy, 226, 229, 254
higher education, 193, 194

Egypt, 201, 269, 329

Einstein, Albert, 25, 269

elections, 71, 93, 120, 145, 147, 148n97, 149, 149n98, 161–62
electoral competition, 148, 148n97
See also voting

Eliot, George, 89

embryos, 298, 300n208, 301–302, 302n209, 303

Emmanuel, Steven, 30

emotion and reason, 26n12, 67, 67n42, 72–73

empiricism, 21–22

Endangered Species Act (ESA), 177–78, 180

End of Blackness, The (Dickerson), 290n202, 297

End of Faith, The (Harris), 74, 316n216, 332

end of history, 341

ends justifying means, 41n28, 155

energy consumption, 260n176

Enlightenment, 121, 121n81, 330, 336

Enron (company), 235n160

entitlements, 144n94, 162, 163, 178, 180

entropy, 269

environmental issues, 74–76, 93n57, 135n90, 198n137, 218–19n149, 254n172, 264
doomsayers, 252, 252n171, 253–55, 257–62, 257n175, 261n178, 268n185
environmental fascism, 135
extremism, 268

Environmental Protection Agency (EPA), 139, 140–41

Epicureanism, 33

equality, 28, 28n15, 32, 129, 210, 215, 338
See also inequality

Erhard, Ludwig, 165

Erin Brockovich (movie), 231

Eritrea, 244

Ethical Ambition (Bell), 150

Ethiopia, 244

ethnicity, 277, 287–97
ethnic strife, 188, 247, 247n170, 282, 295
ethnic cleansing, 197, 247n170

ethnocentrism, 89

Europe, 56, 56n36, 154n102, 173, 288, 334n221

"European social model," 165

European Union, 241, 247

euthanasia, 319–20, 320n218

Everything You Always Wanted to Know about Sex (movie), 61

evil, 85–86, 86n55, 87, 90, 93nn57-58, 94
See also good and evil

Evil: An Investigation (Morrow), 86n55

evil scum, 231–40

evolution, 16–17, 44, 62, 82, 96–97, 96nn59-60, 133, 322
  cooperation needed for, 31, 36, 246, 338
  genetic replication as purpose of, 17, 17n6, 50, 109, 115, 271
  natural selection, 24, 36n25, 96
  technology and, 265–66, 265n182
existentialism, 65
experimentation using animals, 308–309
exploitation of workers, 121, 165, 206–208, 224, 307
expression, freedom of. *See* speech, freedom of
Exxon Mobil (company), 176n118, 232
eyes, evolution of, 96n59

faith, 11, 22, 24, 80, 81
fame, 48–49, 48n31
family violence, 103n66
farm subsidy program, 146–47, 148, 149n98, 222, 240
fascism, 122, 122n82, 135, 159
fathers, absence of black fathers, 296
Faulkner, William, 273
FDA. *See* Food and Drug Administration
Federal Reserve, 204n142
fetus, 299–300, 299n207
"fifteen minutes of fame," 48, 48n31
"Fifth Symphony" (Beethoven), 117
Finn, Huckleberry (fictional character), 26–27

First Amendment to Constitution, 280, 284n198, 285
first cause, 95
Fitzgerald, F. Scott, 185
Flaubert, Gustave, 78n48
flight, first, 275–76
flying, fear of, 105–106, 276n188
Food and Drug Administration, 143–44
food chain, 306
Ford, Henry, 205, 239, 267, 272
foreign policy of US, 200–201, 333
fossil fuels, 260
Fourteenth Amendment to Constitution, 319
Fourth Amendment to Constitution, 318
France, 245, 334n221
Frank, Anne, 9, 29
"Frankenfood," 104–105
Frankenstein (fictional character), 266
Frankl, Viktor, 43, 44, 342
Fraser Institute, 230
freedom of religion, 179
freedom of speech, 149n98, 152n99, 179, 280–86, 286n200
freedom of the press, 179
free market, 79, 123, 164, 165–66, 202–16, 222, 237, 309–10, 340
  invisible hand, 133, 203, 204, 206
  success of, 144, 145n96, 218, 226, 233, 234, 341
free trade, 124, 218
free will, 63–65, 68
French Revolution, 120
Freud, Sigmund, 68

Friedman, Benjamin, 218–19n149
Friedman, Milton, 164, 167, 173n115, 204n142, 342
Friedman, Thomas, 226, 335
Fukuyama, Francis, 341
fundamentalism, religious, 124, 195
    See also Islamic extremism

Gaia, 135n90
game theory, 29–30n17
Gandhi, Mahatma, 220
garbage, 233, 233n158
Garden of Eden, 269
Garfunkel, Art, 111
Gates, Bill, 237
gay marriage, 325–26, 326n220
gays and lesbians. *See* homosexuality
GDP. *See* Gross Domestic Product
gender differences, 114, 114n75, 284n197, 322
genetically modified food, 104–105, 105n69, 107, 257n175, 268
genetic replication, 17, 17n6, 109, 115, 271
genetic similarities of humans, 277n190, 287–88
Germany, 165, 198, 200, 225, 243, 245, 275, 295, 334n221
germs, 96n60, 103, 103n67, 107
gerrymandering, 148n97
ghettoization, 247, 294n203
"ghost in the machine," 59
Gingrich revolution and Newt Gingrich, 161, 162
Give Me a Break (Stossel), 145n96, 172, 176n118

"giving something back," 34, 34n24
global cooling, 261n178
global warming, 261
GM food. *See* genetically modified food
God, 15, 21, 32, 32nn20-21, 63, 84n52, 95, 266
Goering, Hermann Wilhelm, 257
Goethe, Johann Wolfgang von, 89, 90
"golden rule," 29, 29n16
Golding, William, 127n86
Goldwater, Barry, 123, 124
good and evil, 63, 84, 84n52, 85n54, 89, 339
    See also evil
good Samaritans, 35–36, 209n145, 303
government, 137–51, 182–201, 186n125, 239–40, 241–50, 306–10
    core functions, 125, 166
    growth of, 152–58, 159–68
    paternalistic government, 159–68, 172, 182, 213
    regulations, 137–51, 152–58, 228
    role of, 127–28, 169–74
    See also bureaucracy; politics
graduated income tax, 157n106
Grasso, Richard, 235n160
gravity, 98–99n64
Gray, John, 114
Great Depression, 122–23, 204n142, 272
Great Pyramid of Giza, 269
Greece, 321
greed, 68, 202, 233–34, 235n161, 265

"green revolution," 257n175
gridlock, 213
Gross Domestic Product, 230,
  230n155, 254–55n173
group survival, 36, 36n25
"groupthink," 69–70, 79
Guantanamo detainees, 200
guaranteed annual income, 173n115
Guevara, Che, 268
guilt, 39, 64, 65, 66n40, 224, 264, 338
  and innocence, 290n202,
    313n213, 315
  and shame, 36, 63, 66, 87
Gujarat, 295
gulags, 200
Guns, Germs, and Steel (Diamond),
  288

Haiti, 200, 228
half-empty vs. half-full glass, 42, 54
Hamlet (Shakespeare), 117
handicapped. *See* disabled
happiness, 33–41, 42–50, 50n32,
  53, 54, 57, 86, 111
  measuring, 39–40, 39n27
  and pleasure, 34, 34n22, 38, 40
"harassment codes," 284n198
Harris, Sam, 74, 332
Harvard University, 55n35, 114n75,
  265n181, 284n197
Hayek, Friedrich A. von, 164
Head Start, 169–74
healthcare issue, 157–58, 157–
  58n107, 178–79, 213, 214
hedonism, 41
Hemings, Sally, 274n187
hermaphrodites, 322

higher education, 193, 194
highway congestion, 213
highway death rate, 106, 107,
  107n72
Hippocratic Oath, 320n218
Hirst, Damien, 83, 83–84nn50-51,
  92
history, lessons of, 272–79, 341
Hitler, Adolf, 26, 26n11, 88, 269,
  282, 295n206
Hobbes, Thomas, 127, 127n86, 129
Hoffer, Eric, 187n126
Hofstadter, Richard, 93n58
holism, 135
Hollywood and blacklisting, 285–86
Holmes, Oliver Wendell, 281
Holocaust, 25, 86, 252, 274–75
"holy war," 332
homelessness, 77, 142
Homer, 89
homosexuality, 321–27
Hong Kong, 165, 218, 246
Horowitz, Vladimir, 176
housing codes, 142
Howard, Philip, 141, 145, 180
Hoyle, Fred, 97n62
hubris, national, 245n169
Hugo, Victor, 89
Human Accomplishment (Murray),
  83–84n51, 271
"Human Development Indicator,"
  254–55n173
human dignity, 208, 293, 320, 325,
  341
human nature, 30, 32, 62
human rights, 60n38, 175–81, 256,
  259, 308

humans, 23, 209n146, 257, 264–71
  genetic similarities of, 277n190, 287–88
human trafficking, 317
Hume, David, 87
Huntington, Samuel, 328
Hurricane Katrina, 139, 186n125
Hussein, Saddam, 198n137, 257, 278n191
Huxley, Aldous, 40
Huxley, T. H., 97n61

ice age, 261, 262
"I have a scream" speech, 71n45
immigration issues, 141–42, 194–95, 247–49, 272, 296–97
immune systems, 103n67
imperialism, 187, 196, 197, 197n136, 198, 330
imprisonment. See prison
impulses, 68
incarceration rate, 319
incentives, 29, 51, 211, 216
  economic incentives, 56n36, 160, 164, 207, 212, 214, 236, 240
incest, 302
income, 190–95, 191n129, 192n131, 253, 254, 254–55n173, 259
"Index of Social Health," 254–55n173
India, 244, 255n174, 259
Indians, North American. See Native Americans
individualism, 131–36, 131n88
individuality, 131n88, 132n89
Indonesia, 244, 295

inequality, 28, 78n48, 202, 216, 217–30, 293, 340
  economic inequality, 190, 191, 192, 193, 202, 207–208, 209
  global inequality, 217, 219, 223n150, 226
  See also equality
infidels, 332
inflation, 191n129
infrastructure, 228
"in-group," 246
injustice, 28, 188, 189, 207
  economic injustice, 202, 217, 219, 223, 224
  See also justice
"inner directed" personality, 70
Inquisition, 284
insects, 96n60, 104n68
institutional racism, 290
insulin, 105n69
insurance, 178–79
integration, 188, 292, 293–94
  See also segregation
intelligence, 78–79, 139, 177
interest groups, 147–49
  See also lobbying
Internet, 239–40, 267
interracial marriage, 325
intolerance, 249
intuition, 22
"invisible hand," 133, 203, 204, 206
in vitro fertilization, 300–301
Iran, 120, 197n134, 329
Iraq, 73, 92, 197, 198n137, 201, 242, 278n191
  Iraq war, 74, 74n47, 93n57, 198, 198n138, 200, 334n221

Islamic extremism, 282–83, 328–36
  See also 9/11 terrorist attacks
Israel, 243, 295, 329, 330
Italy, 288
"ivory tower," 283

James, Henry, 45n30
Japan, 224n151, 225, 245, 275
Japanese Americans, internment of, 189, 198
Jefferson, Thomas, 199, 256, 274n187, 281, 342
Jesus, 82, 85
Jewish tribes, 80
Jews, 295
"jihad," 332
"Jim Crow," 292–93
job security legislation, 173
Johnson, Lyndon B., 138, 172
Joneses, keeping up with, 55, 55n35
Jordan, 223
judgmental thinking, 85, 93
judiciary, 154, 154n102, 188–89
Julius Caesar, 44, 48–49
justice, 27–28, 155, 210, 227n153, 311–20
  See also injustice
Justinian II, 273n186

Kagan, Donald, 273
Kalahari, 92
Kant, Immanuel, 34, 35, 41n28
Kashmir, 244
Katrina (hurricane), 139, 186n125
Kennedy, John F., 81, 149, 200
Kepler, Johann, 24
Khmer Rouge, 199n139

Khomeini, Ruhollah, 197n134
Kida, Thomas, 80
King, Martin Luther, 292
kingship, 126, 126n85
Kinsey, Alfred C., 85
Kinsley, Michael, 124
Kirkpatrick, Jeane, 328
Kitty Hawk, North Carolina, 275
knowledge vs. beliefs, 21–22, 24
Koran, 331–33
Korea. *See* North Korea; South Korea
Kors, Alan Charles, 284n198
Kosovo, 73, 74n47, 197, 200, 295, 329
Kristol, Irving, 124
Kurzweil, Ray, 265n182
Kushner, Harold, 112
Kuwait, 73, 197, 201

labor, division of, 214
labor unions, 121n80, 149
laissez-faire, 122, 125, 164–65, 209n146
language, 64
Latin America, 222, 256
Latvia, 256
Laurel and Hardy, 243–44n166
law, rule of, 226–29, 227n153
law and lawyers, 226–29, 240, 268n185, 311–20
law of supply and demand, 203–204, 212
law of unintended consequences, 140, 150, 164, 199n139
lawsuits, 178–79, 231n156, 240
Lazarus, Emma, 194

LeBlanc, Steven, 265n181
Left (political), 74n47, 79, 90–92, 156n104, 161, 187, 239, 283
　facism and, 122, 122n82
　history of, 120–21, 122, 122n82, 123–25
　and McCarthyism, 284, 284n196
　redistribution of wealth, 202, 208, 210
　See also anti-Americanism; liberalism
legalizing drugs, 317–19
legitimacy, 120
leisure time, 267
Lenin, Vladimir Ilyich, 80, 156, 283, 284
Leopold, Aldo, 134, 135
lesbians and gays. *See* homosexuality
level playing field, 215
Lewis, Bernard, 330
libel, 281
liberalism, 123n83, 163, 189, 194n133, 215
　history of, 121–22, 123–25
　and role of government, 137, 150, 152–58
　See also Left (political)
Liberia, Kuwait, 201
libertarianism, 125, 156, 166
life, 11, 38, 45n30, 234, 314
　beginning of baby's life. *See* abortion issue
　gift of life, 18–19, 33, 43
　the good life, 33–41, 57, 111
　meaning of, 11, 13, 15–20, 21–22
　origin of life, 16–18, 96–97
　quality of life, 44, 52, 56, 102, 190, 234, 254–55n173
　sanctity of life, 308, 313, 313n213
　value of life, 44, 305, 307, 308
life spans, 253
lifestyle, 53, 254n172
light years, 98n63
limited liability, 232
Lincoln, Abraham, 186
Lithuania, 256
litigation, 75, 176, 178–79, 180, 231n156, 232n290
"live and let live," 13, 180, 241, 243, 244, 282, 324
living standards. *See* standard of living
lobbying, 146–48, 161–62, 170, 222
Locke, John, 126
logging industry, 178
logic, 24
Lomborg, Bjorn, 252n171
London, 213
Lonely Crowd, The (Riesman), 70
Lord of the Flies (Golding), 127n86
love, 49–50, 67n42, 109–18
"love thy neighbor," 247n170
Low, Bobbi, 265n181
Lowell, Percival, 22
luck, 28, 46, 171, 193, 215, 319, 340
Luddites, 104–105, 224, 264–65
"lump of labor," 248
lust, 67n42, 68, 321
lynchings, 295n206

MacArthur, Douglas, 198
Macbeth, Lady (fictional character), 275

mad cow disease, 103
majority rule, 145, 154n102, 157, 157n105, 183
Mallaby, Sebastian, 149
Malthus, Thomas, 251, 257
Mandela, Nelson, 269
Man's Search for Meaning (Frankl), 43
manufacturing, 224n151, 233
Mao Zedong, 156, 269
marijuana, 319
market failure, 212
marriage, 50n32, 109–18, 325, 325–26, 326n220
Mars canals, 22
Marshall Plan, 200
Marxism and Karl Marx, 121, 121n80, 191n130, 203, 205, 206, 214, 255n174
Maslow, Abraham, 49
masochism, 39
materialism, 34, 51–52, 58
"maximizers," 54
McCain-Feingold law, 140, 148, 149n98
McCarthyism and Joseph McCarthy, 284, 284n196, 285
McDonald's (fast food), 63
McJobs, 192
McWhorter, John, 294
meaning of life. *See* life
media, 70–72, 71n45, 102–103, 279n193
Medicaid, 162
medical malpractice, 178–79
Medicare, 162, 170
"melting pot," 247

Men Are from Mars, Women Are from Venus (Gray), 114
Mencken, H. L., 34
Merchant of Venice, The (Shakespeare), 277
Mexican War, 197n136
Michelangelo, 83, 83–84n51, 92, 117
middle class, 121n80, 157–58n107, 192, 193, 297
Middlemarch (Eliot), 89
military and gays, 324–25
military-industrial complex, 150
military spending, 205–206n143
Mill, John Stuart, 39, 83, 166, 342
Millionaire Next Door, The (Stanley and Danko), 53
Milosevic, Slobodan, 257, 295n206
Milton, John, 89
mind, 59, 60n38
  See also brain
minimum wage, 173
minority rights, 157n105, 157n106
mirror neurons, 37n26
misanthropy, 27
mobility, social, 194n133
Mobutu, Joseph, 229
Model T car, 267
mohair, subsidy for, 162n112
money, 214, 223n150, 230, 254, 267
monkeys, 97
monopolistic practices, 210, 225
Moral Consequences of Economic Growth, The (Friedman), 218–19n149
morality, 26–32, 32nn20-21, 34–36, 41n28, 87n56, 88, 273, 306, 338–39

moral relativism, 64, 82, 85, 85n54, 93n57
Mormons, 80
Morrow, Lance, 86n55
mortality, 19–20, 19nn8–9, 26n13, 46
Mozart, Wolfgang Amadeus, 78n48
Mugabe, Robert, 227, 229
multitasking, 267n184
murder, 87, 312–15, 315n215, 318
Murray, Charles, 83–84n51, 271
Muslims. *See* Islamic extremism
mutations, 96
mysticism, 22, 25

NAFTA. *See* North American Free Trade Agreement (1993)
"nanny state," 159–68
nationalism, 189, 243
nationalization of industries, 165
National Socialists. *See* Nazism
nation-states, 241–50, 243n165
Native Americans, 80, 172, 188–89, 249
natural laws, 31
natural resources, depleting of, 252, 258, 259–60
natural selection. *See* evolution
nature, tampering with, 104–105, 105n69, 264–71
Nazism, 26, 26n11, 31, 43, 69, 78, 90, 122, 200, 243, 282
  as movie/TV bad guys, 231, 239
Nebuchadnezzar, 245n168
"negative income tax," 173n115
neoconservative, 124
New Coke, 239
news media. *See* media

Newton, Isaac, 23, 342
New York Stock Exchange, 235n160
Nichomachean Ethics (Aristotle), 30
Nigeria, 228, 295
"nigger," 281, 286, 296
9/11 terrorist attacks, 85, 88, 139, 186, 334
  and civil liberties, 195, 283
  and flying, 105–106, 108, 276n188
  See also Islamic extremism
Nineteen Eighty-Four (Orwell), 119
Nixon, Richard M., 66n40, 71
"noble savage," 265, 265n181
nonjudgmentalism, 64, 72, 82–94, 85n54
nonviolence, 313
North American Free Trade Agreement (1993), 222–23
North Korea, 73, 74, 119, 120, 197, 220
North Vietnam, 199
Norway, 228
Nostradamus, 81
nuclear power, 101–102, 104, 106, 106n71, 107, 261n177
nurture vs. nature, 322

obesity, 254n172
objectivism, 12, 38
Occam's (Ockham's) razor, 80–81
Occupational Safety and Health Administration, 141, 159
offensive speech, 281–83, 282n194, 284–85, 284nn197-199
Oil Age, 260
"oil-for-food," 242
oil reserves, 252, 260, 331

Old Testament, 247n170
Olympics, 279
Onassis, Aristotle, 47
optimism, 42, 46, 50, 54, 339
orgasm, 116
origin of life. *See* life
Origin of Species, The (Darwin), 24
Orwell, George, 119, 284
OSHA. *See* Occupational Safety and Health Administration
Oswald, Lee Harvey, 81
"other directed" personality, 70
outsourcing, 224–26, 225n152
overpopulation, 255n174

pacifism, 73–74, 74n47, 265
pain, 37n26, 39–40, 108, 111, 253, 307, 319
  and suffering, 38, 39, 42–43, 135, 271, 277, 338
Paine, Tom, 184n122
Pakistan, 244
Palestine, 243, 295, 330, 333
Panama, 197
Panama Canal, 185n124, 197n136
Papua New Guinea, 236
Paradox of Choice, The (Schwartz), 54
"Paranoid Style in American Politics, The" (Hofstadter), 93n58
parental notification requirements, 299
parenthood, dual, 326–27
Parks, Rosa, 151, 342
parsimony, principle of, 80–81
patriotism, 184n122, 187, 189, 283n195

pay to play, 148
peace, 73–74, 199n139, 219, 253, 265n181
pedophiles, 324
"people power," 256
personal responsibility, 59–68, 303
personhood, 299
pesticides, 76, 96n60, 104, 104n68, 105n69, 107
pharmaceutical factory, bombing of, 71–72, 274
Philippines, 197n136, 198
Pirsig, Robert, 83
planets, 98–99n64
Plato, 67, 90, 182
"playing God," 266
pleasure, 33–34, 34n22, 36, 38, 39, 40, 41, 79, 307
Poland, 256
political correctness, 93, 114n75, 283–85, 284n197, 292, 330–31
politics, 28n15, 70, 93n58, 117n79, 119–25, 149, 203, 294n205
  "pork barrel," 161–62, 162n111
  See also government
pollution, 139, 140–41, 212, 234, 254n172, 260n176
Pol Pot, 88, 295n206
pop culture, 279n193
population control, 218
population growth, 251, 255–56, 255n174, 260, 260n176, 341
"pork barrel" politics. *See* politics
postmodernism, 84n53
poverty, 164, 169–74, 190–92, 230, 297
  causes of, 165, 193n132, 234

impact of redistribution of wealth on, 155, 202, 207, 208–209, 216, 218, 340
War on Poverty, 138, 172
world poverty, 217–30, 222, 254, 255–56, 258, 259, 268, 331
power, lust for, 245
power lines. *See* utility companies
prayer, 195
precautionary principle, 108
premature infants, 299
press, freedom of, 179
price system, 203, 204, 212–13, 239
principle of parsimony, 80–81
prison, 311, 313, 314n214, 318, 319
"prisoner's dilemma," 29–30n17
privacy rights, 150
private property, 227–28, 230
privatization, 144, 202n140, 212
probability theory, 106n71
procreation, 50, 321, 324
procrustean bed, 114, 114n76
productivity, 160, 218, 248, 267
profits, 206, 207, 233–35, 238, 340
progressive, 124, 137, 152–58, 265n180
Prohibition, 317, 318
promiscuity, 117n79
Proper Study of Mankind, The (Chase), 267
property rights, 209, 227–28, 227n153, 230, 303n210
prosperity, 55, 55n35, 246
prostitution, 316–17, 317n217
protected sex, 304n212
protectionism, 220–22, 225n152
Proudhon, Pierre-Joseph, 227

psychics, 81n49
Public Service Commission, 143
Puerto Rico, 197n136
Punic Wars, 273
punishment, 311–20
puritans, 34
pursuit of happiness, 32, 51, 52, 155, 160, 200, 327
Putnam, Robert, 166n114

quantum fluctuations, 98, 98–99n64

race and racism, 153n101, 188n127, 287–97
railroad tracks, 62, 69
accident on, 76, 140
Rand, Ayn, 38
rape, 116n77, 299, 302
Raphael, 78n48
Raspberry, William, 297
Rawls, John, 215, 216
reactionary, 123
Reagan, Ronald, 29, 123, 124, 137, 161, 187
reality, 21, 21–22n10, 22–23, 66, 274
reason, 21–32, 67, 67n42, 72–73, 78–79, 80, 337
reciprocity, 29, 35, 37, 40
redistribution of wealth
impact on poverty. *See* wealth
red tape. *See* bureaucracy
Reeve, Christopher, 43–44
regulation by government, 137–51, 152–58, 228
and corporate self-regulation, 237
relativism, 82–94, 330–31

religion, 11, 32, 63, 67n42, 70, 95, 166, 273, 316n216, 324
  freedom of religion, 179
  fundamentalism, 124, 195. *See also* Islamic extremism
  and meaning of life, 15–16, 21–22
  and mortality, 26n13
  theocracy, 195
rent control, 142
"rent seeking," 148–49, 164
reparations, 294n204
reproductive success as goal of nature, 17, 17n6, 50, 109, 115, 271, 324
republic, 120
research animals, 308–309
resources, natural. *See* natural resources, depleting of
responsibility, 159n109, 180
  corporate social responsibility, 236, 236n162
  personal responsibility, 59–68, 303
reverse discrimination, 290, 293
Revolutionary War, 184–85, 185n123, 272
Ricardo, David, 219
rich, 52n33, 191, 207, 208–209, 216, 217–18, 259, 267, 340
  See also affluence; wealth
Riesman, David, 70
Right (political), 79, 120, 122
  See also conservatives
right and wrong, 30, 84, 85n54, 89, 339
righteousness, 36
rights, 150, 175–81, 210
  animal, 26n14, 306–10

  balance of between woman and embryo, 302–303
  against government, 179
  human, 60n38, 256, 259, 308
  individual, 127, 129, 341
  property rights, 227–28, 227n153, 230, 303n210
risk, 102, 106n71, 111, 112
Road to Serfdom, The (Hayek), 164
Robin Hood (fictional character), 155
Robinson, Elizabeth, 10, 16n4
robots and robotics, 266, 266n183
Roe v. Wade, 154
Rolex watches, 52–53, 52n33, 54, 57
romantic love, 109–18
Rome, 183, 196, 321
Roosevelt, Eleanor, 282
Roosevelt, Franklin Delano, 123
Roswell, New Mexico, 81
Rousseau, Jean-Jacques, 126–30
rule of law, 226–29, 227n153
Russia, 227, 245, 274, 275
  See also Soviet Union
Rwanda, 73–74, 242, 295

"satisficers," 54
SBC (company), 240n164
scare messages, 101–108, 251–63
Schlesinger, Arthur, 272
Schumpeter, Joseph, 211
Schwartz, Barry, 54, 55
Science of Good and Evil, The (Shermer), 32n21
scientific method, 23, 24, 84
Scrooge, Ebenezer (fictional character), 38

searches and seizures, freedom from, 318
secularization of the West, 330
segregation, 91, 289, 292–93
    See also integration
self-awareness, 60–61, 64–65, 307
self-centeredness, 132
self-esteem, 49
self-expression, 280
selfishness, 34, 36n25
"selfless" acts, 37
self-realization, 13, 38, 112, 136
self-sacrifice, 38, 41
self-sufficiency, 220
Semaritan, good, 35–36, 209n145, 303
Serbia, 69–70, 73, 74n47, 78, 329
serial killers, 87, 314–15n214
service economy, 206
sex crimes, 312
sexual abuse, 77
sexuality, 85, 109–18, 117n79
    homosexuality, 321–27
    protected and unprotected sex, 304, 304n212
Shadow University, The (Kors and Silverglate), 284n198
Shakespeare, William, 89, 90, 269, 277
shareholders, 232, 235, 235n160, 236n162
Shaw, George Bernard, 56, 161
Shermer, Michael, 32n21, 87n56, 247n170, 265n181
Shoreham Nuclear Power Station, 101–102
Shylock (fictional character), 277

Silverglate, Harvey A., 284n198
Simon, Paul, 111
Simpson, O. J., 71, 290n202
"single-payer" system in healthcare, 158
sins, 67n42, 316n216
Sistine Chapel, 92
Skeptical Environmentalist, The (Lomborg), 252n171
skin color, 287–97
slander, 281
slavery, 73–74, 91, 188, 274n187, 289, 291–92, 294n204, 325
slippery slope, 155, 156, 281
Slobovian widgets, 220–21, 223, 224
Smith, Adam, 41n29, 203, 206, 221–22, 234, 342
Smithsonian Institution, 275
smoking, 143
social consciousness, 134, 166
social contract, 28–29, 35, 79, 126–30, 209, 282, 314, 339
    government role in, 137, 152, 154, 157n105, 183
Social Contract, The (Rousseau), 126
social cooperation, 31, 31n18, 36–37, 246, 308, 338
social Darwinism, 97n61
socialism, 121, 122n82, 165, 202n140, 209, 230
socialized medicine, 158
social justice, 28, 155, 210
social mobility, 194n133
social responsibility, corporate, 236, 236n162
social safety net, 173n115

Social Security, 153, 162, 170, 213
Socrates, 15, 69, 76, 283
software, 60, 61–63, 70, 78
Somalia, 200
Sontag, Susan, 37
South Korea, 73, 74, 197, 201, 218
South Vietnam, 199n139
sovereignty, 120
Soviet Union, 90, 187, 200, 203, 274, 278n191, 329
   communism and, 121, 134, 164, 283
   fall of, 211, 245, 256, 279
   state control of, 160, 164, 184
   See also Russia
space-time barriers, 98, 98n63, 99n65
Spain, 197n136
Sparta, 298, 299, 304
speech
   freedom of, 149n98, 152n99, 179, 280–86, 286n200
   offensive, 281–83, 282n194, 284–85, 284nn197-199
"speech codes," 284
spirituality, 25
Spock, Mr. (fictional character), 67
sports, 278–79, 278n192
spotted owl, 178
Stalin, Joseph, 156, 269, 282, 283, 284
standard of living, 55, 160, 166, 192, 209, 218–19n149, 225, 230n155
Stanley, Thomas J., 53
Star Trek (TV show), 67, 121
statistics, manipulation of, 77–78, 252n171, 264

Statue of Liberty, 194
status, 47, 49, 52, 208
"steady state," 97n62
steel imports, 222
stem cells, 301–302
stereotypes, racial, 293
stock market, 232, 235n160
stoicism, 33–34
Stone Age, 260
Stossel, John, 145n96, 172, 176n118, 192, 285
subatomic physics, 98
subsidies, 220–22
suburban lifestyle, 189–90
Sudan, 71–72, 201, 242, 274, 277, 277n189, 278
Suez Canal, 329
suffering, 42–43, 86
   in animals, 307, 308–10
   and pain, 38, 39, 42–43, 135, 271, 277, 338
suicide, 320
sulfur dioxide, 212
Summers, Lawrence, 114n75
"summer soldiers" and "sunshine patriots," 184n122
Super Bowl, 278, 279
supermarkets, 211
supernatural sources, 21, 21–22n10
supply and demand, law of, 203–204, 212
supply side economics, 160–61n110
Supreme Court, 154, 195, 279n193
survival, 18–19, 36, 36n25, 44, 63, 338
   social cooperation and, 31, 31n18
   survival of the fittest, 97n61

"sweatshops," 224, 226
syllogisms, 24
symbiosis, 133

Tacitus, 245
Tailhook scandal, 325
T'ai-p'ing Rebellion, 252
Taiwan, 244–45, 245n167
tariffs, 220–22
taxation, 154–55, 157, 158, 158n108, 160–61n110, 170–71, 230
   "negative income tax," 173n115
   way to redistribute wealth, 154, 157n106, 160, 170, 207
"tax freedom day," 160
Taylor, Charles, 257
technology, benefits of, 257–58, 260, 264–71, 341
"telephone game," 77
Tennyson, Alfred, 111
Terence, 84
territoriality, 241–50
terrorism, 71–72, 92, 108, 162n111, 328–36, 334n221
   See also 9/11 terrorist attacks
Thatcher, Margaret, 132n89, 161, 165, 202n140, 209n145
theocracy, 195
thinking. See thought
third world, 76, 225n152, 236, 262n179
Thirty Years' War, 252
Thomas Aquinas, Saint, 32n20
Thomson, Judith, 303
Thoreau, Henry David, 167
thought, 59–68
   vs. actions, 65, 67, 67n42

black and white thinking, 84, 86, 88–89, 93
"think for yourself," 69–81
Thought as a System (Bohm), 61
"thrill of the hunt," 56
tobacco, 143, 319
Tocqueville, Alexis de, 55, 166n114
Tojo, Hideki, 257
tolerance, 82–83, 85, 91, 94, 249, 281, 282
Tolstoy, Leo, 89, 90
Torquemada, Tomás de, 80
totalitarianism, 122, 153, 159, 216, 256
trade, global, 219–26
trade, unfair, 221
trafficking in humans, 317
train wreck, 76, 140
transactional politics, 149
Trenton, Battle of, 184–85, 185n123
trial lawyers, 240
tribalism, 241–50
"trickle-down economics," 171
"trust but verify," 29
Turkey, 275
Twain, Mark, 26–27
Twentieth Century Capitalist Revolution, The (Berle), 210–11
Tyco (company), 235n160

UFO abductions, 81
Ukraine, 256
"Umma," 331
UN. See United Nations
unconscious, 68
underclass, 290
"unfair trade," 221

unintended consequences, law of, 140, 150, 164, 199n139
United Nations, 74n47, 242–43
universal medical insurance, 157–58
universe, beginning of, 95–100, 97n62, 98–99nn64-65
universities. *See* colleges and universities
University of Maryland, 285
University of Michigan, 191, 265n181
unpatriotic views, 283n195
unprotected sex, 304
Urban League, 297
utilitarianism, 39–40, 41n28
utility companies, 137n92, 235n161

vanity, 52, 66
Veblen, Thorstein, 52
vegetarians, 306, 310
Venezuela, 227n153
vengeance, 313
victimhood, 294n205
victimless crimes, 316–20, 316n216
victims, 292, 294, 294n205, 312, 315n215
Viet Cong, 199
Vietnam, 198–99, 199n139
violence, 102–103, 103n66, 313
visual-spatial skills, 114n75
voting, 145, 183–84, 183n121, 188n127, 236n162, 294, 294n205
  See also elections

wages, 173, 192, 205, 223, 223n150, 224

Wal-Mart, 186n125
war, 73–74, 74n47, 93n57, 247
Warhol, Andy, 48n31
"war on drugs," 317–19
War on Poverty, 138, 172
"war on terror". *See* Afghanistan; Iraq; terrorism
Washington, George, 184–85
wastage, 205–206n143, 240
water, bottled, 237n163
water, pricing of, 212–13
"water buffalo," 284n199
Watergate, 71, 140
wealth, 53, 53n34, 190–95, 191n129, 205–206n143, 217–18, 267
  effect of redistribution of on poverty, 155, 202, 208–209, 216, 218, 340
  taxation and, 154, 157n106, 160, 170, 207
  See also affluence; rich
Wealth of Nations, The (Smith), 222
weapons of mass destruction, 198
Weber, Max, 232n157
welfare system, 140, 169–74
West, opening of, 272
wheelchairs, 175–77, 175n117, 177n119, 180
white supremacy, 289–90
Will, George, 192, 273
wine, 52
work ethic, 55–56, 56n36
World Bank, 254
world government, 242
World Series, 279
world's policeman, 197n135

World War I, 198
World War II, 162n112, 195, 252, 272, 274
  Axis powers in, 73, 198, 200, 245
  US in, 74, 189, 198, 334n221
worry, 44–48
Wright brothers, 275–76

xenophobia, 124, 247

Y2K computer problem, 105
Yale University, 273

Yamani, Sheikh, 260
Yeltsin, Boris, 244

Zambia, 218
Zelig (movie), 70n44
Zen and the Art of Motorcycle Maintenance (Pirsig), 83
zero-sum game, 205, 217, 225, 248, 311, 340
zero tolerance, 142n93
Zimbabwe, 227, 229